F.V.

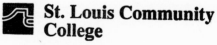

St. Louis Community College

Forest Park
Florissant Valley
Meramec

Instructional Resources
St. Louis, Missouri

Springer Series on
LIFE STYLES AND ISSUES IN AGING

Series Editor: Bernard D. Starr, PhD
Marymount Manhattan College
New York, NY

Advisory Board: Robert C. Atchley, PhD;
M. Powell Lawton, PhD; Marjorie Cantor, PhD (Hon);
Harvey L. Sterns, PhD

Mildred M. Seltzer, PhD, is a Senior Fellow in the Scripps Gerontology Center and Professor Emerita in the Department of Sociology and Anthropology, both at Miami University in Oxford, Ohio. She has held national offices in the Gerontological Society of America and the Association for Gerontology in Higher Education. She is also active on committees and boards of other professional and community organizations and serves as one of the Disinterested Trustees for several of the Scudder, Stevens and Clark AARP Funds.

Dr. Seltzer's research activities are eclectic. Topics include humor and aging, older women, academicians' decisions to retire early, along with academic administrators' perceptions about the effectiveness of early retirement programs and factors affecting the decision to purchase long-term care insurance. She is particularly interested in academic gerontology programs in institutions of higher education and has served as consultant to a number of colleges and universities about their programs. Dr. Seltzer has published several books and a number of articles.

The Impact of Increased Life Expectancy

Beyond the Gray Horizon

Mildred M. Seltzer, PhD

Editor

 Springer Publishing Company

Springer Publishing Company, Inc.
536 Broadway
New York, NY 10012

95 96 97 98 99 / 5 4 3 2 1

Library of Congress Cataloging-in-Publication Data

The impact of increased life expectancy: beyond the gray horizon/
   Mildred M. Seltzer, editor.
            p. cm.—(Springer series on life styles and issues in aging)
      Includes bibliographical references and index.
      ISBN 0-8261-8760-9
         1. Life expectancy.   2. Social prediction.   3. Quality of life.
   I. Seltzer, Mildred M.   II. Series.
   HB1322.3.I437   1995
   304.6'4573—dc20   94—36331
                                                                              CIP

Printed in the United States of America

As always, to my circle of four
that has grown to one of eight: George, Judy, Sarah
Lisa, Jay, Rob, Ben, and Will (in order of entry)
and to the memory of my parents,
Lafe B. and E. Libbie Glickman Murstein.

Contents

Foreword

Children do it all the time. Think back to your own childhood or recall your children or grandchildren growing up. The phrase "let's pretend," or some variation of it, will be a familiar refrain. Academicians, too, sometimes let their imaginations wander, conceiving of different scenarios and their implications. Philosophers regularly engage in such speculation, calling it "thought experiments." Demographers routinely ask what the consequences will be for population size, composition, or distribution under varying assumptions about vital rates. Yet, gerontologists seem to be less prone to asking such questions. Whatever the reasons for our reticence to confront possible futures, we tend to be far more concerned with describing the here and now, with explaining how we got to where we are. Far less often do we raise, let alone seriously confront, "what if" questions— questions such as the imaginative one posed by Mildred Seltzer, the editor of this provocative book: What if life expectancy were to reach 100?

Rare as these "speculative excursions" (a term used by Seltzer and some of her colleagues in a series of symposia presented over the years at the annual meetings of the Gerontological Society of America) are, there are compelling reasons to remove the disciplinary lenses causing our temporal myopia. In this case, average life expectancy in Western nations has been increasing steadily over the past century. From about 47 years in the United States at the beginning of the century, life expectancy has increased to 76 years now. For white females, the figure is 80 years. Along with the general aging of the older population—what has been called the aging of the aged—the number of centenarians in the United States has also risen steadily, from an estimated 15,000 in 1980 to a projected figure of over 100,000 at the beginning of the 21st century. Judged by these and a variety of other measures (e.g., median age, the percentage of the population over the age of 65, the percentage of the 65 and older population that is 85 and over), our society is clearly aging. Whether we can reasonably expect the average length of life to reach 100, and when that would occur, are probably unanswerable questions at this time. The fact remains, however, that we are slowly and steadily moving in that direction, and it behooves us to look ahead and seriously ponder the ramifications of increased longevity, both for society and for the gerontological enterprise itself.

To be sure, as the distinguished group of authors in this volume make clear, substantial gains in life expectancy will have profound consequences for our society and for other nations that experience this achievement. Just as clear is the fact that the implications of heightened longevity will depend on the balance of how these gains are distributed between periods of active life expectancy and periods of frailty. If the balance is in the direction of simply adding years to life without appreciably decreasing morbidity and disability, thereby increasing the length of time older persons are beset by frailties and infirmities, the implications for public policy, especially that which concerns the financing and delivery of health care and human services, will be unprecedented. If, on the other hand, we can manage to compress morbidity and decrease disability as we increase life expectancy, other scenarios of consequences, challenges, and even opportunities present themselves. The route by which we get there is all important.

Consider a few examples of the profound implications of a pronounced increase in life expectancy under either of the morbidity scenarios. Despite the population aging hat has been occurring so clearly since the end of the baby boom, and for some time before that, our social and cultural systems lag far behind in developing a repertoire of meaningful roles for our older population. Can we reasonably expect meaningful roles to be available to the vastly larger numbers of older persons whose life expectancy will exceed current longevity by another 20-25 years? Beyond token acknowledgment of their achievement, coupled with the usual request to identify the reasons for their long life, our culture has no particular expectations nor any special place for its centenarians. Would this situation change, and how would it change, if being a centenarian becomes a norm rather than a rare exception?

Another way to pose this question is to inquire about the consequences for the life course distribution of education, work, and retirement? To borrow Matilda White Riley's distinction, will the structure of these roles continue to be largely age differentiated, with education, work, and leisure segmented at separate states of the life course? Or will the added life expectancy lead to a major transformation of the life course, with the age structure of education, work, and leisure roles becoming more fully integrated across the life course? And how will our very conceptualizations of the life course change? Will the added years and the considerably greater heterogeneity of the older population prompt academic and popular reconceptualizations of the life course and of what it means to grow old and be old?

Think of the family. Already we have witnessed the emergence of families composed of four, even five generations. Under the scenario of an average life expectancy of 100 years, four- and five-generation families will be the norm, and there may well be a smattering of six-generation families. What will the implications be for intergenerational family relationships, for intergenerational family transfers, for intergenerational caregiving? Will the added generations diffuse or enhance the potential for the types of intergenerational family support that we have come to recognize as so prevalent and important?

Significant questions about intergenerational relations in such a long-lived society crop up in another context. Recently, concerns about intergenerational equity have been publicly and vociferously raised. Entitlement programs for older persons have come under increased scrutiny and have been challenged by those who believe these programs benefit the elderly at the expense of younger generations. To what extent would substantially added longevity compound these concerns and force a fundamental reexamination of age-based benefit programs? At a more specific level, would pressures on the financing of the Social Security system increase and become so great that the age of eligibility would have to be revised beyond the scheduled changes slated to take effect after the turn of the century? And what would this mean for the labor force participation of older persons whose continued employment has not been greeted, to this time anyway, with universal enthusiasm?

As these examples suggest, and as is further developed by the authors throughout this book, the consequences for a society where becoming a centenarian is the norm, would doubtless by profound and far-reaching. But lest we conceive of these outcomes as being primarily negative, as only presenting problems, it is important to remember that asking "what if" questions may also cause us to envision what could be, to think about opportunities. Unfettered by current structural arrangements, we can give free rein to our imaginations and inquire about the types of social and cultural structures that would be most conducive to supporting a long-lived society.

There is another theme, equally interesting, that the editor and authors develop throughout the book. If life expectancy did increase to 100, what would it mean for the gerontological enterprise? Are there recurring research questions that would take an added significance? Are there new and important research questions that would come to the fore? Surely, questions informed by a life-course perspective would be of considerable interest if persons routinely lived 20-25 years longer than they do now. Questions about the relationship between demographic change and social and cultural change would loom large under this scenario. Questions about political behavior and processes would likely become more central to gerontological research in a society where a substantially larger proportion of the electorate than at present is composed of older persons. Questions about the distribution, organization, delivery, and utilization of health and human services would be critical from both basic and applied perspectives.

These are but a few examples of research areas that would become prominent in a long-lived society, and the list could go on and on. What I believe can be said with some certainty is that funding for gerontological research would increase and that larger numbers of scholars and researchers would turn their attention to issues related to aging. Were it to occur, a decidedly healthy development would be a greater interest among disciplines that have been under-represented in gerontological research—anthropology, economics, political science, biology, the humanities.

Is the premise of this book—achieving and sustaining an average life expectancy of 100—likely to be realized in the near future? Probably not. Does it matter? No, because by posing the scenario and systematically examining its implications, the authors confront and extrapolate from a trend toward greater longevity that has been in evidence over the past century and that will no doubt continue. Whether we actually reach an average life expectancy of 100 or 95 or 90 is perhaps less important than the trend underlying the premise. Anticipating the consequences, challenges, and opportunities posed by greater longevity—whatever number that ultimately turns out to be—can only serve to help us be better prepared for the inexorable aging of our society.

STEPHEN J. CUTLER, PHD
Professor of Sociology and the Bishop Robert F. Joyce
Distinguished University Professor of Gerontology
The University of Vermont

Acknowledgments

Thanks to my Scripps colleagues who generously share their time and ideas; to the late Fred Cottrell and to Bob Atchley for their intellectual stimulation, honesty, and unswerving support. Particular thanks to the Scripps support staff, especially Lisa Haston, who has kept me as organized as it is possible for me to be. Thanks, too, to the chapter authors who responded kindly to my nagging and whose contributions will give this book whatever success it achieves. I have been fortunate in knowing all of these people.

Contributors

Robert C. Atchley, PhD, is Director of the Scripps Gerontology Center and Distinguished Professor of Gerontology at Miami University in Ohio. He has published more than a dozen books and contributed more than 65 articles and book chapters to the social science literature on aging.

Ruth E. Dunkle, MSW, PhD, is currently on the faculty of the School of Social Work at the University of Michigan. Her research interests and publications have been in the areas of mental health, language impairment of the elderly, and service utilization for impaired elders. She has co-authored or edited 6 books and numerous articles on aging.

Hiram Friedsam, PhD, is currently Professor Emeritus in the School of Community Service at the University of North Texas. He has served as Editor-in-Chief of *The Gerontologist* and as President of the Association for Gerontology in Higher Education.

Jon Hendricks, Professor and Chair, Department of Sociology, Oregon State University, has been a long-time contributor to social gerontology. He is the author of a number of articles and books in the field.

Robert B. Hudson, PhD, is Professor and Chair, Department of Social Welfare Policy, Boston University School of Social Work. He has written widely on the politics of aging, federal budgeting and expenditures on aging, and issues in the design and implementation of aging-related programs.

Jennie Keith, PhD, is Provost and Centennial Professor of Anthropology at Swarthmore College. She has written articles and books from a cross-cultural perspective about the experiences of aging and the significance of age as a basis of social differentiation, as well as about anthropological methodology.

Charles F. Longino, Jr., PhD, currently holds the title of Wake Forest Professor of Sociology and Public Health Sciences at Wake Forest University and the Bowman Gray School of Medicine. His interests are the demography of aging, health policy and ideology, and long-term care.

Susan Lynch, MSW, is on the faculty of the School of Social Work at Western Michigan University. She is completing her doctorate in Social Work and Development Psychology for the University of Michigan.

Thomas McRae, MD, is the Director of Education for the Division of Geriatrics and Assistant Professor of Clinical Medicine at the New York University Medical Center. He is also Chief of the Bellevue Geriatrics Clinic and Associate Clinical Director of the Aging and Dementia Research Center. Dr. McRae's major research interest is in Alzheimer's disease, including neuroimaging, molecular biologic, and drug treatment studies.

John W. Murphy, PhD, is currently Professor of Sociology at the University of Miami, Coral Gables, Florida. His interests are sociological theory and social philosophy.

Dena Shenk, PhD, is Professor of Anthropology and coordinator of the Interdisciplinary Program in Gerontology at the University of North Carolina at Charlotte. Her major research interests include social support systems and aging within various cultural contexts. She has incorporated a range of qualitative methods in her aging research, including the use of visual methodologies, social network analysis, and life histories.

Lillian E. Troll, PhD, is Professor Emeritus, Rutgers University, and Adjunct Professor, University of California–San Francisco. She is the author or editor of 9 books, as well as many articles. Her primary interests are life-span developmental psychology with a focus on family and women's issues.

PART I

Establishing a Context for "What If" Questions

Introduction to Part I

This book grew out of a 1992 symposium conducted by a group of social and behavioral scientists to discuss the implications of a possible life expectancy of one hundred years. The title of that session at the Gerontological Society of America meeting was "Doing More with More: Multidisciplinary/Professional Approaches to an Increased Life Expectancy of 20–25 Years." The idea for the original symposium was shaped, in part, by two questions given on graduate student exams some years ago. The first was given in an unknown place and at an unknown time to sociology doctoral students. They were asked to design a social system in which there was no death. The answers, like the name of the professor who asked the question, are lost to memory. The second question was asked more recently of master's level students: "Assuming you continued to do research until you died, what kind of research questions would you ask and what designs would you use if you lived to be one hundred years old?" Answers to the latter question may still be in an unknown filing drawer. In both instances, the questions implied the phrase "what if?" The same premise undergirds chapters in this book. Authors were not asked to predict what will happen, but only to describe what could happen if our society achieved a common life expectancy of one hundred.

When it was decided to use the original presentations as the basis for a book we added to the original group representatives of some professions involved in working with older people, particularly in health-related and human services, areas that would be affected dramatically by increased life expectancy.

A life expectancy of 100 years was selected for this book because it seems an increasingly possible achievement for the future. The original questions continued to influence the authors of this book. Each was asked to focus on two general areas: the probable consequences for society and for individuals if our life expectancy were so increased and the effects of these factors and the researchers'/practitioners' own increased life expectancy on his or her research. In order to enhance consistency among answers to the first general area, authors were asked to focus on similar topics: family, interpersonal relationships, individual development, politics and policy, labor force participation, and retirement.

In responding to the second area, authors were asked how the change in life expectancy, including their own, would change their professional and professions' research agendas, thus blurring the age distinction between observer and observed. What would be the impact of extending one's professional life expectancy along with one's chronological one? Would research be similar to or different from today's research activities? What kind of questions would be asked, what designs and methods used? What might be the areas of interest? Practitioners were asked to discuss how the organization of professional services and characteristic therapeutic techniques would be affected by increased longevity. How would underlying philosophies, ideologies, models, and paradigms of professions and disciplines be affected?

Individual authors answered these questions in varying proportions, some emphasizing one set of questions, others responding to different issues. Each author also based her or his chapter on personal assumptions regarding the reasons for increased life expectancy and was asked to make these assumptions explicit. As a result there is some variability in how each views the probable causes of increased life expectancy and, consequently, in what the resulting salient issues would be.

Authors of this volume represent a range of academic disciplines and professions. They were asked to perform the difficult task of describing a society and their own research agenda in a world where life expectancy is 100 years. They had to be a combination of visionary, science fiction author, and scientist/practitioner. The individual authors have their personal and professional values and attitudes relating to aging. These influence their responses to the "what if?" questions they were asked. Attitudes and values also influence assumptions about the causes and consequences of people living to be 100 years old. Scientists often find it difficult to change the operating rules we take for granted. Instead, we pattern the future after the present; the present then is a shaping template for that future. And yet, to paraphrase an aphorism, there is no science without fantasy and no fantasy without facts. The authors of the following chapters reflect this approach in their descriptions of a long-lived society.

The chapters collectively constitute a multidisciplinary and multiprofessional approach to the topic. The authors represent some of the social and behavioral sciences and the medical and human services professions.

Conspicuous by their absence are economists, humanists, physical and biological scientists. Their omission is not a reflection of disciplinary chauvinism (Hendricks, 1988); rather, it reflects the organization of the original symposium and some practical constraints. Individual authors do not represent the varied approaches within the individual disciplines and professions. Presenting all disciplinary, intradisciplinary, professional, and intraprofessional viewpoints in a single place, let alone a single book, would be an insurmountable task. It might, however, be an interesting challenge to present in other books, the various intradisciplinary and intraprofessional perspectives of single disciplines or professions on these same topics. Individual authors in this book have made and continue to make significant contributions to the field of aging. Each recognizes that the study of aging and practice with an older population are multidisciplinary endeavors; that knowledge and practice are inextricably interrelated.

There are many ways of editing books. One can actually edit the individual papers, bringing a consistency to the volume that might otherwise be lacking. The editor can suggest to the individual authors that each deal with specific topics. The editor can write an individual introduction to each of the chapters or, alternatively, can write an overall introduction that deals with the individual chapters in relation to specific topics or one that synthesizes all of the chapters. He or she can also take the position that each of the authors were invited to contribute because each has significant points to make, and, therefore, they should make their points in their own words. Edited books follow these patterns or some combination of them. In this instance, I have chosen a combination of these, excluding editing the authors' chapters.

This book is organized into four parts. The first part sets the stage for subsequent chapters by describing, in a general way, previous and current efforts to do something about old age and death. Part 2 consists of five chapters, each of which provides a disciplinary perspective of a society peopled by centenarians and discusses a discipline-based research agenda in such a society. Part 3 moves the discussion from academic disciplinary perspectives to three professional perspectives: social work, medicine, and long-term care. Part 4 contains a discussion of a paradigmatic shift in the area of biomedicine and concludes with a chapter summarizing and synthesizing all of the previous ones.

References

Hendricks, J. (1988). Comments made at a leadership retreat of the Gerontological Society of America in June 1988.

Chapter 1

Racing Against a Pale Horse

Mildred M. Seltzer

This first chapter focuses on five themes: ways of thinking about growing older or staying younger, what we want to achieve, a description of some current attempts to achieve what we want, some gerontological efforts to anticipate what could happen if we were successful in achieving the goal of longevity, and some data about current centenarians.

Ways of Thinking about Growing Older or Staying Younger

Our culture values youth. We are fearful of aging not only because of its vicissitudes which we see, read and hear about, but because the old are devalued. These values and related beliefs and attitudes are not new. They have characterized Western society for centuries (see, for example, Hendricks & Hendricks, 1986; Falkner & de Luce, 1989; Achenbaum, 1978; de Luce, 1993; among others). We want to look young, feel young, not age, not die. At the same time, our myths and folklore warn us against asking for the unattainable lest our wishes be granted. Myths and stories, however, reinforce the belief that there are methods, perhaps as yet undiscovered, for achieving long life, perpetual youth, immortality. In some of these stories, longevity is viewed as reward; in others, as a curse. Old age is seen as punishment for those who violate norms or sin against the gods. Some, for example, believe that there was no old age in the Garden of Eden before the Fall or prior to the Flood. Although these beliefs do not necessarily represent mainstream religious groups, they persist and reinforce beliefs that at one point life without aging existed and, therefore, is attainable again.

Literary prescriptions for achieving longevity or immortality are fairly explicit: for vampires, drink blood, and stay out of daylight. For others, stay in your own environment and you will not age in place. Even the perpetually young or immortals can be destroyed, however. Lo-Tsen, the character in *Lost Horizons* (Hilton, 1934), ages when she leaves home, a reminder of the importance both of maintaining your own home and of avoiding pollution. Vampires can be destroyed by hammering a stake through their hearts and burying them at a crossroads. After living 2,000 years, Ayesha died in minutes and shriveled up to the size of a large and hideous monkey, destroyed by the Fire of Life (Haggard, 1957).

A familiar classic frequently cited among gerontologists from Greek mythology illustrating the pitfalls of careless prayers for immortality is the story of Tithonus, Aurora's husband. Aurora asks Zeus to grant Tithonus immortality. She forgets, however, to ask that he remain young. And so, Tithonus grew old doomed to live forever with increasing symptoms of very old age. Aurora shut him up in a room where "…he babbled endlessly…His mind was gone with his strength of body…" (Hamilton, 1942, p. 290). According to one version of the story, Aurora eventually turned Tithonus into a grasshopper, a most noisy insect. This story reinforces the belief that declining physical ability is associated with declining mental ability.

A less familiar mythological story is that of Sibyl. She asks Apollo, who was attempting to seduce her with gifts, to give her one year of life for every grain of sand in a nearby pile. Like Tithonus, she too forgot to ask for eternal youth. Trimalchio claims to have seen her in a bottle where, when she is asked what she wants, answers she wants to die (Seneca, 1977, p. 63; King, 1989). This story is additional evidence of the need to be careful in our requests of the gods and goddesses.

If the story of Tithonus describes what happens to an individual given eternal life, the story of the Strudlbrugs describes what happens to a society in which some members are immortal. In *Gulliver's Travels*, Swift discusses the social consequences of longevity. He describes the Strudlbrugs or Immortals of Luggnuggia. Unlike other Luggnuggians, Strudlbrugs are doomed to live forever. As did Tithonus, they suffer the indignities of old age. Hated by their society, the Strudlbrugs are considered legally dead upon reaching the age of eighty, the typical Luggnuggian life span. Gulliver, after witnessing these Immortals and their lives writes, "The Reader will easily believe, that from what I had heard and seen, my keen Appetite for Perpetuity of Life was much abated" (p. 172). What the contemporary readers may also gain from this story is the persistence of age stereotypes and ageism and the social meaning of death.

Science fiction literature is often a place where authors experiment with changing the rules we take for granted. These writers epitomize constructionism in their creation of new worlds and societies. For example, Pohl (1992) describes a society in which, with rare exceptions, people live virtually forever. Rafiel, the protagonist, on the other hand, is one of the very few humans who grows old and dies. Pohl's characters have different perspectives on careers, relationships, and futures depending upon their life expectancies. In describing these, Pohl also deals with the meaning of separations and losses and the meaning of life in a world of immortals. Francavilla (1984) reviews descriptions of immortals in his review of Zalazny's novels. How do authors create meaningful lives for people who live virtually forever? Is the meaning of life related to the prospect of death? Interestingly, an October 1992, issue of *Life* magazine dealt with the topic of aging. One part contained the description of a world in which longevity injections were available. A major problem people faced was boredom, with the result that many eventually requested euthanasia. One couple's final choice, however, was not death but cloning themselves so that they could live forever (Darrach, p. 43).

These few examples from folklore and novels raise provocative questions about the downside of achieving the various goals of prolongevity and immortality. They express our negative attitudes toward old age and death and our positive ones toward youth, although the stories are often morality tales reminding us of the potential pitfalls of interventions in the "natural world," whatever that natural world is.

Currently there is growing attention to creating a positive image of old age. We see this in the publications of gerontologists from all disciplines and perspectives as well as popular authors who have been focusing on the strengths and competencies of old age. They are giving increasing attention to the potentials of old age, not only its frailties. One possible explanation for this new emphasis is the aging of the baby boom generation; another is the purchasing power of the affluent elderly segments of the older population. Further, there is a cohort of gerontologists who are growing old. Just as in the past, their research interests reflected their stage of life (the "empty nest," caregiving, retirement), now they are focusing on issues of old age. We have also seen an increase in the number of positive role models of older people. This emphasis on the potential of old age constitutes a reaction formation to the emphasis on rejuvenation or youth maintenance.

We can measure this shifting emphasis to the more positive aspects of aging by the popularity of courses about aging gracefully, meeting the challenges of this new stage of life, and by books about successful, healthy, productive aging (Bronte, 1993; Butler, 1993; Friedan, 1993). Popular writers may be learning from scientists, or from their own aging process. In any event, the general public is learning from writers of popular literature what, apparently, scientists have had only limited success in communicating: that menopause is neither unexpected nor devastating, and also that there is life after retirement. There is, however, a downside to all of this—if we do not have to remain youthful, then why must we be stereotypically wise and generative in old age? People, including older ones, need to be careful not to substitute one monolithic goal for another; one sweeping generalization for another. It is as exhausting to be perpetually wise as it is to be perpetually youthful. Descriptions of the potential of old age may be transformed into the prescriptions of how one should behave. The "successful" and proper role for an old person to play is increasingly becoming that of a Goody Two Shoes of old age. Aging successfully and dying with dignity are fast becoming the ultimate achievements of the Protestant ethic.

What Do We Really Want to Achieve: Fantasy and Reality

Peoples' interest in longevity is more than academic: It is an expression of our desire for long life and, perhaps, our fear of death as well. The presence of centenarians among us gives us all hope—if they can do it, so can we.

We begin with the question of what do we really want? Is the goal to prolong life beyond what, at any given time, is to be expected? Do we want to find a way to be rejuvenated, a Fountain of Youth in which to bathe? Do we want only to retard aging? Is our goal the postponement of death or more ambitiously, to achieve physical immortality? Do we want to restore life to the dead? Do we want to remain young until we die—of what? Old age? Maybe we merely hope to prolong middle age until very near the end when we finally succumb to old age.

A succession of generations has tried to give us what we wanted or, at least, to give some select portion of the population what it wanted. Historically, there have always been individuals who attempted to learn, understand, and control the secrets of life, aging, and old age. Where once there were magicians, shamans, and priests, who mixed elixirs and chanted formulae, now there are physicians, other health care providers, biologists, physiologists, sociologists, psychologists, social workers, humanists, and authors of "how-to" books. Where once explorers looked for the Fountain of Youth, now there are the cosmetics industry, plastic surgeons, and travel agents. Present day searches are conducted in different ways and in different places. Where once we sought an elixir or a bath in special waters, now we look for the proper diet, social support, and low-fat fun.

Over time, magic became science and yesterday's alchemist has become today's scientist. Those who once might have practiced magic are today various kinds of technicians, physicians, and other health practitioners. Current methods that seek to increase longevity, prolong youth, or postpone death take place in the laboratories of scientists. The methods are less global and less all encompassing. Instead of concocting a single, longevity-producing drink, scientists examine genetic structure and conduct experiments with animal models of aging. The search is no longer for a magic formula that would prolong life, a "Methuselah enzyme" or genetic locale where aging is "turned on." Once the location is discovered, scientists may be able to intervene, control, manipulate.

The terms used to describe past and current goals include prolongevity, immortality, rejuvenation, delaying death, postponing aging, eliminating diseases. The overriding goal of each of these is the avoidance of the decrements and disadvantages of aging commonly experienced by a majority of people in previous societies. R. C. Atchley (private communication, October 14, 1993) suggests that the goal is to prolong the physical, social, and psychological power of maturity. He believes many would prefer death to a long life if the latter entails facing some of the unavoidable decrements of physical aging. At the same time, continued Atchley, people do not want to die if it means the end of the self. People were and continue to be ambivalent: we want a long life because we do not want to die and we are afraid to live a long life because of the negative aspects of old age. Nothing much has changed since the mythical time of the Titans. There is continuity in our concern with avoiding the negative aspects of old age and death. There is change over time in notions of how to do so and in who controls the means of doing it.

Approaches to Avoiding Old Age

Efforts to prolong youth, postpone aging and its accompanying decrements, and postpone death itself have been characterized by five major emphases: (a) maintaining perpetual youth, (b) restoring youth or rejuvenation, (c) postponing biological aging, (d) prolonging life, and (e) achieving physical immortality. These five approaches are not necessarily mutually exclusive. One can want to be perpetually young and live forever. All are, however, expressions of our negative attitudes toward old age and death and efforts to avoid both. Concurrently, they express the great value placed on youth.

• Maintaining Perpetual Youth •

"How sad it is! I shall grow old, and horrid, and dreadful. But this picture will remain always young...If it were only the other way! If it was I who were to be always young, and the picture that were to grow old!" (Oscar Wilde) And so begins an exemplar of a closed system approach to aging; something must grow old: if not the person, then the picture. Dorian Gray expresses the desire of those who would remain perpetually young and the reasons some fear aging.

Our desire to remain young has both physical and social aspects. We want the appearance of youth accompanied by its vigor and involvements. We want to feel good, and to have the energy and strength to accomplish the same things a young person can. There is a difference between maintaining youth and restoring it after we have aged. Most of us are sufficiently reality bound to recognize that the former is highly unlikely but that the latter is, to an extent, under our control. We can try to do things that will enable us to feel that we are maintaining a youthful appearance and that we look younger than we are. This is particularly important in a youth-oriented society, or in a society which deprecates aging and old people, where continuing to look and act young are held in such esteem. There are articles and books that stress the importance of proper nutrition, exercise, cosmetics, plastic surgery, and preventive medical attention to help disguise, prevent, or retard symptoms and manifestations of aging. Slimness is equated with youth; thick hair, any color but gray, and a taut, tight skin also help convey a youthful appearance. As a result of these values and advances in medicine and cosmetology, it is becoming increasingly difficult to estimate age solely on the basis of physical appearance, including dress. A *New York Times* fashion article was devoted to showing "ageless" clothes that could be worn by people of any age. The models for these fashions were people in their late 80s and 90s (The look of the nineties, 1993).

Subsequent letters to the editor, however, reflected some ambivalence about "the look of the nineties" (Thomson, 1993; Kearcher, 1993). Fashions might appear ageless but bodies do not.

At the same time, because activity is equated with youth, we strive to maintain youthful behaviors as well as appearance. This involves "keeping up" with some activities and avoiding others. Our avoidance behaviors are shaped as much by negative stereotypes of old age as by the positive aspects of being young. Hence, we find it important to keep busy, stay involved, and to avoid behaviors thought to reflect being old. There are even acronyms reflecting this characteristic of activity, "opals" (older people with active lifestyles or "grampies" (growing retired active monied persons in an excellent state) (Crispell, 1990, p. 51).

• Restoring Youth or Rejuvenation •

Rejuvenation connotes restoring the youthful appearance and energy of a young person. The goal of rejuvenation is to transform an old person into a young one. In legend, winding back the clock would be accomplished by drinking a potent liquid, bathing in a magic body of water, or by employing some other, nonliquid, method. More current approaches involve plastic surgery, Retin-A, or one of the various rejuvenation treatments available in European spas such as injections of sheeps' placenta or Gerovital.

If we have not found a Fountain of Youth, we can, nonetheless, with the assistance of these current techniques plus the efforts of beauty parlor technicians, restore a youthful look so valued particularly for women in our society. Rodeheaver and Stohs (1991, p. 145) refer to "...a culturally accredited set of rituals of rejuvenation . . ." and point to the "implicit marketing of hope." Cosmetics are marketed with claims that they can remedy cellular changes that accompany aging and thus restore a youthful appearance. Aging itself may be irreversible but malfunctioning cells might be reversible. In this fashion, the use of cosmetics is said to be therapeutic and it becomes almost obligatory for one to take the responsibility for restoring one's youthful appearance. The issue becomes one of control and individual responsibility and, if we cannot reverse the internal clock of aging, maybe we can replace or reinstate external conditions. While we seek youth, however, we add the proviso, "If I knew then what I know now," suggesting we want the youthful appearance of the past and the knowledge and experience of maturity.

If we were to become the age irrelevant society Neugarten (1982) calls for, the emphasis on youth and hence on rejuvenation in its many connotations would be less of a goal for many of us.

• Postponing Biological Aging •

Delaying aging is different from both the maintenance of perpetual youth or its restoration. One of the goals of biological research is to delay aging; to learn what causes aging and how these causes can be manipulated. At another level, the postponement of aging focuses less on looking and acting young and more on delaying some of the typical characteristics of aging. Although some of the methods may be similar to those involved in maintaining youthfulness, the goal differs. Through diet, exercise, good medical attention, and various other social, biological, and psychological interventions, we hope to postpone the physical problems, visible signs, and symptoms of aging. We have achieved, on a societal level, relative success in this goal. People in their 60s are less apt to be considered old; we have moved aging up decade by decade.

In recognition of our efforts to postpone symptoms of aging and accomplishments in this area, gerontologists have developed a vocabulary to reflect the fact that symptoms of aging do not occur at a specific chronological age. Chronology, in fact, is not a good predictor of many things, particularly about specific individuals. Moreover, old age itself is not an all or nothing condition at any stage of life. Gerontologists, therefore, use physical functioning as a modifier for chronology in describing our older population. Thus, the gerontological language distinguishes among various categories of old people using words such as "young old," "old," "oldest old," and "frail elderly." There is aging and there is aging and not all aging is the same. Furthermore, there is aging and there are diseases. Disease is not the same as aging, although disease may interact with other physiological and social aspects of aging. A distinction between aging and disease is one that, as yet, not all medical practitioners maintain. Disease may hasten physiological characteristics of aging; physiological aging may accelerate the progress of specific diseases.

• Prolonging Life and Postponing Death •

In his comprehensive review of pre-nineteenth century European and non-European thinking about prolongevity, Gruman writes that he coined the term prolongevity, using it for the first time in 1955 (Gruman, 1966). He defines prolongevity "...as the significant extension of the length of life by human action" (p. 6). The term encompasses two phenomena: life expectancy and life span. Although he does not specify whether the human action is conscious, one presumes that some human action can increase life expectancy as an unintended but beneficial consequence of attempts to achieve other goals. If life span is really species specific and controlled by genetic programs, then human progress can affect life span through genetic alteration.

In this book, the term prolongevity is used more inclusively. It incorporates the goal of increased life expectancy with the investigation of whether there is a finite species specific life span as distinguished from life expectancy and if so, whether we can manipulate it and thus implicitly postpone death.

On an intuitive level, there is a distinction between extending life and postponing death. The former refers to factors that result in greater life expectancy. It suggests more positive images than the latter. The postponement of death connotes the medical care and its related technology that enables us to "put death off." It conjures up pictures of the terminally ill replete with tubes and other accouterments of medicine that are successful in postponing or delaying death if not in enhancing life. As a society, we are unsure about the extent to which we want to postpone death and are increasingly concerned about those instances in which "Death takes a holiday" (Ferris, 1931). Concern often focuses on issues of quality rather than quantity of life.

There is an intrinsic ambivalence about prolongevity if it means postponing death. This ambivalence is particularly obvious when postponement of death is at great personal and social cost. Our concerns are increasingly evident in the attention we give to the consequences of deaths delayed. It is apparent in our current emphasis on biomedical ethics, advance directives, durable powers of attorney, living wills, death with dignity, hospice programs, and to an extent, discussions regarding health care rationing for the older population. Obviously there are limits on the circumstances under which we want to extend life by postponing death.

Cryonics claims to offer an alternative to dying now from a terminal illness. On the assumption that our descendants may find cures to illnesses that are presently terminal, an individual can be frozen and, presumably, resuscitated in the future when a cure is at hand. There is, then, the possibility of life after life. Should cryonics become successful, it would certainly change the conventional meaning of life expectancy. It would also change the ways in which a person thinks and is treated in terms of age. It would result in a redefinition of dying and death, with legal ramifications that would delight a group of attorneys.

• Achieving Physical Immortality •

Physical immortality presupposes the total elimination of death and, for purposes of our discussion, does not include ideas about reincarnation and resurrection. The closest we have come to describing a scientific method that would enable humans to become physically immortal has been in some of the attempts to discover the genetic basis of aging. Theoretically, if we find this, we can intervene to create immortals. Curtsinger and colleagues' statement "...that the limited life-span paradigm is not supported by observations on genetically homogeneous populations of *Drosophila*" (Curtsinger, Fukui, Townsend, & Vaupel, 1992, p. 463) is not, however, evidence that biological immortality is within immediate reach, nor does it necessarily reflect the consensus of everyone.

Some Current Attempts to Achieve Our Goals

• Background •

Current day scientists can be identified with one or more of the five approaches described above. Some biogerontologists are engaged in research that would result in increased life expectancy; others are attempting to discover what the ultimate human life span is. Life expectancy refers to the average number of years a population age category might live after reaching a specific age. Current or projected age-specific mortality rates are used to compute the average number of years of life that could be expected given the mortality rates assumed. Life expectancy changes at different ages, reflecting the average number of years of life remaining to people who have already survived to a given age. Life expectancy figures are aggregate ones and do not speak to what a specific person's age will be at the time of her or his death. We act fairly confident, statistically, about life expectancy data although our confidence is based on all kinds of assumptions, among them a belief that the future will not be too dissimilar from the past. Life expectancy depends on assumptions about mortality rates, that is, the probability of death. Thus, the postponement of death alters assumptions about mortality and, in turn alters life expectancy figures. The term *life span* refers to a specific biological limit to life. As will be discussed below, there is no definite agreement about the limits of the human life span. Some believe it to be about 120 years, citing the case of Shigichio Izumi, who lived in Japan, as one example of a man who lived to be 120 years old (Smith, 1993). Countries may differ in life expectancy rates, but theoretically, humans may not differ in life span potential.

We have been successful in extending life expectancy beyond what our ancestors believed possible. We have accomplished this by democratizing life expectancy (Butler, 1993). It has been achieved without the magic elixir thought to be necessary by the forerunners of current day scientists. Public health measures and improved medical practices resulted in reduced infant and maternal mortality rates, and reduced death rates in late life. Life expectancy—considered without factors such as war or "ethnic cleansing"—has increased in virtually every industrial nation in the world.

Changes in life expectancy and in mortality rates have a greater impact on our thinking when we realize how these changes affect individual lives. In today's society, for example, most women do not expect to die in childbirth. The death of a child has become a nonnormative event. Although at the beginning of this century, 20% of white children and about 33.3% of nonwhite children died before age five, now between 1% and 3% do, the rate depending on race and social class (Taeuber, 1993, p. 3-2). Women born in 1900 had a life expectancy of almost 51 years; men, almost 48 (Smith, 1993, p. 120). Now, most infants can be expected to live until their 70s or older. Usually married men do not expect to be widowed, although married women do. Most people entering retirement now can look forward to at least a decade or more in retirement; whereas people born in 1900 usually did not live long enough to spend much, if any, time in retirement. We are, however, often fearful about future disabilities and frailties as well as the nature and cost of health care in old age. Because our life expectancy is greater than our grandparents', we are more likely to survive to ages at which chronic and disabling conditions are more prevalent, and when we die, we are more likely to die from disabling chronic conditions than they were. These changes result in our having quite different life experiences than those of our grandparents.

In the past the remarkable increases in life expectancy were the result of declines in infant and maternal mortality rates; in recent years, the marked declines in mortality have occurred in the later years of life (Olshansky, Carnes, & Cassel, 1990). Earlier estimates of age-related rates of decline in late life mortality rates were probably too high (Manton, 1992). Earlier estimates were based on assumptions that may prove faulty and limitations on then current research methods. Many physiological functions may decline more slowly than originally thought or many of the declines occurred just prior to death. Manton suggests the possibility of still more gains in the future both in years and in active life expectancy. Some, however, have suggested that we have gone almost as far as we can go in extending life expectancy. Others are interested in whether we have approached the limits of our life span. If there is neither a finite life span or it is considerably longer than we have yet realized, then the possibility remains that we can continue to increase life expectancy beyond today's.

Our success in achieving prolongevity is not without its costs. Newspapers articles are filled with reports and dire warnings about the economic and social consequences of our extended life expectancy. Schools develop academic programs to educate students about living in an aging society and working with an aging clientele. Special programs are developed for our older population. Heated political debates deal with issues of intergenerational equity, entitlement programs, medical care, and the potential of "gray power."

Moreover, despite the democratization of life expectancy, at the present time there is still considerable inequality in life expectancy rates in the United States. Social class, race, ethnicity, gender, and other social structural variables continue to play a role in influencing the adequacy and availability of health care throughout the life cycle and consequently affect life expectancies for various social categories within the population.

A Brief Review of Some Biogerontological Findings

The variety of research foci and the range of interests among biogerontologists is as varied as it is among social and behavioral scientists. It ranges from intrinsic processes of aging to extrinsic ones; from biochemical factors to genetic ones. On the one hand, some of the research about manipulating longevity is based on animal models. The extent to which we can project these findings onto humans is almost as questionable as the extent to which experiments using introductory psychology students can predict how middle aged and older adults will behave in "real life." On the other hand, as Barinaga (1992) points out, findings based on animal research could influence discussions about aging and mortality.

There appears to be no greater agreement among biogerontologists than among other categories of scientists. For example, there is no agreement about whether or not there is a limited human life span. The limited life span paradigm in biogerontology is based on the assumption that there is a genetically fixed maximum life span for humans. It assumes that if an individual does not die prematurely, he or she will die a "natural death" preceded by a sharp decline. We can improve the environment to reduce premature death but we are unable to delay senescent death.

Writing from another perspective vis-à-vis increased longevity, Rose (1993), urges us to examine factors other than reduced mortality rates in late life. He urges us to consider what he calls evolutionary gerontology. This approach is based on the "...conviction that the fundamental cause of aging has nothing whatsoever to do with any ineluctable biochemical mechanism" (p. 67). More specifically, he states, "To us, the search for biomedical or cellular theories that might fundamentally explain aging is as cogent as quantum mechanical theories of linguistics" (p. 67).

Rose's discussion of the postponement of aging is cogent and supports the presumption of this book, a world in which we can achieve a life expectancy of 100. He writes, "One of the most powerful corollaries of the evolutionary theory of aging is that it should be feasible to postpone aging if one alters patterns of natural selection, given the rejection of any simple biochemically determinate aging" (p. 69). For example, experiments suggest that postponing reproduction can eventually result in postponed aging.

Rose does not doubt that given sufficient time and resources we will be able to postpone aging somewhat. He recognizes, however, that there may be some problems in achieving this goal. For example, if, as a society we want to achieve longevity, and, if in order to do so it is necessary to postpone reproducing ourselves, whose reproductive activities shall be postponed? On what basis? Under what circumstances? Although Rose is aware of all of the political ramifications of these issues, he is nonetheless optimistic in pointing out the prospect for gerontology as a discipline if we are able to achieve increased longevity. "For example, the problem of postponing human aging will be transformed from a mystery mostly discussed by quacks into a technological project with delimitable methods, costs, and benefits" (p. 65).

Scientists have long been interested in the function of postreproductive years. As Medvedev (1975) pointed out, "The main question gerontology must answer is how the duration of this period of life between sexual maturity and death is controlled" (p. 196). His answer was to bring mean life span closer to maximal life span by attacking diseases associated with aging, such as heart diseases, cancer, and arthritis. He also asks a philosophical and, as yet, unanswered question. Is it really necessary to increase life span?

Kastenbaum (1992) summarizes current bipolar thinking about the foregoing and related issues. Debate centers on three topics: (a) Aging is detrimental vs. aging is adaptive; (b) The rate of aging can/cannot be modified and, therefore, longevity can/cannot be extended; and (c) The biological limit on the human life span is real/illusory (pp. 289–291). Kastenbaum's discussion is prefaced by the caveat that "these controversies are best followed by those who are willing and able to speak the language of biogenetic research" (p. 289).

• Another Perspective •

Although my focus until this point has been on biological and physical sciences, behavioral and social scientists have dealt with similar issues. Hamlin (1967), for example, outlined a psychological version of an evolutionary theory of aging over 25 years ago. He asked two questions: "Who needs the old person?" and "Why does the individual need old age?" (p. 37). He discussed the possibility that "... utility determines the life span" (p. 37). Of the three programs shaping humans—physiological, social, and behavioral—the physiological program is salient in the early stages of development. In later years, the behavioral one becomes dominant. According to Hamlin, behavioral programs are fixed by culture, mediated by language, and as long as culture grows, behavioral programs grow as well. Breakdown is not inevitable at a specific age and only occurs when culture prevents the individual from participating in social activities and tasks.

Hamlin's emphasis is upon the individual, not society. In asking his primary question, why the individual needs old age, his organizing principle is the task, operationalized as the "...meaningful use of time or energy" (p. 40). This is the definition of utility or order—he sees these as synonymous (p. 44). As cultures become more complex, utility also increases. In his words, "If a given culture grows and develops needs for abilities that do not appear until late in life, then the life span increases" (p. 39) "...If one is needed, one lives longer. Darwinian evolution and physiology control the first half of life. Cultural evolution and behavior control the last half" (p. 45). He does not address the social and cultural factors that affect pregnancy, childbirth, survival of childbirth, or other related factors. He goes on, however, to point out that "Man [sic] is made in infancy. In old age, Man makes himself" (p. 45). Presumably, the same can be said for Woman.

Anticipatory Scenarios

Gerontologists, epidemiologists, futurists, demographers, and others among the scientific literati have been looking at how various societies would be affected by the presence of more people achieving longer lives. Some efforts focus on preparing for the future; others describe the age composition of that future. Their perspectives and assumptions often differ from one another. This book is not the first to describe the possible impact of changing life expectancy on our society.

It was certainly evident in the earlier 1969 Committee on Research and Development Goals in Social Gerontology (CoRAD) report (Havighurst, 1969). That project also focused on research on specific topics that related to social policy aspects of an aging society: (a) work, leisure and education; (b) living arrangements of older people: ecology; (c) social services for the aged and aging; and (d) economics of aging. The committee also recommended specific areas of research "...as especially worthy of support by public and private funding agencies" (Havighurst, 1969, p. 1). Participants deliberately avoided the areas of basic research in sociology and psychology primarily because these were not topics of interest to the funding agency. Interestingly enough, a special subcommittee was appointed for this project consisting primarily of younger colleagues or those new to social gerontology in order to "...help correct any over-conservative 'establishment' biases of members of the main committee" (Havighurst, 1969, p. 1), an early precursor of deconstructuralism and an illustration of latent ageism in gerontology. Value judgments and biases, if not always so explicit as those of the CoRAD committee, continue to characterize a great deal of current gerontological thinking.

About two decades ago, Neugarten edited a special issue of *The Gerontologist*, entitled *Aging in the Year 2000: Aging in the Future* (1975a). In that publication, she differentiated those who predict what the future will be like into three categories: visionaries, science fiction writers, and scientists engaged in "futures research." Others writing in that same volume made different kinds of distinctions. For example, Kahn (1975) distinguished between predictions about what *will* happen and those that describe what *should* happen. Such a distinction is essential because it differentiates between probabilities on the one hand and ideology and hope on the other. Beatty (1975), also writing for that same volume, is a willing participant in shaping the future. He describes the other authors in that volume as having "...identified themselves with the scientific futurists rather than the literary Utopians or the science-fiction writers." He writes:

> *I would suggest that their efforts must be placed within a normative frame-work of what ought to be, as well as within an international framework of anticipated change. We must be careful to avoid straight line projections of the past in forecasting the future. We must relate past and present knowledge of aging to give "shape" and, if you will, "bend" the future, so as to remove many unacceptable conditions confronting today's older persons as we look ahead to the aging population of the year 2000. (Beatty, 1975, p. 40).*

Beatty discards a linear version of time; the past is not necessarily prologue to the future; rather we have a responsibility to shape the future. Discarding Kahn's distinction, Beatty would have us be, if not Utopian seekers, then certainly value biased in some as yet undefined fashion in order to eliminate the so-called "unacceptable conditions." Predictions, in general, rely on values.

The goal of those involved in that symposium was

> *...to select several of the most salient issues related to the personal and social effects of increased life expectancy, to survey what is known about these issues and how they are related, then to identify the research questions that should be pursued in clarifying policy issues that will develop over the next few decades. In short, our intention has been to develop a research needs assessment program. . . . By needed research we mean not only new types of data, but new ways of organizing existing data, and new social experiments. (Neugarten, 1975b, p. 3).*

This is not unlike the charge to the authors of the current volume.

The 1975 call for research in the service of social policy is not unusual within the Gerontological Society of America. It has been reiterated in one fashion or another since the founding of the society.

At the time the CoRAD report was issued, there were 20 million Americans over 65. The estimate at that time for the year 2000 was a population of 28.2 million over 65 (p.5). Papers in "Aging in the Year 2000" (Neugarten, 1975) were based on the assumption that there would be no drastic increases in life expectancy (in 1970 it was 71); rather, increases would be slow. In 1990, however, there were already 31.1 million people over 65 and 3 million 85 and over (Taeuber, 1993, p. v).

Planning for the year 2000, 2040 or a "what-if" world in which the life expectancy is 100 is, obviously, an "iffy" undertaking dependent, in part, on underlying assumptions. Different assumptions result in different predictions, descriptions, and scripts.

Other efforts to anticipate and/or prepare for the future of our aging society can be found in such publications as the National Institute on Aging's, *Our Future Selves* (Neugarten & Maddox, 1980) and Jarvik's, *Aging in the 21st Century* (1978). This present book is less an effort to anticipate or prepare for a world in which life expectancy is 100 than an attempt to describe, from a disciplinary or professional viewpoint, what our society might be like in such a world.

Current Centenarians

Although this book asks the question What if the average life expectancy were 100?, it is not a totally unrealistic question. There are centenarians among us, although there is some uncertainty about their exact number. We know, then, that a life expectancy of 100 is not completely unimaginable or unrealistic, particularly given current demographic changes. Not all demographers agree, however, about the number of centenarians in the United States and elsewhere. Birth certificates were not always registered or required. Sometimes records of vital statistics have been destroyed. Often the old were thought to have exaggerated their ages for any one of a number of personal and social reasons (see, for example, McKain, 1967; Medvedev, 1974).

In the United States, estimates of the number of centenarians in 1990 range from 22,000 (Kestenbaum, 1992) to 54,000 (Poon, 1993). A more detailed discussion about the demography of centenarians can be found in Atchley's chapter in this book, "The Longevity Revolution." Regardless of the specific numbers, a major point is that there are data problems for a number of reasons.

During the 20th century, government agencies, demographers, gerontologists, and the popular press have devoted considerable time to studying and reporting the aging of our population as well as that of other nations. The resulting publications have ranged from books and articles divulging secrets of longevity, to advice on how to reach a 100th birthday, to simple descriptive studies of centenarians. Others have interviewed the very old and published the results of these interviews. But, as Hendricks (1992a) notes in a review essay of four recent books about the research endeavor, we learn little from these books other than that centenarians do not differ significantly from other old people. He claims that we "...have scarcely moved past chronological age as an explanation" (p. 138).

Any discussion of reports on centenarians would be remiss if it neglected mentioning Belle Boone Beard, one of the first social scientists interested in studying centenarians. Her research lasted over the 40 years prior to her death in 1984. Her book, Centenarians: The New Generation (Beard, 1991), was published posthumously and its bibliography is a testament to scientific and lay interest in the prospects of becoming and being a centenarian.

The Georgia Centenarian Study (Poon, 1992) continues Boone's works. Poon and an interdisciplinary team of associates are engaged in an effort to develop a conceptual framework to study "master survivors" and "expert survivors," the former being "successful agers" in their 80s and the latter in their 100s. The purpose of the Georgia group's work is to develop "... a theoretical rationale, hypotheses, models, and methods and procedures ..." for their research of these extremely old people (p. 1). Their preliminary findings constitute a valuable resource for those interested in this topic.

Conclusions

As is evident from the foregoing, there are two levels on which literature, both scientific and nonscientific, discusses issues of longevity: the personal and the societal. On an individual level, many people, including those in the field of aging, tend to look forward to a longer rather than shorter life expectancy. Gerontologists discuss what we believe are the consequences of longevity for the individual. What does it mean to grow old in a society where people live so long? How is aging experienced? How defined? What does age mean? How does age structure the life cycle? We ask what will happen if we are able to increase life expectancy, particularly with reference to health-related issues. We examine how the increased life expectancy since World War II has affected our social institutions and personal lives. As we talk at meetings and write in our literature, the specters of the Strudlbrugs and Tithonus hover in the background. We express our concerns in common gerontological platitudes and aphorisms that guide our continued discussions and research and relate to our concern with improving the quality as well as the quantity of life. "We need to add life to years not only years to life."

Gerontologists are not unique in expressing ambivalence about the prospects of a very long life or of immortality. Our mixed feelings have been reflected in scientific and nonscientific literature over the ages. It is seen in the pronouncements of our politicians and policy makers, philosophers and novelists. We are persistently reminded that the costs of having our prayers answered may be greater than we anticipated or are willing to pay as individuals and as a society.

In general, earlier gerontological studies paid little, if any, attention to how the aging of the population included ourselves as researchers and how an increased life expectancy could affect our own research agenda. The authors in this book took exactly this path. They describe issues that, from a disciplinary point of view, they would expect to arise. They discuss how increased longevity could affect their disciplinary-based research activities with respect to issues examined and questions raised. Their chapters evidence their scientific imagination in describing what would happen if there were additional years added to life. I have been stressing the word *our* in order to draw attention to the fact that scientists as well as their research subjects will live longer. Increased longevity becomes a personal issue as well as a research one, thus blurring the line between the observer and the observed.

In a field in which replication is rare, in which many of us age along with the subjects of our research, the increase in our own life expectancy has profound professional as well as personal implications. Thus, the authors describe not only what our society might be like but also what our professional activities and concerns might be.

When, in the present, we look at similar past attempts to describe what would happen with the aging of our population, we are reminded of the difficulties in predicting, forecasting, anticipating the future consequences of present events. Fitzpatrick writes, "…I think experts—that is scholars, scientists—just don't think carefully enough about the premise underlying prediction" (1993, p. 47). After discussing chaotic and complex situations, she goes on to write: "It finally justifies that peculiar claim of historians, disdained as illogical by many social scientists, that while you can't predict events, you can explain them after the fact—not immediately, only after a certain time has elapsed" (p. 47). Another way of saying this is "History is lived forward but understood backward" (Kushner, 1993, p. 42). Twenty years from now, *if* our average life expectancy has increased to 100 years, and *if* people read this book or *if* they recall the original symposium on which this book is based, it will be interesting to see whether some of the ideas presented in this book are transformed into predictions by gerontological historians. Hendricks, at the original symposium during which early versions of some of these chapters were given, described a future Gerontological Society of America meeting at which "a panel of bright young gerontologists" were convened to discuss "Why our forebearers failed to anticipate the social consequences of an extended life cycle?" (Hentricks, 1992b). Those panelists, at least, will understand this book is not predictions of things to come but rather responses to what-if questions.

Acknowledgement

I want to thank Jon Hendricks and Judith A. Seltzer for their invaluable editing assistance.

References

Achenbaum, W. A. (1978). *Old age in a new land: The American experience since 1790*. Baltimore: Johns Hopkins University Press.

Barinaga, M. (1992). Mortality: Overturning received wisdom. *Science 258*, 398–399.

Beard, B. B. (1991). (Eds.) In V. K. Wilson & A. J. E. Wilson III, *Centenarians*. Westport, CT: Greenwood Press.

Beatty, W. M., Jr. (1975). Discussion. *The Gerontologist, 15*, (1, Pt. 2): 39–40.

Brontë, L. (1993). *The Longevity Factor*. New York: HarperCollins.

Butler, R. L. (1993). *Who is Responsible For My Old Age?* New York: Springer.

Carey, J. R., Liedo, P., Orozco, D., & Vaupel, J. W. (1992). Slowing of mortality rates at older ages in large medfly cohorts. *Science 258*, 457–461.

Crispell, D. (1990). Guppies, minks, and ticks. *American Demographics 12* (6), 50–51.

Curtsinger, J. W., Fukui, H. H., Townsend, D. R., & Vaupel, J. W. (1992). Demography of genotypes: Failure of the limited life-span paradigm in *Drosophilia melanogaster*. *Science 258*, 461–463.

Darrach, B. (1992, October). The war on aging, p. 33–43.

de Luce, J. (1993). Ancient images of aging. *Generations, 17*(2), 41–45.

Falkner, T. M., & de Luce, J. (1992). A view from antiquity: Greece, Rome and elders. In T. R. Cole, D. D. Van Tassel, & R. Kastenbaum (Eds.), *Handbook of the Humanities and Aging* (p. 3–39). New York: Springer.

Falkner, T. M., & de Luce, J., (Eds.). (1989). *Old age in Greek and Latin literature*. Albany: State University of New York Press.

Ferris, W. (1931). *Death takes a holiday*. New York: French.

Fitzpatrick, S. (1993). Things happen. *The University of Chicago Magazine,* *85,* 48–49.

Francavilla, J. V. (1984). These immortals: An alternative view of immortality in Roger Zelazny's science fiction. *Extrapolation 25* (Spring), 20–33.

Friedan, B. (1993). *The Fountain of Age.* New York: Simon and Schuster.

Gruman, G. J. (1966). A history of ideas about the prolongation of life: The evolution of prolongevity hypotheses to 1800. *Transactions of the American Philosopohical Society New Series 56,* 5–97.

Haggard, R. H. (1957). *She: A history of an adventure.* London: Collins.

Hamilton, E. (1942) *Mythology: Timeless tales of gods and heroes.* Boston: Little, Brown.

Hamlin, O. M. (1967). A utility theory of old age. *The Gerontologist,* 7, (2, Suppl.): 37-45.

Havighurst, R. J. Chair. (1969). Research and development goals in social gerontology: A report of a special committee of the Gerontological Society. *The Gerontologist,* 9, (4, Suppl.): 1–90.

Hendricks, J., & C. D. Hendricks, (1986). *Aging in Mass Society: Myths and Realities.* Boston: Little Brown and Company.

Hendricks, J. (1988). Comments made at a leadership retreat of the Gerontological Society of America in June 1988.

Hendricks, J. (1990). Personal resources and successful aging [Review of *Becoming and being old: Sociological approaches to later life, Eighty-five plus: The oldest old,* and *Snowbirds in the sun belt: Older Canadians in Florida*]. *The Gerontologist,* 30, 273–274.

Hendricks, J. (1992a). Paths of virtue? [Review of *Ageism: Negative and positive, Centenarians: The new generation, Centenarians in Hungary: A sociomedical and demographic study,* and *Life after ninety*]. *The Gerontologist,* 32, 136–138.

Hendricks, J. (1992b). Taking a longer view: Methuselah as metaphor, and as social gerontologist. Paper presented at gerontological Society of America's 45th Annual Scientific Meetings, Washington, DC.

Hilton, J. (1934). *Lost Horizons.* New York: William Morrow.

Jarvik L. F. (Ed.). (1978). *Aging into the 21st century.* New York: Gardner.

Kahn, R. L. (1975). The mental health system and the future aged. *The Gerontologist,* 15, (1 Suppl.): 1–40.

Kearcher, L. (1993). Letter to the editor. *New York Times Magazine,* October 10, p. 10.

Keeton, K. (1992). *Longevity.* New York: Viking Penguin.

Kestenbaum, B. (1992). A description of the extreme aged population based on improved Medicare enrollment data. *Demography,* 29, 565–580.

King. H. (1989). Tithonas and the Tettix, In T. Falkner & J. de Luce (Eds.), *Old Age in Greek and Latin literature* (p. 6-89). Albany: State University of New York Press.

Kushner, H. S. (1993). *To Life! A celebration of Jewish being and thinking.* Boston: Little, Brown.

Manton, K. G. (1992). Mortality and life expectancy changes among the oldest old. In R. M. Suzman, D. P. Willis, & K. G. Manton (Eds.), *The oldest old* (p. 157-182). Oxford: Oxford University Press.

McKain, W. C. (1967). Are they really that old? *The Gerontologist, 7,* 70-72, 80.

Medvedev, Z. A. (1974). Caucausis and Altay Longevity: A biological or social problem. *The Gerontologist, 14,* 381-387.

Medvedev, Z. A. (1975). Aging and longevity: New approaches and new perspectives. *The Gerontologist, 15,* 196-201.

National Institutes of Health (1993). *In search of the secrets of aging* (NIH Publication No. 93-2756). Washington, DC: Department of Health and Human Services, National Institutes of Health, National Institute on Aging.

Neugarten, B. L. (Ed.). (1975a). Aging in the year 2000: a look at the future. *The Gerontologist, 15,* (1, Suppl.).

Neugarten, B. L. (1975b). The future and the young-old. *The Gerontologist, 15,* (1, Suppl.): 4-9.

Neugarten, B. L. (Ed.). (1982). *Age or need: Public policies for older people,* Beverly Hills, CA: Sage.

Neugarten, B. L. & Maddox, G. L. (1980). *Our future selves: a research plan toward understanding aging* (NIH Publication No. 80-144). Washington, DC; U.S. Government Printing Office.

Olshansky, S. J., Carnes, B. A., & Cassel, C. (1990). In search of Methuselah: Estimating the upper limits of human longevity. *Science, 250,* 634-640.

Pohl, F. (1992) *Outnumbering the Dead.* New York: St. Martin's.

Poon, L. W. (Ed.). (1992). The Georgia centenarian study. *International Journal of Aging and Human Development, 34,* 1-89.

Poon, L. (1993). Centenarians. In R. Kastenbaum & S. Kastenbaum (Eds.), *Encyclopedia of Adult Development* (p. 63-64) Phoenix, AR: Oryx.

Rodeheaver, D., & J. Stohs (1991). The adaptive misperception of age in older women: Sociocultural images and logical mechanisms of control. *Educational Gerontology, 17,* 141-156.

Rose, M. R. (1993). Evolutionary gerontology and critical gerontology; Let's just be friends. In T. Cole, W. A. Achenbaum, P. L. Jakobi, & R. Kastenbaum

(Eds.), *Voices and visions of aging: Toward a critical gerontology* (p. 64-75). New York: Springer.

Smith, D. W. E. (1993). *Human Longevity*. New York: Oxford Press.

Swift, J. (1958). *Gulliver's travels and other writings*. New York: Random House Modern Library. (Original work published 1735)

Taeuber, C. M. (1993) *Sixty-five plus in America*. Valletta, Malta: International Institute on Aging.

The look of the nineties. (1993). *New York Times Magazine*, September 12, pp. 73-81.

Thomson, D. (1993). Letter to the editor. *New York Times Magazine*, October 10, p. 10.

Wilde, O. (1992) *The Picture of Dorian Gray*. New York: Random House Modern Library. (Original work published 1891)

PART II

Disciplinary Perspectives

Introduction to Part II

Five academic disciplines are represented in this section: demography, sociology, psychology, anthropology, and political science. Each chapter is written from the author's disciplinary perspective. The section begins with Robert C. Atchley's demographic description of the longevity revolution and its implications for individuals and society. He stresses the increasing diversity of the old population on virtually every sociodemographic characteristic from chronological age to the experiences of aging. As we read his chapter, we are reminded that demographic data provide us with a mirror of social life reflecting but not necessarily describing individual lives. Atchley alerts us to the changes that will occur in every social institution, in our thinking and in the way we lead our lives. These are themes we see repeated in various ways in different scenarios throughout the rest of this book.

Jon Hendricks, a sociologist, anticipates the need to redefine life stages and life events. He points out that longevity requires that we rethink and reconceptualize aging processes, the life course, life stages, development and other constructs. Certainly, under the conditions postulated, our temporal perspectives would change as would the priority levels of various social and political issues.

Lillian E. Troll, a psychologist, draws on data from a study of adaptation among the very old in San Francisco as well as on personal reflections regarding her own aging. She focuses on three perspectives important to consider in the what-if? society of many centenarians: peoples' own feelings about reaching the age of 100, the views of those with whom centenarians interact, and, the perspectives of outsiders, the observers. We know less about the first of these than the latter two. Present-day centenarians are survivors: would being a survivor at 100 have the same meaning in a society in which that age is relatively common? What can we speculate about self-concept, cognitive abilities, and the meaning of work for people 100 years old?

Dena Shenk and Jennie Keith, anthropologists, reinforce Hendricks' emphasis about reconceptualizing life course constructs. Along with others, they stress that meanings and definitions of old age would change considerably in a world of centenarians. Life expectancy increased to 100 would affect not only the end of life but the entire life cycle, offering more options to play different roles with different temporal norms throughout life.

Robert B. Hudson is a political scientist. He describes eight different scenarios based on different combinations of three dichotomized variables. He addresses sources of strain that can occur in societies and the policy implications of these strains. The development of our current aging policies and practices are examined and provide the context within which to anticipate policies in a long-lived society.

All of these authors implicitly or explicitly suggest and/or design research projects that deal with issues they raise in their chapters. They introduce us to the many possible worlds of a centenarian society. Several make the point that if living to be 100 becomes common, we would then have another, even older age category, to examine as unusual survivors.

Chapter 2

The Longevity Revolution

Robert C. Atchley

T he increases in life expectancy at the oldest ages that occurred in the 1980s were unprecedented. If these trends continue as expected, the numbers of older Americans in the oldest age categories—those in their late 80s, those in their 90s, and centenarians—will increase dramatically. The goals of this chapter are to look at: a) the demographic projections for the oldest-old and what they imply for increased demographic heterogeneity within the older population, b) potential effects of greater longevity on the inner life of aging individuals, c) social changes that could stem from a growing proportion of very old people, and d) research challenges posed by these social and demographic trends. Each of these topics could be the subject of a separate chapter, but for now we will briefly examine them as a context for many of the chapters that follow.

Trends in Longevity and Demographic Diversity in the Older Population

In its most recent projections of the population of the United States, the U.S. Bureau of the Census (1992) laid out three scenarios of future mortality. The high life expectancy scenario assumes a continuation of the longevity gains of the 1980s and would result in a life expectancy at birth of 87.6 by the year 2050. The medium life expectancy scenario projects a slower increase in life expectancy, from 75.8 in 1992 to 82.1 in 2050. The low series held current mortality rates constant, with an increase over the next 15 years in deaths due to AIDS. Under the low scenario, life expectancy at birth would drop slightly to 75.3 in the year 2050.

Table 2.1 shows the three series of projections for the total population, the population age 65 and over, the population age 85 and over, and the population age 100 and over. For all three series, the projected population in the oldest age categories increases much faster than the population as a whole or even the general 65-and-over population. The population of centenarians is projected to grow the most dramatically. Note also that the pattern of increases in population fluctuates, especially for the oldest population categories. This reflects mainly the effects of fluctuating birthrates in the past. The medium series projects a more than 5-fold increase in the 85-and-over population from 1990 to 2050 and more than a *32-fold increase* in the population of centenarians over this time span, while the overall population is expected to grow by only 53%. This is a demographic change of monumental proportions, one that has never occurred before in recorded history. The new and unprecedented survival rates are expected to cause the oldest age categories in the population to rapidly fill with the survivors of the large birth cohorts that made up the baby boom.

We can also look at the projected change in the proportion of people entering the older population that survives to reach very old age. Table 2.2 shows the proportion surviving for successive age cohorts expected to enter the older population between 1990 and 2020. For men, the proportion of the age 65–69 population expected to survive to age 95–99 increases steadily from 4.3% of those who were 65–69 in 1990 to 8.7% of those who are expected to be 65–69 in 2020. For women, the proportion surviving from their late 60s to their late 90s increases from 11.2% for those 65–69 in 1990 to 18.7% of those who are expected to be age 65–69 in 2020. The proportion surviving from their late 60s to their late 90s is projected to nearly double in the period between 1990 and 2050. Thus, not only will the very old population increase as a result of high birthrates during the baby boom, but the survival rate during later life is expected to improve substantially.

One interesting facet of the above projections is the change expected in the sex ratio. In 1990, there were 81 men for every 100 women at age 65–69. By the year 2020, this ratio is expected to be much closer—92 men for every 100 women. A similar narrowing of the gender gap in survival isexpected to occur at age 95–99, from 31 men per 100 women among

TABLE 2.1. Projected Population Age 65 and Over, Age 85 and Over, and Age 100 and Over: U.S. 1990–2050

	Total Population		Population Age 65 and Over			Population Age 85 and Over			Population Age 100 and Over		
	Number (Thousands)	Decade % Change	Number (Thousands)	% of Total	Decade % Change	Number (Thousands)	% of Total	Decade % Change	N (Thousands)	% of Total	Decade % change
Low series											
1990	249,415		31,224	12.5		3,050	1.2		36	0.0	
2000	268,108	7.5	33,968	12.7	8.8	4,055	1.5	33.0	66	0.0	83.3
2010	278,078	3.7	36,694	13.2	8.0	4,852	1.7	19.7	103	0.0	56.1
2020	285,200	2.6	47,182	16.5	28.6	4,820	1.7	-0.6	130	0.0	26.2
2030	286,710	0.5	58,027	20.2	23.0	5,569	1.9	15.5	152	0.1	16.9
2040	282,286	-1.5	57,560	20.4	-0.8	7,933	2.8	42.4	167	0.1	9.9
2050	275,647	-2.4	55,157	20.0	-4.2	9,228	3.3	16.3	250	0.1	49.7
Medium series											
1990	249,415		31,224	12.5		3,050	1.2		36	0.0	
2000	274,815	10.2	34,886	12.7	11.7	4289	1.6	40.6	77	0.0	113.9
2010	298,109	8.5	39,705	13.3	13.8	5,702	1.9	32.9	160	0.1	107.8
2020	322,602	8.2	53,627	16.6	35.1	6,480	2.0	13.6	278	0.1	73.8
2030	344,951	6.9	69,839	20.2	30.2	8,381	2.4	29.3	435	0.1	56.5
2040	364,349	5.6	75,588	20.7	8.5	13,221	3.6	57.7	620	0.2	44.2
2050	382,674	5.0	78,876	20.6	4.3	17,652	4.6	33.5	1,170	0.3	88.7
High series											
1990	249,415		31,224	12.5		3,050	1.2		36	0.0	
2000	281,306	12.8	35,534	12.6	13.8	4,484	1.6	47.0	82	0.0	127.8
2010	317,895	13.0	41,790	13.1	17.6	6,473	2.0	44.4	196	0.1	139.0
2020	360,123	13.3	57,855	16.1	38.4	8,028	2.2	24.0	407	0.1	107.7
2030	405,130	12.5	77,731	19.2	34.4	11,083	2.7	38.1	746	0.2	83.3
2040	453,687	11.2	88,857	19.6	14.3	18,374	4.0	65.8	1,198	0.3	60.6
2050	506,740	11.7	97,926	19.3	10.2	26,160	5.2	42.4	2,491	0.5	107.9

Source: Compiled by the author from the U.S. Bureau of the Census (1992).

TABLE 2.2
Trends in Survival from Age 65–69 to Age 95–99

Year Age 65–69	Number (In Thousands)	Year Age 95–99	Number (In Thousands)	Percent Surviving to 95–99
Males				
1990	4,508	2020	194	4.3
1995	4,521	2025	223	4.9
2000	4,369	2030	247	5.7
2005	4,709	2035	302	6.4
2010	5,733	2040	406	7.1
2015	7,340	2045	576	7.8
2020	8,444	2050	732	8.7
Females				
1990	5,558	2020	619	11.2
1995	5,427	2025	667	12.3
2000	5,100	2030	691	13.5
2005	5,388	2035	803	14.9
2010	6,457	2040	1,043	16.2
2015	8,133	2045	1,417	17.4
2020	9,225	2050	1,723	18.7

Source: Compiled by the author from the U.S. Bureau of the Census (1992).

those who were 95-99 in 1990 to 42.5 men per 100 women at age 95-99 in the year 2020. This narrowing of the gender gap is expected because of gains in longevity for older men due to reductions in heart disease and a slower rate of increase in longevity for older women as a result of increasing rates of heart disease.

As dramatic as the above projections are, we should also note that over the past 20 years the Bureau of the Census projections have consistently underestimated gains in longevity. The actual numbers of Americans age 85 and older by the year 2050 may exceed even the seemingly unbelievable 26.2 million projected by the high series in Table 2.1.

The growing age disparity within the older population will be accompanied by wide variations in health status, income, and living arrangements. Health status is strongly but not perfectly correlated with chronological age. The concept of *active life expectancy* was developed to distinguish between the average number of years of life remaining and the number of years remaining in a nondisabled state (Rogers, Rogers, & Belanger, 1989). As the age of a population cohort increases, so does the proportion with chronic disease and functional disability. For example, Kunkel and Applebaum (1992) estimated that in 1986 the proportion of elders with no functional disability dropped from 90% at age 65–74, to 79% at age 75–84, to 50% at age 85 and older. At the other end of the functional continuum, the proportion with severe disability increased from 4% at 65–74, to 10% at age 75–84, and to 29% at age 85 and over. Functional disability in this study was measured by deficits in a combination of activities of daily living (ADL), instrumental activities of daily living (IADL), and cognitive impairment. Because of the aging of the older population and increased survival, Kunkel and Applebaum projected that the number of disabled elders would increase from 5.1 million in 1986 to 16.3 million in 2040.

However, recent evidence indicates that age-specific rates of disability may be declining in the older population. For example, based on an analysis of National Long-Term Care Survey longitudinal data for 1982 through 1989, Manton, Corder, and Stallard (1993) found that when the 1982 to 1984 period was compared with 1984 to 1989, the probability of remaining nondisabled for 2 years increased significantly at all ages and the proportional increase in probability of being nondisabled was greatest at age 85 and over. They suggested that medical advances used to increase life expectancy, such as treatment for congestive heart failure, also increased active life expectancy. Even when they adjusted their data for mortality and change in age distribution, there were significant declines in the probability of becoming disabled or becoming an institutional resident. Thus, growing variability on health and disability measures even among the oldest-old seems a likely prospect. The good news is that the trend seems to be in the direction of increases in the proportion of the oldest-old who are not disabled, or in the direction of greater active life expectancy.

Most sources of retirement income do not keep pace with inflation and general levels of wages and salaries. As a result, economic resources of the oldest age categories within the older population usually compare very unfavorably with the incomes of those just entering the older population. For example, in 1988 the proportion of elders with income at or below 125% of the poverty level increased from 24% at age 65–74 to 45% at age 85 and over (Schulz, 1992). Whatever the oldest-old do in terms of lifestyle adaptations usually has to be done with less income.

Living arrangements also vary systematically by chronological age (Coward, Cutler, & Schmidt, 1989). For example, among elders living in the community in 1980, at age 65–69 most elders (52.6%) lived with a spouse in an independent household and 19.9% lived in multigenerational households. At age 65–69, older people in multigenerational households were very likely to be the household head or the spouse of the household head. Among those age 90 and over, only 13% lived with a spouse in an independent household, 46.6% lived in multigenerational households. The very old were unlikely to be the head of a multigenerational household. The proportion living alone showed an inverted U-shaped pattern. At age 75–79, 36% lived alone; at age 80–84, 41% lived alone; and at age 90 and over, 33.5% lived alone. At age 65–74, only 1.3% of elders lived in nursing homes in 1985. The proportion that lived in nursing homes increased to 5.8% at age 75–84 and 22% at age 85 and over (National Center for Health Statistics, 1989). These patterns of living arrangements are largely a reflection of age differences in the functional capacity to live alone, often coupled with the death of a spouse caregiver.

As more oldest-old parents require ongoing care from their children, who themselves may be retired, there may also be a reduction in interstate migration connected to retirement. On the other hand, to accommodate increased disability, more elders can be expected to make local moves within communities to find more service-rich living situations.

As the degrees of physical health, physical and mental frailty, and functional disability become increasingly diverse within the older population and as objective circumstances such as income and living arrangements diversify, the common ground that comes from being older together can be expected to diminish. When the older population spans an age range from 65 to 105 or more and an enormous variety of life circumstances, it is probably unrealistic to expect that being older would have any specific meaning. Nevertheless, there are some dimensions of increased longevity and active life expectancy that suggest ways that the experience of aging may change.

Increased Longevity and the Nature of Inner Life

The unprecedented increases in longevity over the next 60 years can be expected to alter the time horizon for life planning, create greater uncertainty about the nature of aging as an experience, increase the incidence of anxiety and depression connected to functional disability and fears about aging in the face of uncertain outcomes, and provoke more interest in active, managed death.

As a collection of culturally ideal sequences of roles and transitions, often specific according to gender, social class, and ethnicity, the life course is poorly charted beyond age 70 or 75. Following Levinson's (1990) theory about the 5-year cyclic build-up and decay of life structures, we might expect that elders in their late 80s and beyond would still be confronting changing circumstances and the need to think ahead to a new life struc- ture of activities, relationships, and environments. Instead of a planning horizon around age 85, as Fries (1980) encouraged, realistically we should think in terms of the possibility that we could live to be 105 or so. This means that at age 75 we might have another six or seven reorganizations to make in our life structure, each with their own assumptions about capa- bilities, limitations, goals, and resources.

Although there are distinct advantages to the flexibility of later life as a do-it-yourself enterprise, there are also disadvantages to not having a well- articulated cultural map. The greatest disadvantage is probably uncertainty with regard to what roles are possible for the oldest among the old. What do the oldest-old see as their "possible selves" (Markus & Nurius, 1986)? Elders currently confront the realities of ageism and age discrimination as early as age 45 or 50, and we know very little about the experience of ageism and age discrimination among people who are in their 90s or among centenari- ans. How do the very old fashion a life for themselves and negotiate approval of it by the people around them? Is this necessary? The challenge of trying to anticipate which roles are available and which are proscribed can lead to ambiguous visions and awkward interactions. For the young-old, a privatized social world of household and long-standing relationships with family and friends may buffer this ambiguity, but the oldest-old are often coping with life in an institution and friendship and family networks deci- mated by death.

Langer and Rodin (1976) were among the first to call attention to the powerful effects that a sense of personal control or efficacy might have on the experience of later life and indeed on longevity itself. For the oldest- old, this issue often comes down to how one maintains a sense of sover- eignty over one's life and at the same time acknowledges the need for assis- tance. Elsewhere (Atchley, 1983), I discussed the need to use an "assist the capable" model of service delivery to frail elders rather than a "help the helpless" model. Given the many gradations of dependency and the wide variations in age of onset and slope of change, there is little hope that a large number of very old people maintaining a strong sense of highly personalized control could lend itself to the development of culturally prescribed lockstep versions of the advanced stages of the life course. Our overly simplistic conceptions currently do more harm than good. Fending for oneself or living in a nursing home is about as far as the average adult can get in trying to conceive of how to cope with being a centenarian. Thus, all too often those who would provide social support to the oldest-old have impoverished ideas about how to go about it.

Our social institutions are not much better. The actuarial assumptions built into retirement pension financing generally have not taken increased longevity into account. As long as interest rates were relatively high, capital appreciation provided a cushion against miscalculation. But in the late 1980s and the 1990s, interest rates were very low, which reduced pension fund managers' degrees of freedom in coping with the need to continue pensions for unexpected survivors. These same increases in longevity are also part of the stated rationale for the panic about the future of Social Security that began in the late 1970s and early 1980s. The Social Security plan for insuring the system's capacity to deliver promised benefits incorporates periodic updates to the latest projections of survival rates, and as a result the system's revenue needs can be adjusted to maintain benefits should the projections show unexpectedly high survival rates. But the unexpected nature of the gains in longevity continuously raise the specter of a system that is out of control. Finally, unexpected longevity makes individual financial planning for later life very difficult. This is one reason that the "life-cycle" theory of saving during the working years and spending savings in retirement (Ando & Modigliani, 1963) did not fit the facts. Because of the financial uncertainties of later life, a large proportion of elders are reluctant to spend their savings and indeed continue to save in retirement. But with increasing longevity and the costs of health care and long-term care that are a prevalent part of the lives of most people in the oldest-old category, even with prudent management, more elders can be expected to outlive their contingency reserves. And with the current climate of public opinion against any kind of taxes for public expenditures, the prospects seem dismal that national, state, or local governments will provide secure financial back-up for the oldest-old who need it. Thus, economic uncertainty is another important part of the uncertain experience of being part of the oldest-old in the future.

Anxiety and depression are likely outcomes of both the chronic disabilities, especially those accompanied by physical pain, that often occur among people in their 90s or people age 100 or over and the uncertain life structure, social roles, and financial well-being of these people. Our mental health "system" is currently in disarray and in the process of rapid contraction. How can this system be expected to be able, much less willing, to respond to the special needs of the oldest-old?

One way to reduce uncertainty is to take control over one's own death. As the proportion of oldest-old increases dramatically, programs of planned suicide and assisted suicide may also increase. Right now, there are no accepted social arrangements for permissible suicide, and this is perhaps another area where social structure could be expected to emerge over the next decades.

One thing seems certain. The amazing growth in the oldest age categories is bound to bring a variety of changes.

The Longevity Revolution and Social Change

In addition to some of the cultural patterns mentioned in the previous section, the longevity revolution can be expected to change our cultural definitions, influence family structure, exert pressures to change our rules about employment and retirement, change our concepts about disability and its relation to aging, and inspire new maps of the life course.

Already we are having difficulty separating the older population into meaningful categories. In the 1950s and 1960s all older Americans tended to be lumped together into the older population. In the 1970s, Bernice Neugarten (1974) and others (Cain, 1974; Harris, 1978) began to speak of the young-old and the old-old. Then came the young-, middle-, and old-old (Atchley, 1985). Then we had a flurry of program initiatives concerning the oldest-old, the "frail" old and the "vulnerable" old.

Our statistics tend to group the older population into five-year age intervals, usually beginning at age 65 because that was the most common retirement age historically. The young-old are defined as those age 65–74, the middle-old are those age 75–84, and the old-old are those age 85 and over. There are many differences in the life situations of people age 85 compared to people age 105, yet they are all lumped together into the old-old in many analyses. Indeed, very few analyses consider detailed age breakdowns within the older population at all.

With retirement ages dropping closer to age 60, the old convention of beginning the older population at age 65 is questionable. When the general public discusses age, the language used refers to decades: people are in their 60s, 70s, 80s, 90s, or are centenarians. This simple approach has as much merit as the program-driven definitions we have been using in gerontology, and it has the virtue of separating the older population into at least five categories.

In addition to developing language to differentiate the older population into meaningful chronological categories, we have also developed concepts of frailty and vulnerability to differentiate the older population with more disability and less reserve capacity from those whose bodies and minds are basically sound, if somewhat creaky and occasionally muddled. As we learn more about vulnerability and frailty, the language we use to discuss these issues will be elaborated, giving us more jargon (excuse me, technical language) to teach and learn. Kidding aside, these conceptual refinements could be an important and necessary tool for targeting services in a nation that includes 2.5 million centenarians.

Our cultural definitions concerning later life are not merely statistical or practical matters. Because the concept of old age is tied to certain moral entitlements to aid in our societal moral framework, if we do nothing to change our definitions of old age, then we could be overwhelmed by the responsibilities imposed by our moral system as a result of the longevity revolution. At the very least we need to begin clearly to separate the concept of retirement as a life stage from the concept of old age as a life stage (Atchley, 1994). The retired do not usually need help nearby, the old do. People in their late 80s and older are much more likely to have the culturally defined characteristics of old age as a life stage than are people in their 60s or 70s. The current practice of combining age and functional definitions of need for service will become more prevalent, and we may reach the point that very few benefits apart from retirement income go to those who are simply chronologically old. Of course, the longevity revolution may be used to call into question our moral commitment to health and social care for the old. This is occurring now; what will it be like when we have 32 times more centenarians and more than 5 times more people age 85 and over? Draconian rationing could be a real possibility (see Callahan, 1987). Finally, euthanasia for social reasons rather than for mercy is a frightening possibility that should cause us all to remain alert.

The longevity revolution will also have a profound effect on the generational structure of families and the capacity of families to meet the needs of older members. Bengtson, Rosenthal, and Burton (1990) called attention to the emerging family structure of four and five generations, with each generation containing fewer members than in the past. In ethnic groups and social classes in which early marriage and/or childbearing is the norm, the longevity revolution could result in families with as many as eight generations. For example, in a family in which the members bear children at around age 15, a 107-year-old could be expected to have great-great-great-great-great-grandchildren. It boggles the mind. In the middle class, with its increasing age of childbearing, the number of generations will be much smaller. For example, for families that bear children at 28, to get to five generations the oldest generation would be aged 112.

Family ties in America have both morally compulsory and voluntaristic qualities. There is no doubt that a majority of adults provide care to parents who need it. However, obligations to grandparents and certainly obligations to great-grandparents may be seen as ambiguous and as voluntaristic. This could become significant when a very old person's adult children are themselves disabled. For example, with a generational interval in the family of 25 years, a person age 105 could need assistance from an adult child who is 80. The longevity revolution could drastically reduce the predictability of family support to a very old, frail elder. Centenarians have a high probability of outliving their spouses and even their adult children.

The longevity revolution could also have profound effects on the rules governing employment and retirement. If the population of oldest-old gradually comes to be viewed as the older population of concern, then the population under age 75 could experience increasingly conflicting economic pressures with regard to employment and retirement. To keep pension and health care financing systems solvent, the pressure will be on continued employment in order to maintain a larger base of people paying payroll taxes. On the other hand, continued high unemployment among young and middle-aged adults exerts strong pressure to retire older adults (workers in their 50s or older). Ageism and age discrimination are firmly rooted in our culture and our efforts to reduce them through legislation and education have thus far proved ineffective, which means that elders will in all likelihood continue to be at a disadvantage in labor markets. The most likely scenario, in my opinion, is an employment pattern in which younger adults and workers over age 50 are concentrated in jobs with low pay and benefits, with workers age 35–50 holding the most desirable jobs. Because our systems of financial support for retirement are becoming increasingly problematic, more elders will be forced to stay in the labor market, often in less desirable jobs. Even though retirement from "career jobs" may occur in the early 60s, many elders will remain in the labor force well into their 70s and some into their 80s or 90s.

The longevity revolution may also shift the moral justification for retirement. Morally, retirement has been justified on several grounds. First, retirement was historically justified in terms of providing income to people who were no longer physically or mentally able to work. Second, the labor movement, in particular, justified retirement as deferred wages. Kohli (1987) pointed out that in the "work society" in which all benefits are tied to employment, not all of a worker's compensation comes in the form of current wages. Part of the worker's compensation comes in the form of pension credits. Third, retirement can be justified as an *earned right*. The pension credits generated as a part of employment allow workers to legitimately choose retirement as a reward for their service in the economy. Fourth, retirement is justified on the grounds that in a work society with a limited number of jobs, there is a need to connect people with jobs, which means that people who have had jobs for a long time have an obligation to move aside to provide opportunities to new people coming into the labor market. In this conception, retirement is a societal good, and this justifies spending public resources on retirement pensions. Of these justifications, the image of elders as being hard pressed by the physical and mental demands of employment is perhaps the most compelling. As active life expectancy has increased well beyond the traditional retirement ages, there has been increasing discussion of whether retirement of capable elders can be justified. The point seems to be that as long as the economy is generating huge economic surpluses, we can afford to provide socially adequate public retirement benefits to relatively young retirees, but when the economy sours and pressures on public revenues increase, spending increasingly scarce tax dollars on public retirement benefits to capable persons who are still in middle age is seen as potentially unjustified. This is an example of situation ethics at the national level.

The longevity revolution will also call into question our concepts about disability. Right now, the public conception of the oldest-old involves significant disability. What will happen to this image if the proportion of able elders increases substantially among the oldest-old? We are currently ambivalent about providing rehabilitation to people in their 70s, in part because of the idea that these people do not have enough life remaining to justify the expense. But what happens when we realize that a 75-year-old may be around for another 30 years or so? Is it to our advantage to rehabilitate a disabled individual in order to eliminate or significantly reduce the expense of long-term care? Probably. However, the sheer number of disabled elders who could benefit from rehabilitation could swamp our capacity to provide it, and the result could be a de facto rationing system, probably tied to age.

A major question mark concerns the future course of dementia in the older population. At current age-specific rates, Alzheimer's disease and related dementias are very prevalent among the oldest-old and prevalence increases with age even within this population. If medicine succeeds in developing prevention or treatment of dementia, the positive effect on the life situation of most people age 85 or older could be enormous. The impact on the social definition of what it means to be very old could also be significant.

The longevity revolution could also produce better definitions of life course paths beyond age 85. Just as the increasing prevalence of retirees who were living out various alternatives helped to crystallize our cultural images of what retirement could be, both positive and negative, so the increased numbers of people creating life structures at very old ages could bring the potentials and liabilities of these life stages into better focus.

All of the changes discussed in the previous sections represent opportunities for research. Speculation is a good source for research questions. The nature of the changes brought on by the longevity revolution also has implications for how we think about research on aging.

The Longevity Revolution and Research on Aging

As the characteristics of the older population change and as the process of aging extends to a significantly farther time horizon, we will need to begin to think about research on adult development and aging in some new ways. The longevity revolution has important implications for how we think about adult development, social structure in relation to aging, social processes such as communication and politics, and social change in relation to aging.

GERONTOLOGICAL RESEARCH

The most widely-used theory of adult development and aging takes a linear, incremental, deterministic approach (Erikson, Erikson, & Kivnick, 1986). However, given the levels of uncertainty about physical and mental capability among the oldest-old, we need to devise theories that can provide effective diagnostic tools for describing development in those stages of life and at the same time allow for uncertain inputs and outcomes. Levinson's life structure theory (1990) and Atchley's continuity theory (1989, 1993) both are constructed as feedback systems theories that allow a great deal of flexibility within a general framework.

If development is seen as the continued evolution of adaptive capacity, then development could be expected to continue to the very end of life. However, almost no attention has been paid to the unique developmental challenges of extreme old age. The effort here should probably begin with carefully designed descriptive studies on successive cohorts of people living at the oldest ages. For example, how does being age 100–105 in 1995 differ from being age 100–105 in 1985 or 1975?

Given the enormous amount of variation in capabilities and circumstances within the oldest-old population, shifting the research emphasis away from studies designed to look at control and prediction toward studies designed to support understanding and adaptation makes sense. Deterministic theories and models have not worked well even for the young-old.

SOCIOLOGICAL RESEARCH

The longevity revolution also has numerous implications for how we study social structure. For example, how does the functioning of social support networks change as individuals move from their 80s to their 90s to over age 100? How does community involvement change as people move through the oldest ages? Does extreme old age effectively isolate elders from involvement in groups and organizations?

The increased span of the older population could reduce the capacity for communication within the older population itself. Is there a diversity of meanings attached to the language used by various age cohorts? How might this affect the advocacy process?

If we see social structure as a negotiated order (Buckley, 1967), then the exchange resources the oldest-old bring to their social interactions will be an important research question. Does the public see anything of value in potential social exchange with the oldest-old? The answer we get to this question today may be very different from the answer we get in the year 2020.

POLITICAL SCIENCE RESEARCH

To the extent that decentralization of political decisions is associated with a rise in the influence of various forms of prejudice, the politics of the future could combine with the longevity revolution to produce a very adversarial political situation for the oldest-old. In addition, the situation could vary widely from state to state. For example, as the numbers of very old people increase dramatically, the struggle over the right of the oldest-old to drive an automobile could become ugly. The danger is that these decisions will be based more on age prejudice than on research data.

The longevity revolution could also produce intergenerational conflict within the older population. The resources available to meet the needs of older people have almost no chance of keeping up with the rapid increases in the population. Resources per capita will shrink. This may spark conflict among different need factions within the older population.

This catalog represents the barest hint of the richness of research topics connected to the longevity revolution. It may seem that we have plenty of time to organize ourselves to address these issues, but to understand the effects of the longevity revolution we need to begin our research *now*.

Summary

Demographic projections of the older population clearly predict a revolution in longevity in which increasingly large cohorts enter the older population and survive to very old ages in increasingly large numbers. From 1990 to 2020, the probability of surviving from age 65 to age 95 will nearly double. From 1990 to 2050 the number of elders age 85 and over is expected to increase more than 5 times over and the number of centenarians is expected to increase more than 32-fold. And these projections probably underestimate the numbers who will actually survive. In all likelihood, by 2050 there will be more than 26 million Americans aged 85 and older and they will represent about 5% of the total population. Of that 26 million, more than 2.5 million will be centenarians. This enormous shift in age structure within the population will have profound social repercussions.

The growth in population at the oldest ages will dramatically increase the diversity within the older population with respect to the prevalence of chronic disease and functional disability, the variety of living arrangements, long-term care needs, and income security. The direction of most of these trends is toward greater ambiguity and uncertainty.

The longevity revolution will increase the horizon for making life course plans but as yet there is no clear cultural map for identifying the life course choices available at the oldest ages. The oldest-old will be forced to adapt without much help from our culture. Uncertainties will stem from poor definitions of the roles appropriate for the oldest-old, the challenges of combining the need for control over one's own life with the need for assistance, and poor anticipation of the longevity revolution by our systems for financing retirement and health care. These uncertainties may increase the incidence of anxiety and depression among the oldest-old.

The longevity revolution will also challenge how we think about aging. Our customary ways of categorizing various chronological or functional segments of the older population may need to be refined. We may also be forced to revisit our moral and ethical beliefs about such issues as the justification for retirement and entitlement to health or social care.

Changes in the structure of the family coupled with the longevity revolution may cause family caregiving environments to become more problematic for the oldest-old, who will have a greater likelihood of outliving their spouses or adult children. How grandchildren or great-grandchildren will respond to dependency needs of the oldest-old within the family remains to be seen.

The longevity revolution may also call into question the institutional arrangements that currently support retirement for the population younger than age 85. If active life expectancy continues to increase, then the moral justification of retirement that comes from the notion of providing income to people who are no longer physically or mentally able to work could be gradually eroded. At the same time, unless we find effective ways to change attitudes and beliefs about the negative effects of aging on employability and to enforce age discrimination legislation, ageism and age discrimination cannot be expected to diminish. As a result, the young- and middle-old may be forced by circumstances to remain in an increasingly hostile labor market.

The longevity revolution may also alter our views about the efficacy of rehabilitation for the disabled. As the number of years that a person must endure disability increases, the perceived benefits of rehabilitation may also increase.

The longevity revolution can also be expected to have significant implications for research on aging. The uncertainties of extreme old age should lead us in the direction of process theories of adult development that allow for more flexible, less deterministic outcomes. At the same time, models aimed at control and prediction of development are likely to collapse under the weight of the enormous variation to be found at extreme old age.

All of our current approaches to studying the relationship between aging and social structure, social process, and social change will have to be reexamined in light of the dramatic changes in life circumstances in the oldest-old population and in the structure of the older population itself.

References

Ando, A., & Modigliani, F. (1963). The life-cycle hypothesis of saving. *American Economic Review, 53*, 55–84.

Atchley, R. C. (1983). *Aging: Continuity and change*. Belmont, CA: Wadsworth.

Atchley, R. C. (1985) *Social forces and aging* (4th ed.). Belmont, CA: Wadsworth.

Atchley, R. C. (1989). A continuity theory of normal aging. *The Gerontologist, 29,* 183-190.

Atchley, R. C. (1993). Continuity theory and the evolution of activity in later adulthood. In J. R. Kelly (Ed.), *Activity and Aging* (pp. 5-16). Newbury Park, CA: Sage.

Atchley, R. C. (1994). *Social forces and aging* (7th ed.). Belmont, CA: Wadsworth.

Bengtson, V. L., Rosenthal, C., & Burton, L. (1990). Families and aging: Diversity and heterogeneity. In R. H. Binstock & L. K. George (Eds.), *Handbook of Aging and the Social Sciences* (3rd ed.). (pp. 263-287). New York: Academic Press.

Buckley, W. (1967). *Sociology and modern systems theory*. Englewood Cliffs, NJ: Prentice-Hall.

Cain, L. D., Jr. (1947). The growing importance of legal age in determining the status of the elderly. *The Gerontologist, 14,* 176-174.

Callahan, D. F. (1987). *Setting limits: Medical goals in an aging society*. New York: Simon & Schuster.

Coward, R. T., Cutler, S. J., & Schmidt, F. E. (1989). Differences in the household composition of elders by age, gender, and area of residence. *The Gerontologist, 29,* 814-821.

Erikson, E. H., Erikson, J. M., & Kivnick, H. Q. (1986). *Vital involvement in old age*. New York: W. W. Norton.

Fries, J. F. (1980). Aging, natural death, and the compression of morbidity. *New England Journal of Medicine, 300,* 354-359.

Harris, C. S. (1978). *Fact book on aging*. Washington, DC: National Council on the Aging.

Kohli, M. (1987). Retirement and the moral economy: An historical interpretation of the German case. *Journal of Aging Studies, 1,* 125-144.

Kunkel, S. R., & Applebaum, R. A. (1992). Estimating the prevalence of long-term disability for an aging society. *Journal of Gerontology, 47,* S253-S260.

Langer, E., & Rodin, J. (1976). The effects of enhanced personal responsibility for the aged: A field experiment in an institutional setting. *Journal of Personality and Social Psychology, 34,* 191-198.

Levinson, D. J. (1990). A theory of life structure development in adulthood. In C. N. Alexander & E. J. Langer (Eds.), *Higher stages of human development* (pp. 35-53). New York: Oxford University Press.

Manton, K. G., Corder, L. S., & Stallard, E. (1993). Estimates of change in chronic disability and institutional incidence and prevalence rates in the U.S. elderly population from the 1982, 1984, and 1987 National Long-Term Care Survey. *Journal of Gerontology, 48*, S153–S166.

Markus, H., & Nurius, P. (1986). Possible selves. *The American Psychologist, 41*, 954–969.

National Center for Health Statistics. (1989). The National Nursing Home Survey: 1985 summary for the United States. *Vital and Health Statistics* (Series 13, No. 97). Washington, DC: U. S. Government Printing Office.

Neugarten, B. L. (1974). Age groups in American society and the rise of the young-old. In F.R. Eisele (Ed.), *Political consequences of aging* (pp. 187–98). Philadelphia: American Academy of Political and Social Sciences.

Rogers, R. G., Rogers, A., & Belanger, A. (1989). Active life among the elderly in the United States: Multistate life-table estimates and population projections. *Milbank Quarterly, 67*, 370–411.

Ruhm, C. J. (1990). Career jobs, bridge employment, and retirement. In P. B. Doeringer (Ed.), *Bridges to retirement: older workers in a changing labor market* (pp. 92–107). Ithaca, NY: ILR Press.

Schulz, J. H. (1992). *The economics of aging* (5th ed.). New York: Auburn House.

United States Bureau of the Census. (1992). Population projections of the United States, by age, sex, race, and Hispanic origin. *Current population reports* (Series P-25, No. 1092). Washington, DC: U. S. Government Printing Office.

Chapter 3

Taking a Longer View: Sociological Perspectives on Longer Life

Jon Hendricks

Picture this: It is the second quarter of the next century and the annual meeting of the Gerontological Society of America is being held in Hayward, the largest city in mainland California. A panel of bright young social gerontologists has been convened to discuss the topic: "Why Our Forebearers Failed to Anticipate the Social Consequences of an Extended Life Cycle." The moderator introduces the topic by asking why, with medical breakthroughs always bearing the foreshadowing of themselves, did not the gerontologists of the late 20th century begin to anticipate the social consequences of what is now an "established fact"?

Undoubtedly everyone sitting there that day might contribute something about how their elderly dissertation advisor had remarked that when the century was ending he or she had been part of a team that had focused on a harbinger of the current issue. Fantasy aside, there have been few projects addressing increasing longevity, and those there were seldom had much salience. Other than the Jarvik (1978) volume published in the late 1970s, that decade paid little heed. In the 1980s, Neugarten and Maddox (1980a) edited the behavioral and social sciences portion of a National Institute of Health research plan called *Our Future Selves*, which enjoyed some currency but passed from view far too soon. When seen in retrospect, that report contained some seminal recommendations for reshaping the research agenda of social gerontology and our conceptual approach to living longer. Despite improved vigor among older persons, the need for a broad range of supportive and restorative services was forecast for the years after the turn of the century. One of the real contributions of the report came through a series of subtle challenges to how the aging process is conceptualized. A simple question will make the point: Is there much in our theorizing in social gerontology about life course transitions that is independent of people's involvement in other institutional spheres? Elsewhere I have noted that the way we conceive of life's script cannot help but color everything else we say about it (Hendricks, 1984). If all we have to say about old age derives from the existence of federal laws and a variety of entitlement programs, will anything social gerontologists assert be taken as more than journalistic reflection?

Some of the contentions made in the Neugarten and Maddox (1980a) volume are helpful for thinking about how our theorizing and our research can accommodate the future. The authors were almost alone in recognizing that continuous revisions in what we provide, how we provide it, and how we think about the target population will be necessary and far different as we move into the next century and longer living populations. They asserted, and rightly so, that social gerontology must be more analytic, less descriptive, and more innovative in its conceptual approaches if social gerontologists are to make a difference.

Obviously some solace for the lack of foresight can be found in the fact that 100,000 years of history have witnessed little change in the maximum life span but, as Richard Cutler (1975) pointed out twenty years ago, that doesn't mean the potential did not change. Cutler asserted that an increase in the number of cortical neurons is concomitant to an increase in the life span of a species (he used the phrase *maximum life span potential*); meaning, as our species has become smarter it has also been living longer. The late George Sacher made a similar point and was unequivocal when he asserted that the brain may be the central organ of longevity (Sacher, 1978). Both Cutler and Sacher were speaking as life scientists, but the relevance of their point pertains equally to the behavioral sciences.

If some predictions based in molecular biology are correct, we may be on the verge of breakthroughs that will make it possible for tomorrow's children to celebrate their 100th birthdays (Prentice, 1989). Assuming it is true, realistically it will still take the better part of a century, at least 85–100 years, for patterns of mortality to change for the population as a whole (Olshansky, Carnes, & Cassel, 1993). Though elusive, the recognition that what kills people is not aging per se, but rather age-related diseases, is itself news. Whether these diseases are genetic, environmental, or have some other type of etiology remains a matter of some debate. Although there are no magic bullets that will strike down the things that kill us, there may be prospects for real gains, nonetheless. As work advances on any of the possible fronts, the potential will also be there to improve the quality of life; the question that remains is whether we can in fact do so (Cassel & Neugarten, 1991; Palmore, 1986). Breakthroughs and optimism in one realm do not automatically lead to breakthroughs or optimism in another and the challenge will be to extend the number of years of active life.

As we move through the 1990s, the prospects for a longer life is being debated on the front pages of *The New York Times*, the *Los Angeles Times*, and other mainstream and mass circulation publications. A great deal of attention has been focused on the species' genetic potential. Yet, as is frequently pointed out, genetics explain only about 2%–3% of the variance in life expectancy. That genetics per se does not explain much about long-term survivability should not be too surprising. In times gone by, so few people survived into old age that there was little opportunity for genetic selection to play itself out. Now that people are living longer, it is still the case that the most important factors for survival may not become relevant until after reproductive potential has been realized. With this being so, how could longevity be selected for by natural evolution? It may be, however, that pleiotropic genes—those implicated in more than a single biological process—that are operative earlier in life may have secondary and beneficial effects for survival. If the contention that genetics does not explain a significant amount of the variation in longevity is not an invitation to behavioral scientists to contribute to the debate, then I have never seen one. In fact, Gavrilov and Gavrilova (1991), among others, asserted in their discussion of the biology of the human life span that attitudinal and behavioral factors play a major role in explaining why rates of improvement in life expectancy have slowed in recent years and why any possible gains that appear on the horizon will be linked to behavioral factors.

Substrates and Social Outcomes

Is extending life a medical, social, or political process? As social gerontologists discuss the prospects of a dramatic increase in life expectancy, one of the pressing questions with which we must deal is, How will the explanatory frameworks employed reflect the changes? A corollary to that basic question is, Who should participate in the discussion of possible consequences—either positive or negative? What if medical progress does make it possible to extend the average life expectancy to close to the century mark? Will other facets of our lives benefit equally?

In *Extending Life, Enhancing Life: A National Research Agenda on Aging* (Lonergan, 1991), published on behalf of the National Institute of Medicine, an attempt was made to establish priorities to meet the needs of a growing population of very old individuals, those over the age of 85. As one assays that compendium, one of its most notable features is the absence of any rethinking of ways to approach the "problem." Behavioral scientists are no less culpable than any other group and share the responsibility for providing new perspectives; we have a great deal to offer. To do so, however, we must rethink our understanding of our own explanatory frameworks. First on the agenda is the need to explore the ways our frameworks are themselves reflections of societal involvements hinged to current life expectancies.

Early in the 18th century, Benjamin Gompertz formulated a mathematical model to predict age-adjusted mortality rates for use in his insurance business. So exact were his projections that until recently his theoretical doublings every 8 years of the number of people from a given cohort who will die in the interval have been the standard against which theories of mortality are measured. The mortality curve Gompertz plotted has remained surprisingly accurate for most of the adult life span. What sometimes gets lost, however, is the fact that the gains in survival rates we have seen have come about primarily among infants, children, and women of childbearing age. Over the years the shape of the curve has not changed much, only the slope has been pushed back some. For additional gains to be evident, some new inroads will have to be made. Relying on recognized statistical techniques, Olshansky, Carnes, and Cassel (1990) asserted a 55% decline in mortality from all causes would have to be realized for life expectancy at birth to reach 85 years. When gender is taken into account, females will need to realize a 50% reduction while among males a 70% decline would have to occur. To reach an average life expectancy at birth of 100 years, an overall reduction on the order of 85% would have to occur at every age. Prior to age 30, death rates would have to approach zero for significant long-term gains to come about. These same authors point out, however, that it is hardly reasonable to expect everyone to adopt lifestyles free of most known risk factors. It does not take much perspicacity to begin to see why many experts assert that social science has a major role to play.

Nevertheless, we are on the verge of a society in which most of those who are born will live long enough to become old. Many of the acute conditions that used to afflict people in the first few years of their lives are under some semblance of control in the industrialized world. The next great task is to come to grips with chronic conditions. We have postponed the age at which degenerative diseases take their toll, but not the toll they ultimately take. Nor have we postponed them equally for all segments of society. Obviously two questions emerge. The first concerns why any improvements are unlikely to be equally distributed. The second is more global. Were such a change to occur, and extensions to the second half of life to take place, how would we, as social scientists, conduct meaningful research into the aftermath?

The substrate mechanisms are far more complicated than the lay public realizes. As we prolong life, will morbidity be compressed or expanded? With added years, it may only be that age-related debilitating diseases will have sufficient time to manifest symptoms (Olshansky, Carnes, & Cassel, 1993). If disability and limitation await, who among us will want the "benefit" of a longer life? However, even if small increments are realized, imagine the actuaries and the insurance companies trying to manage their liabilities and annuities to strengthen their reserves in the face of beneficiary populations 2 to 5 times greater than today's (Olshansky, Carnes, & Cassel, 1993). Imagine medical schools dealing with a whole new client population, with emergent patterns of morbidity and mortality, or imagine the health care industry facing health expenses some have estimated might be as high as $1.6 trillion annually (in 2002) with annual expenses per employee of $8,500 (Modern Healthcare, 1992). Imagine, too, private enterprise responding to consumer potentials. Wilford Brimley touting Quaker Oats while driving postholes will be just the tip of the iceberg.

Now, imagine the role of social science research. What do we have to contribute? How might we adapt and, more important, how will our explanatory frameworks have to change?

We know about the compression of morbidity that might be accomplished given recent medical advances (Fries, 1984). But what if medical science makes its breakthroughs and all we net is an extension of the period of dependency? That is, we live longer but not necessarily in better health. The social policy implications of any gains in life expectancy are staggering and mere tinkering will not serve society well. In light of what Riley (1990) referred to as "structural lag," wherein changes in individuals' lives occur more rapidly than social institutions can adapt, the prospect for human suffering becomes palpable. Crews (1993) pointed out that the rectangularization of the survival curve has outstripped cultural definitions of the elderly and attitudes toward them. With this asynchrony, the game of catch-up will be waged at the expense of human suffering and much hand-wringing about the shortsightedness of the national agenda. On a global scale, the pressures will be even greater than in the industrialized world alone because the most dramatic increases in populations of older persons are going to occur in countries just entering a period of industrialization. If the resources available to them do not keep pace with the growth of their populations, it is likely the hue and cry will be heard beyond the benign realm of diplomacy and international aid and may have devastating potential.

What will daily life be like? Does it make sense to say it will be essentially the same then as it is today? Should we look to technology and other interventions to have immediate and visible effects on lifestyles? Like medical breakthroughs, the so-called labor-saving devices of the second half of the 20th century were heralded for the liberation they promised. We remain in a quandary, however, over how much they actually delivered and to whom. Whatever their role in our personal lives, are any changes in longevity likely to alter what we have heretofore referred to as a person's *productive life*? Will the portions of the human life cycle that were historically devoted to any given set of tasks, be they education, childbearing and child-rearing, work life, retirement, and so on, be indexed to gains and changed only as a function of those changes, or will they be fundamentally altered and recast? There are other pressing questions as well, questions of social policy and social practice.

A Peek in the Crystal Ball

There are questions aplenty. My focus, however, is confined to what social gerontologists need to think about in terms of restructuring our conceptual perspectives. There are very real questions about what attitudinal changes must occur and how those changes can be effected. But to answer the questions, social scientists need to move beyond thinking about the life course as a series of definite phases. Will age be as relevant to the way society is organized if these extensions are realized? Under one possible scenario age discrimination could become a more serious problem. Under another set of circumstances, as Neugarten (1982) suggested, the problem might go away, either because the population structure will grow top-heavy or because age per se will not play as definitive a role as it has in the past. Either way, the route between birth and grave is likely to change its course, much the way a river does when the distance traversed and rate of descent change together. Social scientists face the need for sweeping reformulations.

To make sense of the potential impact increased longevity will bring, we must assume that as researchers our own productive lives will be extended and our research opportunities expanded accordingly. Beyond that, other assertions are equally plausible. I, for one, am assuming that the individualistic philosophy that is part and parcel of the moral economy that undergirds our worldview and that has characterized our approach to problem solving and social policy to date is not going to vanish overnight whether people are living longer or not. One outcome of this assertion is that long-lived elderly, or their families, may be expected to shoulder an even greater part of the responsibility for their own well-being. Unfortunately, one of our value structure's assumptions is that hardships are spread equally across the entire life course and are no more likely to settle at one point than another. Historically, although exceptions have been granted for children, an inability to cope with hardship has been interpreted as evidence of personal shortcomings. Of course, the paradox of stipulating age limits for certain forms of social participation and the consequent reduced availability of resources for dealing with life's troubles is usually underplayed. As we contemplate increased life expectancy we must assume that all social institutions will be fundamentally restructured to accommodate the changes.

To make sense of what people encounter, we must understand how individual lives are intertwined with social institutions. Riley (1993) employed the term *dynamism* to refer to the interrelationship between individual life courses and structural features of our society. Her point is evident if we consider what life extension will mean for social institutions.

Take education for example: Will it make sense to have all education compressed into the first quarter of life? Using current averages there is a 50 year interval between the age at which most people leave the classroom and the time they go to their graves. The array of possibilities for altering the way education can be delivered has yet to be realized. What might some of the options be? Begin later and extend longer; attain basic competencies with lifelong reinforcement opportunities; provide nonstop education with sequential foci; retrain for replacement career tracks at some intermediate point or even at multiple points; mix liberal arts and professional-vocational educational opportunities throughout the decades; or even leave things as they have been to nurture scarce resources. Then there is the question of what to do with dropouts in the face of life extensions. Think for a moment about the compounding effect dropping out will have. Just as the world's economy will have an effect on labor practices and job prospects, so, too, will it have an impact on education. Knowledge will be globally based and arrayed competitively, so dropping out will cease to be simply a local issue. Nationally, basic skill levels will have to be upgraded at regular intervals lest the work force of any particular country fall behind in international competition. Computational and information management skills provide a ready illustration of skills which must be refreshed at increasingly frequent intervals.

What about marriage and family life? On the one hand, there is a genuine possibility of multigenerational families—with all their attendant stress and support possibilities. On the other hand, should we assume that because people are living longer families are remaining intact longer? Divorce already claims two-thirds of all first marriages and brings a realignment of family responsibilities that social scientists of a generation ago would have had a hard time imagining. If families do remain together, what responsibilities will be assigned to each generation? With families available, social integration may be sustained for older people for far longer than it might be if families are sundered or absent due to disruption. Of course there is a flip side to the family picture. Insightful investigators are saying that what has emerged already is a mid- to late-life pattern of divorce due in part to the fact that marriages are surviving the departure of the last child, enduring long enough for the partners to want to seek alternatives. Living up to 100 years is not going to reduce that tendency. In fact, what may happen is that serial marriages could become the norm. What about the children? If children leave and come back, do extensions in life expectancy imply that they might leave again and come back again several times over? Then there is the question, Who helps whom when both parent and child are over 65? Another facet of the same question is locating responsibility. Should people be held personally accountable for providing for their own old age? Perhaps a "particularistic" focus should replace the "universalistic" focus that has characterized programs for the aging heretofore (Shindul-Rothschild & Williamson, 1991).

The workaday world may pose questions which are certainly as complex as family issues. It is quite possible that men who are nearing retirement in the 1990s may represent the passing of a normative pattern that became institutionalized over the course of the 20th century. It requires a greater leap of faith to assume things will remain constant than it does to predict something different. No one should be nonchalant about the growth in service-sector employment and what it spells for retirement. Already, over 50% of the workers of today work in the service sector. As jobs in service industries grow, agricultural and manufacturing jobs will continue to wane, as they have been throughout the 20th century. Educational requirements will shift, wage structures will decline, career tracks may be foreshortened, and a lifelong series of dead-end jobs may become the norm. Whether the same is true for the information processing industry is debatable, but many experts forecast a compression of most occupational hierarchies.

Another work-related question facing society as a whole is, When do people retire? At the traditional age, an age established when relatively few people lived long enough to retire? Or should retirement slide 10 or 20 or more years to a nice round number of, say, 85? Maybe the whole framework should be abandoned and functional criteria imposed instead of chronological age. If so, behavioral scientists will face the Herculean task of developing new operational definitions not only of old age but for many job-related transitions that presage retirement and denote passage. If we alter retirement we most likely alter occupational mobility as well. If retirement shifts to a later age, what happens to occupational mobility for younger workers? Are new hires confined to their initial entry-level position for 30 years while they await openings on higher rungs of an already compressed organizational ladder? With the growth of employment in service industries, upward mobility may not be such a pressing issue after all. Then too, vast numbers of people working at an array of numbing jobs for minimum wage portends a far different retirement experience for individuals and for society as a whole, than the vision held by the original Social Security legislation. Add to the experiential changes to retirement a vastly different funding base from the historic Social Security and pension system, and new concerns proliferate rapidly. On the one hand, people may look forward to exiting the labor force as early as possible. On the other, a flat and relatively low wage profile may make it necessary to delay exit as long as feasible in order to underwrite Social Security payments when they do begin. Factor into the equation the global distribution of assets, and the negotiation process for worker benefits promises to become far more complicated than it is presently.

By 2020 over half of all workers in the industrial countries will be middle aged and older. (Whatever demographic transitions occur in the United States, or any of the other industrialized countries, they will be dwarfed by changes in developing countries.) The question will be, Can the domestic economy absorb that many older workers? At a time when free trade agreements are being hotly debated, and global free trade zones touted as an economic boon for international commerce—witness the existence of the Mexican *maquiladoras*—what awaits a nation of older, more highly paid workers? Without major investments in and reaffirmations of the importance of human capital, the prospects are not immediately enticing. Job obsolescence may portend the need for watershed accommodations as extensions in life expectancy occur. A dedicated young researcher might have opportunities to follow a cohort's movement through any number of career changes. Likely as not, each one will carry a diverse array of fringe benefits linked, in part, to developments elsewhere in the world where comparable tasks could be performed. What if a move offshore is more attractive than employer obligations and the attendant contributions to retirement packages?

There is a concept we rely on a great deal to explain differential situations—the concept of *age status*. As Neugarten and Maddox (1980a) pointed out, it is a multidimensional concept, one that entails control over personal and social resources and the power and prestige that accrue to those who possess valuable resources. What type of age status will accrue to people whose situation is increasingly insecure or openly challenged? A parallel issue is that of age norms. Fundamental changes will occur in the way age norms are defined and the way they affect individuals. We have been fortunate that explicit age norms are more typically the case than not. If a blurring occurs, social scientists will have to rethink the use of that concept to plot transitions and analyze the congruence among potentially diverse social roles. Is asynchronism likely to be more prevalent than presently? As each of these changes occurs how will the life course be depicted? Do we simply tack on to the further reaches of the life course the added years, or will each of the normative stages be expanded or redefined in some other way? In the absence of clear benchmarks stemming from role involvements, it is likely that so fundamental a concept as age norms will become increasingly ambiguous. That is the real meaning of an age-irrelevant society.

These are more than academic questions, they are questions that anticipate a fundamental restructuring in the way we ply social gerontology.

There is also another facet to the implicit question of generational succession and people's anticipation of what the future holds. If future prospects are fraught with insecurities, will people be willing to defer gratification? What would happen if, to accommodate the advances in retirement age, a pattern of regular sabbaticals scattered through the work cycle was implemented and paid? What then becomes of some of our precious definitions of variables like "working," "in-school," "adulthood," or "retirement" and the use of age norms or age status to explain behavior?

The Shape of Things to Come

In contemplating future life extensions we have to ask what will life be like for those over 85. The mix of elderly will be different, there will be far more immigrant elderly, the cohort as a whole will be better educated, more used to dealing with governmental bureaucracies, and in better health than their counterparts of the 1990s. Their needs, their resources, and society's responses, add up to a conundrum that is easier to anticipate than to solve. Unprecedented changes will occur and magnify adaptations that sweeping changes in the experience of old age over the last quarter of the 20th century have already necessitated. One issue not touched on above is, Shall we assume that differentials between female and male life expectancy will continue? There is more to that question than meets the eye; think about the nature of medical breakthroughs and where they are likely to be focused. Think, too, about an even larger population of older women and what that might portend. Gendered consequences are not an insignificant component of anticipating what extensions to life expectancy may bring. Add the prospect that not all ethnic or racial categories may benefit equally and there is further cause for concern.

Traditionally what seems to have happened is that the evaluation of any needy group ebbs and flows in response to the strength of the national economy. During the 1970s, for example, as the economy deteriorated so too did the country's willingness to provide generous benefits to older persons (Shindul-Rothschild & Williamson, 1991). Certainly the "trial balloons" of the 1980s could lead one to surmise that Social Security itself becomes less sacrosanct during difficult economic times. When the economy flows, the legitimacy of groups in need of assistance seems to be readily acknowledged, only to be challenged when an ebb occurs. With these shifts in our notions of moral economy, of what is fair and just, people are redefined and their social worthiness scrutinized in terms of emergent social priorities.

There is no gainsaying the fact that the shape of our lives is inextricably linked to our membership in important social categories. Leading the list are race, gender, and social class—important for their normative patterning and their meaning-giving potential through the social structuring of the life course. Each of these, in turn and in total, colors the way life unfolds (Hendricks, 1993). While we are accustomed to thinking about the role of social context in shaping early life experiences, it is no less relevant in later life. With any significant gain in life expectancy, structural factors are potentially even more significant still (Kohli & Mayer, 1986).

Institutionalized pathways and opportunity structures are the vehicles by which we arrive at old age. Without an understanding of their conveyance we have faint prospect for understanding how old age or very old age will play out. It is these factors that will provide the commonalties of experience and the "normative timetables" of life (Hagestad & Neugarten, 1985; Guillemard, 1982; Featherman, 1986; O'Rand, 1990). As phased transitions occur and are noted, they provide both the medium for and the behavioral outcomes of the process of growing older (Giddens, 1981; Neugarten & Maddox, 1980a; Riley, 1993). Without attempting to understand how each aspect of the process effects how the other components are realized, we are not likely to contribute much in the way of insightful commentary. Riley, Foner, and Waring (1988) made the same contention in their discussion of age stratification theory. What has heretofore been missing is any explicit attention to the process involved in the transitions.

I have previously written about the intertwining of personal resources necessary to ensure successful aging (Hendricks & Hendricks, 1986; Hendricks, 1993). What is needed now is far greater attention to the arraying of those resources among various social categories. An implicit tenet of a resource-based explanation of adjustment is that structural location colors how a person's personal resources are defined. In their volume, *Eighty-Five Plus: The Oldest Old*, Bould, Sanborn, and Reif (1989) utilized their own version of a personal resource model appropriate for maintaining the well-being of a burgeoning population over the age of 85. As they so cogently noted, as resources available to individuals become increasing limited in four distinct areas—physiological, social-familial, personal-psychological, and economic—the problems of living are inevitably compounded. What needs to be stressed, however, is that the process is not merely additive. It is cumulative, to be sure, but the effect of shortfalls are compounded as vital functioning is compromised.

There is no denying that the politics of demography has yet to emerge into mainstream discussions of social problems. Bould, Sanborn, and Reif

(1989) asked a question we will have to face: By extending life are we entering into a social contract that the necessary resources will be made available? Clearly there currently exists a mismatch between the resources needed for maintaining optimal functioning and those available. That there are risks associated with living longer cannot be denied, but we also need to be mindful that present support services and patterns of allocations reflect earlier times and earlier needs. It would be a shame if longer life meant only increased dependence and hardship because our moral economy was rooted in patterns of the past. We know already that advancing age exacerbates risk of poverty and medical indigence. A prevalence rate of 10% for poverty among the young-old climbs—by close to 80%—to 18% among the oldest-old. Among minority populations, the rate may be up to 3 times greater than among the mainstream population. The same is true for women. As they outlive their partners, women's risk of poverty is close to 4 times greater than for their married counterparts. Of course, structural changes in the labor market, both the involvement of women and minorities and the shift to a service-based economy, will alter current patterns but probably will not change the fact that Social Security and Supplemental Security Income make up the vast majority of the income received by the oldest-old.

For the purposes in this chapter, it is important to point out that there is also a mismatch between the consequences of extensions in life expectancy and the way social scientists conceptualize the life course. Let me make the point by example: Transitions into adulthood, middle-age, and old-age, are not merely chronological—we say so all the time. Nonetheless, we customarily use recognized societal benchmarks, celebrated as hallmarks, to denote transition from one phase or status to the next. These benchmarks have been socially constructed and their meanings reflect historical patterns of life expectancy. At the same time, each of these transitions is also linked to other socially salient categories of group membership, something far fewer of us are able to work into our discussions, research designs, and findings. Unless we use event-history analysis, far too often we resort to categorical definitions and manage to sidestep many of the more thorny issues. We have all the evidence needed to say with certainty that the gap between the richest and poorest citizens is widening, and widening not just in terms of income but in terms of fundamental life cycle characteristics such as morbidity (acute and chronic), transitions to old age, dependency, and to any number of less desirable states. If life expectancy is extended will the problems of social class disparity in the way people experience age be compounded as well?

Augmenting the Conceptual Possibilities

One of our major shortfalls as gerontologists is a failure to develop conceptual frameworks that are truly reflective of the life course. We insist on linearity, ordinality, and incremental change because that is what our models handle best. Imagine the changes a life expectancy of 100 years or more will require. Consider for a moment the way we think of middle age. As I read the literature, middle age is defined in terms of role involvements or by losses that occur or are expected to occur—it is the middle of a sandwich with young adulthood on one side and old age on the other (as if either of those two had firm definitions). How can we possibly focus our research if we cannot do better than that? Neugarten and Maddox, in their summary statement in *Our Future Selves* (1980b), asserted that our sociological and social psychological theories have very little real power to explain why some people age well and others do not. I would add that, for the most part, our theories in social gerontology describe what happens when the contexts in which we are embedded change rather than anything about the aging process per se.

Perhaps that is as it should be, or as it must be, insofar as so much of a person's identity is contingent on their being "in-the-world." By itself, recognizing that simple fact may provide a valuable avenue for examining what factors structure the "life-worlds" of older people regardless of how many years they live. Heinz (1991) speaks of the life course as a sequence of status passages differentiated by key socioeconomic conditions (Heinz, 1991, p. 12), which carry "disequilizing" transitions bringing forth new or reconfigured social risks. Hareven and Masako (1988, p. 275) refer to these same transitions as "turning points." Turning points are transformations that require subsequent adjustment, bring forth unintended consequences or crises, or are unanticipated. I would amplify their definition and say that even the anticipated transformations require a reconfiguration of personal resources to regain equilibrium, so they too constitute turning points. With each turning individuals have to realign their behavior, reassess their strengths and weaknesses and reintegrate according to the new order.

Human agency has the potential for mastering the risks that the transformation poses but the converse, failure, is also a possibility. As Stubbs (1989) noted, the resources that serve as signifiers of social relations and age boundaries are the same ones that effect the opportunities for mastery. Thus, as greater portions of the population reach very old age, it will not be chronology or biology that differentiates among them but ability to exert a degree of mastery over their situation. For those whose resources survive along with them, life will have a rosy complexion. Unfortunately, fragmentation and discontinuity are going to exacerbate the disadvantages of being old when resources are in short supply. As Bould, Sanborn, and Reif (1989) pointed out, something happens to octogenarians that spells fundamental change in their ability to exert control over their own lives. If we have a fourth age, must we necessarily have a population of mendicants as well?

With prolongevity, innumerable transformations may yield new status groupings or class categories created as the very old themselves stand apart from cultural or life cycle mainstreams. Changes will be taking place on two levels simultaneously: structural contexts of living and individual life courses. The permutations of these interactive changes revolve around the need to develop a new equilibrium following whatever transformations occur. To the extent that equilibrium and integration are reestablished, parity and a personal sense of recognizable identity will endure. Without reintegration, crises of one type or another will likely develop. Explanations of either the duration or disruption of personal well-being must incorporate a context-based perspective on the transformation—whether it be one or several—and not a pseudo-age-based explanation. The difference will be that the former follows any type of transition, among people of diverse ages and their abilities to reassert control over a new situation through a reconfiguration of the personal resources at their disposal. I would go so far as to assert that definitions of social age are based on exactly these issues.

Conceptualizations of developmental patterns during the adult years have recently received close attention and substantial refurbishing. In the *Encyclopedia of Adult Development and Aging* (Kastenbaum, 1993), the point was made repeatedly that situational involvements deflect whatever intrinsic development imperatives may exist. What is often referred to as adult development may actually be nothing more than a reflection of career and family transitions and other involvements in the world. Put someone in a different social environment and the framework that worked before could be useless in the new culture. As Neugarten and Maddox pointed out, "We need to know a great deal more, therefore, about the significance of both environmental and personality factors. . . ." (Neugarten & Maddox, 1980b, p. 11). In the process of seeking that information we must also be cognizant of the likelihood that comparable events have different effects, depending on the point in the life course at which they occur and the level of functioning on other relevant variables—the interaction is dynamic and highly variable.

Perhaps what we need are new perspectives altogether. The suggestion above by Neugarten and Maddox (1980b) points to some lively possibilities. For example, the introduction of chaos theory into aging research may aid us in our effort to explain why something has one effect at one point in time and a different effect at another time. Increasingly, natural scientists are recognizing that what were previously thought to be chaotic or nonrational actions may in fact be part of an as yet unrecognized pattern. One example may help label the kernel of the idea. Borrowing from Lorenz (1963), natural science has identified a "butterfly effect," which occurs when relatively small actions result in greatly amplified effects which may become apparent if examined carefully enough. Chaos theorists are also attending to "sensitive dependence" on initial circumstances to help explain why phenomena occur very differently than expected following what might have been thought to be an insignificant effect.

Such perspectives need to be infused into the way we think about aging (Schroots, in press). Perhaps there is a place where what is called "emergent computation" can be grafted onto our thinking about the meaning of adulthood in order to better handle what we have previously dealt with as isolated instances of instability or irrationality and closed systems. The expanded perspective can increase our understanding of how contingencies occurring during the middle and later years of life play out.

A related point stemming from the kind of thinking chaos theory is bringing to social science is that in the lives of individuals there are many nonlinear interdependent systems; yet our theorizing and much of our methodology has stressed linearity, incremental change, and limited interaction across units of analysis. Our acceptance and understanding of the whole focus on fractals, dynamic systems theory, catastrophe theory and all the rest, is not the question. The point is, with extensions in life expectancy, events beyond the realm or the ken of individual actors, or events occurring early in the life course, may have relatively greater effect than they presently appear to have because people will live long enough for potential effects to be realized. With the appropriate interpretative framework, the ramifications of some of these possibilities can be made apparent. There can be new potential for intervention, for early warnings to avert late-life crises. Converging all observations toward the mean because of the logic implicit in our statistical models will not, however, yield what we think of as insights. Perhaps attending to the process of transformation, the turning points of life may enable gerontology to intervene in exactly those arenas where crises, disequilibrium, and isolation seem to emerge from a dissipation of personal resources.

Conclusion

In the course of the 20th century there have been sea shifts in the analysis and conceptualization of the nature of the process of aging. The field has come a long way from the "you can't teach an old dog new tricks" dogma of the Freudian era through at least three generations of theorizing (Hendricks, 1992). Along the way gerontology has passed through a number of phases—and with those phases we have also seen shifts in policies, programs, and projected futures. What was once thought set in stone, has become progressively more socially constructed and malleable. The field may be on the verge of another theoretical step forward in understanding the social aspects of aging, in the cognitive sciences in general, and even in the medical sciences. I will stop short of saying basic biological aging mechanisms, be they in our genes, molecular structure, or ubiquitous tumor viruses, shift with the sands of time or place. But stay tuned. Rowe and Kahn (1987) in their oft-cited manuscript in *Science, "Usual and Successful Aging,"* illustrated the way physical, health-related dimensions of aging may actually be tied to a range of socially-based variables. If they are correct, basic mechanisms may themselves be subject to some limited displacement.

To continue to progress, the conceptual enterprise must grapple with the integration of environmental factors, individual attributes, and societal changes—not an easy task. Whether we label it contextualized research, or eschew labels all together, our search for generalizability has impaired our ability to explain very much of the variance we find and often misses individual variation entirely.

Another point to keep in mind about how we conceptualize: Though we like to think we establish our research agenda on the basis of important questions, it is also true that "pocketbook issues" often provide the nucleus of our research endeavors. Even with the extensions to life expectancies being prognosticated, we cannot assume all behavioral scientists will become caregiving researchers, or will focus almost exclusively on the implications of national health insurance. Yet a funding bias towards these particular examples can influence how we investigate dependencies, health status, and so on. The social construction of old age is, in large measure, a result of wide-ranging policy decisions and those decisions must be recognized for the role they play in shaping the research agenda.

If we perpetuate the way social gerontologists think about the middle and later years, and merely extend these periods to cover any gains in life expectancy, we are likely to be faced with quandaries not unlike those we already face. Paradoxically, our very successes in postponing death, combined with our cultural values, may be exactly the forces that set old people apart. We need innovations in the way we think about later life, the factors that influence it, and their relative impact at various turning points along the way, to improve the prospect of aging for our generation and those to come.

References

Bould, S., Sanborn, B., & Reif, L. (1989). *Eight-five plus: The oldest old*. Belmont, CA: Wadsworth.

Cassel, C. K., & Neugarten, B. L. (1991). The goals of medicine in an aging society. In R. H. Binstock & S. G. Post (Eds.), *Too old for health care* (pp. 75-91)., Baltimore: Johns Hopkins University Press.

Crews, D. (1993). Cultural lags in social perceptions of the aged. *Generations, 27,* 91-93.

Cutler, R. G. (1975). Evolution of human longevity and the genetic complexity governing aging rate. *Proceedings of the National Academy of Science, 72,* 4664-4668.

Featherman, D. (1986). Biography, society and history: Individual development as a population process. In A. Sorensen, F. Weinert, & L. Sherrod (Eds.), *Human development and the life course: Multidisciplinary perspectives* (pp. 99-152), Hillsdale, NJ: Erlbaum.

Fries, J. L., (1984). The compression of morbidity: miscellaneous comments about a theme, *The Gerontologist, 24,* 354-359.

Gavrilov, L. A. & Gavrilova, N. S. (1991). *The Biology of Life Span*. London: Harwood.

Giddens, A. (1981). *A contemporary critique of historical materialism: Vol. 1. Power, Property and the State*. London: Macmillan.

Guillemard, A. M. (1982). Old age, retirement, and the social class structure: Toward an analysis of the structural dynamics of the latter stage of life. In T. K. Hareven & K. J. Adams (Eds.), *Aging and life course transitions: An interdisciplinary perspective* (pp. 221-244). London: Tavistock.

Hagestad, G. O., & Neugarten, B. L. (1985). Age and the life course. In R. L. Binstock & E. Shanas (Eds.), *Handbook of aging and the social sciences* (pp. 35-61). New York: Van Nostrand Reinhold.

Hareven, T. K., & Masako, K. (1988). Turning points and transitions: Perceptions of the life course. *Journal of Family History, 13,* 271-289.

Heinz, W. R. (Ed.). (1991). *Status passages and the life course: Vol. 1.Theoretical advances in life course research.*Weinheim, Germany: Beutscher Studien Verlag.

Hendricks, J. (1984). Lifecourse and structure: The fate of the art.*Aging and society, 4,* 93-98.

Hendricks, J. (1992). Generations and the generation of theory in social gerontology. *International Journal of Aging and Human Development, 35,* 31-47.

Hendricks, J. (1993). Social class and adult development. R. Kastenbaum (Ed.), *Encyclopedia of adult development* (pp. 467-472). Phoenix: Oryx.

Hendricks, J., & Hendricks, C. D. (1986). *Aging in mass society: Myths and realities.* Boston: Little, Brown.

Jarvik, L. F. (Ed.). (1978). *Aging into the 21st century: Middle-agers today.* New York: Gardner.

Kastenbaum, R. (1993). *Encyclopedia of adult development.* Phoenix: Oryx.

Kohli, M., & Mayer, J. W. (1986). Social structure and the social construction of the life stages. *Human Development, 29,* 145-156.

Lonergan, E. T. (Ed.), (1991). *Extending life, enhancing life: A national research agenda on aging.*Washington, DC: National Academy Press.

Lorenz, E. N. (1963). Deterministic non-periodic flow.*Journal of Atmospheric Science, 20,* 130-141.

Modern Healthcare (1992, July 27).The hospital of the future. *Modern Healthcare, 22,* (30), 47-65.

Neugarten, B. L. (1982). *Age or need?* Beverly Hills, CA: Sage.

Neugarten, B. L., & Maddox, G. L. (1980a). *Our future selves: a research plan toward understanding aging,* (NIH No. 80-144).Washington, DC: U.S. Government Printing Office.

Neugarten, B. L., & Maddox, G. L., (1980b). Behavioral and social science research. In *Our future selves: Summary reports.*Washington, DC: U.S. Government Printing Office.

Olshansky, S. J., Carnes, B. A., & Cassel, C. K. (1990). In search of Methuselah: Estimating the upper limits to human longevity. *Science, 250,* 634-640.

Olshansky, S. J., Carnes, B. A., & Cassel, C. K. (1993, April).The aging of the human species, *Scientific American,* pp. 46-52.

O'Rand, A. (1990). Stratification and the Life Course. In R. L. Binstock & L. K. George (Eds.), *Handbook of aging and the social sciences* (pp. 130-148). San Diego: Academic Press.

Palmore, E. (1986). Trends in the health of the aged. *The Gerontologist, 26,* 298-302.

Prentice, T. (1989). Slowing down the march of time. *World Press Review, 36,* (2), 31-32.

Riley, M. W. (1990). *Aging in the twenty-first century.* Bryn Mawr, PA: Boettner Research Institute.

Riley, M. W. (1993). *The coming revolution in age structure.* R-110, Working Paper Series, Pepper Institute on Aging and Public Policy. Tallahassee: Florida State University.

Riley, M. W., Foner, A., & Waring, J. (1988). Sociology of Age. In N. J. Smelser (Ed.), *Handbook of Sociology* (pp. 243-290). Newbury Park, CA: Sage.

Rowe, J. W., & Kahn, .R. L. (1987). Human Aging: *usual* and *successful, Science, 237,* 143-149.

Sacher, G. A. (1978). Evolution of longevity and survival characteristics in mammals. In E. L. Schneider (Ed.), *The Genetics of Aging* (pp. 151-167). New York: Plenum.

Schroots, J. J. F. (in press). The fractal structure of lives: Continuity and discontinuity in autobiography. In J. E. Birren et al. (Eds.), Biography and aging: explorations in adult development New York: Springer Publishing Co.

Shindul-Rothschild, J., & Williamson, . J.B. (1991). Future prospects for aging policy reform. In M. Minkler & C.L. Estes (Eds.), *Critical perspectives on aging: The political and moral economy of growing old* (pp. 325-340). Amityville, NY: Baywood.

Stubbs, C. (1989). Property rites? An investigation of tenure change in middle age. In B. Bytheway, T. Keil, P. Allatt, & A. Bryman (Eds.), *Becoming and being old* (pp. 6-23). London: Sage.

Chapter 4

Some Psychological Implications of an Explosion of Centenarians

Lillian E. Troll

Centenarians today are often feeble and unique. What would it be like to be a centenarian in a hypothetical future if one were able to be in reasonably good health, and if there were others of one's cohort around, so that one was not unique? At the very least, self-images and perceptions of time should be different. Other people would also be likely to feel differently about you. Psychogerontology as a science or clinical profession might change. Old assumptions and goals could give way to new assumptions and goals to match new demographics. Finally, suppose that some psychogerontologists themselves were centenarians. Would they be interested in different issues from psychogerontologists today or would they continue to be concerned about cognitive functioning, about work (i.e., retirement), and about relationships with family and friends? Is it remotely possible that our society would come to look to centenarians as historians and sages rather than as curiosities?

I am basing the speculations that follow both on reflections from my own aging, on the accumulating data from an ongoing longitudinal study of the adaptations of San Franciscans over the age of 85 (Johnson, 1994), and on recent reports on present-day centenarians (Poon, 1992).

Increased Variability

There is no reason to assume that all people who reached 70 would survive to 100, even in an era with many centenarians. There could still be a large number—perhaps a majority—who would die in younger years. A wide spread of ages among those labeled old—perhaps from ages 65 to 110, as well as a very wide distribution of ages of people alive altogether (see, for example, Suzman, Harris, Hadley, Kovar, & Weindruch, 1992) could alter images and definitions of age itself. To illustrate, a 90-year-old resident of a senior housing development said, "The young people here are in their 70s. They have a group of their own. They laugh a lot and walk around the lake. When I came here, I did the same thing." One of the results of this wide spread of ages should be a declining correlation between chronological age and functional status; functional decline would not automatically be associated with what we now call old age. Our current experience with the AIDS epidemic, where obituary columns are filled with people under 40 instead of over 70, is testimony to this possibility. In other words, the word *old* would not immediately conjure up an image of frailty and imminent death. Just as the word *grandmother* no longer automatically brings to mind an image of rocking chairs, the age of 95 would no longer suggest the image of a nursing home bed.

Differentiation along genetic lines might become dramatic, with those destined to live long distinguished from those destined to die young—or relatively young at age 70. How jealous one would be if one's own forebears only lived to 50 or 60 while one's neighbors had held the prospect of going on and on into the 100s! Will we become more accepting of eugenics and look carefully at whom our grandchildren marry to make sure they come from long-lived stock? Or might we emphasize that "it's not how long you live but how good your life is"? The war between the long-lived and short-lived could be played out in politics, even in education. Longevity prediction could become a lucrative profession. People from short-lived geneologies could be discriminated against. For example, we can imagine right-wingers saying that it just wouldn't be worthwhile for short-lived children to get as much expensive education as the long-lived.

Maybe a larger percentage of research money would go towards looking for ways to alter longevity genes than to treat Alzheimer's disease.

I can see centenarians forming their own associations, since the American Association of Retired People's (AARP) new 65-year-olds and retirees would have different agendas from those 30 or more years older than they. Perhaps there would even be a political backlash, like the present anti-immigration movement, with 65-year-olds pitted against 100-year-olds. The resulting generational equity fight could be as bitter as the 1960s struggle between 20-year-olds and 40-year-olds, or as tense as disputes between today's baby boomers and their elders.

Perspectives

There are several viewpoints to consider in the psychological study of aging in a world with many centenarians. One is the perspective of the very old themselves: What it would feel like to have lived 100 years and more, to be the top of the population pyramid with five or six generations below you? Second there are the perspectives of the people with whom centenarians interact, their families and friends. And third, there would be the perspective of those outside the personal situations: epidemiologists, policy makers, lobbyists, and psychotherapists.

• Self •

The perspective of centenarians themselves is rarely looked at today. Although they may routinely be asked to what they attribute their longevity, they are not so frequently asked what it feels like to be 100. It is commonly assumed that even though they are special, they could not have information that would be useful to the rest of us. Our usual image of very old people is that they are precious but dumb. As one 93-year-old man expressed it, it is the solicitousness of others that lets him know things have changed. He didn't see any change in himself; it was imposed from the outside.

It might feel differently to be 100 years old if reaching that age were to become more common. Presumably, as life expectancy increases, one will be more likely to reach that age with more of body and soul intact (Suzman et al., 1992). At a minimum, I can predict a flood of centenarians'

retrospective interview studies and articles and books that "tell it like it is."
I also foresee hundreds of prospective longitudinal studies looking for con-
tinuities and changes in personality—in self and identity and self-esteem—
as well as in cognitive capacities.

Would one feel oneself to be a different person at 100 from what one
was earlier in life? Would you feel that you had acquired new characteristics, that you had added significant attributes to your persona—or sub-
tracted some? Current research conclusions seem to be that old people
show less personality change than younger people in the same time
frame (Bengtson, Reedy, & Gordon, 1985), and that years of inhabiting
one's self-concept lead to greater satisfaction with self and less effort to
induce change.

Few of Johnson's (1994) oldest-old respondents have reached 100 yet,
though most are now over 90[1], so we must move our speculation base
back a decade. When the 85 to 100-year-olds in Johnson's study were asked
whether they felt they were the same person[2], almost three-quarters of the
150 participants indicated that they didn't believe they had changed significantly. In order to assess the frequency of felt change, I rated both their
perceptions of change in "self" or identity or "I" and their perceptions of
change in self-image or self-attributes or self-concept, their "me," employing
William James' (1892) constructs. (See also Atchley, 1989; 1991; Mead, 1934;
Tobin, 1991; Troll, 1990). Three-point ratings were developed for both self-
constructs. Thus, a rating of 3 for the "I" construct signified no felt change:
"I'm much like I was when I was young." A rating of 1 would be, "You look
back and it seems like you were dreaming and that was another life."
Similarly, a rating of 3 for "me" would be "I've always been very calm, composed, very stylish and independent," while a rating of 1 would be assigned
to, "I'm changing all the time; I'm more comfortable with myself now," or "I
used to be very active; now I'm handicapped so I have to be more passive."

Most of the respondents (71%) received a top rating of 3 for the "I," indicating that they felt they were still the same person. Nobody received a rating of 1 on this variable. An 87-year-old man said, "You really don't realize
that you're getting old. Don't feel that at all, and all of a sudden I'm getting
to be 88." Another, "I'm the same guy." An 81-year-old woman said, "I don't
think you can change." An 86-year-old woman responded, "You'd have to
ask someone who knew me. As far as I'm concerned I've been the same."

Respondents do say, however, that they have "gotten older," "slowed
down," "look different," "can't do as much," "have poorer health," are
"more lethargic," "not as angry," "more lonely," and "more relaxed"—that

things bother them less. In other words, many of their characteristics have changed—the "me" aspect of their "self." Only 18% felt they had stayed the same in every way, while almost two-thirds (61%) felt there had been some change (a rating of 2). On the other hand, only 10% felt their attributes were very much different from what they used to be. Johnson and Barer (1992) have described this shift in self-concept as a form of "disengagement."

The oldest-old today are essentially lone survivors. When they are asked to compare themselves with other people their age, they say, "I don't know any people my age. They're all dead." Although they don't actually say it, many hint that they are proud of their feat of survival. The fact that their morale stays surprisingly high over successive waves of interviews, in spite of increasing chronic illness and disability, supports this conclusion. Some say that their families are proud of them. Those who have children (70%) describe 90th-birthday parties to which children and several layers of grandchildren come from afar and which are celebrated in style. They show off group photographs of these events, with themselves—the matriarchs and a few patriarchs—surrounded by an impressive array of offspring in three and more generations. One-hundredth birthdays get national attention, or at least a telegram from the president, a happy-birthday message from the Hallmark Card company and often a mention on a television show. By the time they reach the century milestone today, people may indeed feel they are extraordinary.

In an earlier study (Troll, 1994b), I found that decade birthdays like 50 and 60 now seem to be painful markers. Spontaneous mentions of older family members by respondents aged from the teens to the 90s showed what I called a *cusp effect*. People in their 49th and 50th years, for example, particularly women, talked a lot more about older family members— living or dead—than those between 51 and 58. The same was true for the 40th, 60th, and 70th decade markers. Facing an imminent birthday that would put them into the next decade of age seemed to produce many more thoughts of forebears than did actually being firmly embedded in the next decade, when they would presumably have come to terms with their age. It seemed that the women[3] who were 49 or 50—just approaching their next decade marker or just having reached it—were thinking about how their parents and other elders they had known coped with getting old. They may have been seeking models for what was coming next for themselves. Or maybe they were tormented by horror or dread!

When a lot more people get to be 100, though, will the same decade milestones remain so significant? The age of 50, for example, would only be halfway through the life span. And will centenarians continue to feel like special survivors? Getting to be 100 could become just another decade milestone and no more special than getting to be 50 or 60 is now. Becoming a centenarian would lose the positive quality of rare significance and remarkable survivorship that it has now and become just another milestone, painful to pass.

At least two factors probably affect the self-perceptions of centenarians. One is the expectations they have had for their own life span—their "expected life history" (Seltzer & Troll, 1986). The other is the numbers in their surviving cohort, which of course is related to "expected life history" (*See also* Whitbourne, 1985.) Most of today's oldest-old say that they never expected to live so long. This is in spite of their subsequent reports that they come from long-lived families, and that their longevity is a result of their "genes." Many list grandparents, parents, and siblings who lived to their 90s or older.

Even if they had relatives who lived long, their primary expectations were based more on national life-expectancy figures and biblical statements about "three score and ten" than on their own family's long-life genes, that is, on how many family members they know who have lived long. Now that they are old themselves, they may acknowledge such genes, but 20 years earlier few would have bet on inheriting them. They are thus as surprised as everybody around them that they have made it, and few really prepared themselves for such an eventuality. (See Johnson & Barer, 1993, for a discussion of coping and sense of control among these respondents.) Their plans for death are more evident than their plans for continued life. They will tell interviewers about their plans for the disposition of their property and where they want to be buried. One 95-year-old commented, "I'm too old to get a loan to repair my house. Time is too short to pay a loan back." But this could change if life expectancy increases significantly, and people start believing they will have a good chance of living to 100. They could start preparing themselves early in life. I can predict floods of how-to books, advice columns, and seminars at every turn, not to mention ads for investment groups in every newspaper and magazine.

Present centenarians are remarkable survivors. They have very few peers left. Their friends are gone. Their siblings are gone. They are alone and often lonely, even those who are embedded in their families, surrounded by their children and grandchildren (Troll, 1994b). After all, it is association with nonkin who are friends and age-mates that adds spice to life, not constant and exclusive association with kin, particularly those a generation or more younger—or so our data tell us (Troll, 1983; Adams & Blieszner, 1989).

But if there were a lot of centenarians around, many of them in suffi-ciently good shape to associate with their age-mates, there would be lots of friends and neighbors growing old together. The onset of losing friends and other age-mates would be significantly later. There could be a culture of the oldest-old, as gerontologists were speculating there would be in the 1960s and 1970s when I entered the field of gerontology and when life expectancy prolongations were arousing attention (Rose, 1968). In a cul-ture of the oldest-old, old people could continue to have fun, not find their companions vanishing one by one—at least, not as much as now (Johnson & Troll, 1994a). They could perceive continuity of values and interests, instead of feeling they were ghosts in their own neighborhoods, the world having changed around them. They could believe, at 60 or 70, or 80, that the "best is yet to be" (Browning [1864], 1961).

The issue of perceived continuity of self involves time perspective. As people get near what they think is the end of their life, they think more about the past and less about the future. (*See* Troll, 1982). Actually, Johnson's oldest-old subjects report that they think most about the pre-sent: "I live one day at a time." Will the progression from future to past to present orientation remain as a function of "expected life history" (Seltzer & Troll, 1986), but shift its age parameters to fit changing life expectancy? When most people would expect to die before 50, orientation to the pre-sent would begin at 40. If most people could expect to stay alive until 90 or 100, future-orientation would remain until age 80, at least. One might not expect to grow up before 50—a slight shift from the perspective of today, when many do not feel impelled to settle on a life career before their 40s. And age of marriage—aside from teen marriages—has been inching back up to where it was earlier in the century. In a world rich in centenari-ans, death before 90 would be consider tragedy, retirement before 80 an abuse. Productivity and achievement would not peak before 65 or 70 or even later. Marriage before 30 would be considered impulsive and prema-ture. It is true that the biological realities of the childbearing clock would still serve as a brake; we can speculate, however, that an extension of fertil-ity might accompany a lengthening of the years of biological fitness.

• Feelings •

It was noted earlier that the morale of the San Francisco oldest-old remained remarkably high and remarkably constant over the first years of the ongoing research in spite of continually increasing physical disability. Bengtson and his colleagues, in their extensive review of self-concepts and personality (Bengtson et al., 1985), noted that a positive correlation between self-esteem and age is not unusual. It has been attributed to several causes, including adjustment of the idealized self-concept downward so that it is easier to satisfy, greater certainty of personal identity, even a better survival rate for those who are more satisfied with themselves or whose temperament is more conducive to good morale. All these explanations are applicable to the oldest-old respondents.

One factor mentioned in the literature that is less applicable to these 80- and 90-year-olds is greater satisfaction with body image. Most of them complain about dissatisfaction with their deteriorating bodies, as reported in the statement above about perceived changes in "me." If physical ability is sustained longer in the future, in proportion to increased longevity postulated, there could be greater satisfaction with one's body and a more continuous body image. Part of body image is the presentation of self to others, and if there were more contemporary others, there could be more acceptance of the lines of age, pride in looking old. Gray hair would be a status symbol and people might color their hair gray at 30 or 40 instead of coloring it blond or red at 50 and 60. Given cohort differences, one might find a 60-year-old daughter with white hair confronting her 90-year-old mother with red hair or a 60-year-old bald son confronting his 90-year-old father with implanted hair. There might also be more effort to look good, or present oneself as looking good, and perhaps even greater morale.

• Friends and Family •

Not only should we consider the perspective of the centenarians themselves, but also the perspective of the people who associate with the centenarians, primarily their friends and family members. What would it feel like to be close to centenarians, especially if one were not a centenarian oneself? A large effect, of course, would be produced by the modeling and the inspiration they would provide. The San Francisco study has not systematically included interviews with the relatives and friends of the oldest-old. Although spouses sometimes sat in on sessions, children and friends rarely did. We cannot, therefore, predict from present data what it would feel like to be an associate of a centenarian. The project interviewers themselves, however, reported, and still report, their feelings of awe and optimism when they think of the competencies exhibited by these respondents. As the oldest of the interviewers, I was particularly buoyed by the thought that I might be like my informants when I reached their age. But our reactions are colored by today's realities, when people over 90 are unique survivors.

The study respondents, in fact, have few friends or family members available to them (Johnson & Troll, 1992). Half of the men and 90% of the women were no longer married at the first round of interviews. Seventy-one percent of the men and 68% of the women had a surviving child; 32% had had a child predecease them. Only half—more women than men—said they had a close friend. Half had lost such a friend during the past year. On the other hand, three-quarters of both men and women said they had weekly contact with someone they named as a friend. In many cases, they had relaxed their definition of "friend" to include neighbors, acquaintances, and even hired help or service workers (Johnson & Troll, 1994a). Some were so isolated that it was depressing to read their interviews (Troll, 1994b). And even those who still had friends and relatives were dependent on someone, usually their child or children, for transportation necessary for getting together with others. This dependency increased over the 5 years of the study. Some had substituted telephone calls for face-to-face visiting.

If there were more centenarians than there are today, there could be more age peers available and they could spend more time interacting with each other, with the members of their *convoy*, to use Kahn and Antonucci's (1980) term, instead of interacting primarily with people a generation or two younger, as they do now. There would be less need to turn to younger family members and friends for emotional and social support. More important, if health deteriorates later than it does now, instrumental help from families would not be needed for a correspondingly longer period of time. Associations with relatives would, thus, be more for expressive functions. Children and grandchildren could spend their time visiting and sharing ritual occasions, for example, like holidays and birthdays, instead of chauffering and cleaning.

Family gerontologists are already thinking about the implications and complications of multiple generations in the family. If there were no change in childbearing patterns, five- and six-generation lineages might become common. Life in the modified extended family (Litwak, 1960a, b), where family nuclear units live apart but near each other and in communication with each other, would be so complex, it could boggle the mind and tax the skills of "kinkeepers," those family members who spread the news, see who needs help, and arrange get-togethers (Rosenthal, 1985; Troll, 1986). The parent-child relationship might continue to be the most salient (Troll, 1991), but grandparents could continue to enjoy the births, graduations, weddings, and successes of grandchildren and great-grandchildren and great-great-grandchildren. And although, when old people need it, they usually get help now mostly from spouses and children with little substitution on the part of other relatives (Johnson & Catalano, 1981; Johnson & Troll, 1992), they might then be more likely also to get help and attention from multiple layers of descendants.

Long-term relationships would be the norm. One could coexist with children for 80 years, with grandchildren for 60. There might be successive waves of generations pulling away from each other for a time and then returning to the fold, just as youth does today. The relations between a mother and daughter when the mother is 40 and the daughter 20 could be very different from when the mother is 80 and the daughter 50 or 60 and very different again when the mother is 100 and the daughter 70 or 80. On the negative side, people could just get bored with each other over so many years and repetitions of rituals and conversations and might drift apart. On the positive side, old rivalries and hostilities, which Hess and Waring (1978) predicted would become exacerbated over the years of adulthood, might alternatively become smoothed out over many years.

From the perspective of younger generations, the stretching of generations onward and upward should lend an almost biblical feeling of continuity over time. Young people would face an awesome assemblage of models (both positive and negative) during their own quest for identity.

If more friends live longer together, friendships can also be more enduring than they are for the present oldest-old, among whom so many have lost their friends to death or to infirmities that prevent contact and communication. Long-term friendships, like long-term family relationships, could develop in complexity over the years—or, alternatively, lose their charm.

Cognitive Conditions

Cognitive development is a top concern for today's psychogerontologists, as it has been since the beginning of gerontological research. When does intellectual ability reach its peak and when does it decline? The tracing of different curves for different abilities has led to some of the most creative research in the field (See Schaie, 1965). Schaie has pointed to the confounding of developmental and historical effects in comparing people of different ages at the same period of time. Cross-sequential research, which separates developmental from historical changes by measuring people of different ages at the same time and the same people at different times is pertinent to the task of trying to predict for future centenarians on the basis of present-day centenarians who have grown up and grown old under different economic and cultural circumstances.

Existing rules of thumb are that general ability (measured by IQ) remains relatively constant at least through the ages of 60–70 (Baltes, 1993). But fluid intelligence, including creative problem solving, declines earlier than crystallized intelligence, which involves the accumulation of information, and which persists at least into the 60s and 70s (Poon, 1985; 1992; Reese & Rodeheaver, 1985; Labouvie-Vief, 1985). But we know that fluid intelligence is related to biological fitness, and it could be that a longer living population could look forward to high competence to 80 years of age or more. Certainly, many of the oldest-old in Johnson's study appear remarkably competent cognitively . Half of the 91-year-olds even manage their own affairs, including financial matters and income tax preparation, sometimes with help from others. The problem-solving abilities of the centenarians in Poon's (1992) Georgia study compared favorably with the 60- and 80-year-olds in that study.

Crystallized intelligence might continue to grow over more years among future centenarians, and their accumulated information would therefore boggle the mind. But we would have to see whether human capacities for recording and integrating information could keep up with these demands. It might be difficult to learn from or make sense of the experiences of a century. Are we programmed for dealing with so much information?

From another slant, if many people live a century or more, centuries as units would be diminished in importance. What happened 100 years ago would be part of one's own memories, not just hearsay. Centenarians could tell their great-great-grandchildren, "When I was young..." and refer back to at least 20 presidents and 25 presidential elections!

And what of work and achievement? Would we see more late than early retirement and later peaking of achievement? There is evidence that scientists who publish the most before they are 60 years old continue to be highly productive after 60 (J. E. Birren, personal communication, August 1980). If there are lots of productive very old people around, would younger generations delay their productivity until the age of 30 or 40? Would these early decades become, then, the leisure or playboy or playgirl years? Alternatively, people might start working about the same time, at the end of their teen years, for example, but pass through cyclical burnouts and multiple careers, with alternating periods of reeducation and retraining. What would career counseling be like? What might be the effect on universities, technical schools, and business organizations? With extended life expectancy, would the 1970s phenomenon of returning adult students be even more prevalent in the future? Or would there be a transformational development process resembing the Buddhist model of shifts in life focus at particular ages, so that the age of 100 would be a time for significant new endeavors?

Old Gerontologists

Let us consider the possibility of an increase in age of both research and clinical psychologists. First, would research questions change when the psychologists themselves got close to 100? (I will assume that these very old psychogerontologists would still be asking questions and running experiments and not all opting for early retirement to spend 40 years or more traveling, playing golf, or writing memoirs.) Would they still want to concentrate on Alzheimer's disease, the burdens of caretaking, or procedures for reversing senility? Or would they become more interested in issues of personality, self-esteem, and control?

My own experience is relevant in formulating these questions. I completed my Ph.D. and became a gerontologist when I was almost 50, although I had worked in one or another field of psychology for 30 years before that. Since I was just starting a new phase in my career, I did not want to be judged feeble or in need of care. It is not surprising, therefore, that my early post-degree research pursuits combined an interest in age bias and age discrimination with an interest in similarity between generations. I wanted to be treated as an equal by young women and by men of all ages. Since I did not want to be ignored because I was a woman or an old person, I did not want to be involved in polarizing people by either age or gender. (In the 1960s, women were just starting to fight again for equal opportunities.) It seems to me, therefore, that as many more gerontologists get older, they will be more likely to see other old people as subjects rather than objects, in a phenomenological sense, and become more interested in subjective issues than in caregiving, even though more could have aged parents still alive. Of course, some psychogerontologists would themselves need care, but I expect that in their work they would emphasize the importance of care with dignity and want a share in the control of their treatment. I am assuming that there will always be new, young gerontologists around to be interested in generational equity and in helping their feeble elders.

Conclusion

Considering psychological implications of living longer means considering implications for the feeling of self and self-continuity, for work and family relationships, for friendship, and for cognitive functioning. But first we need to consider a caveat: These factors will only be important if we do, in fact, live longer and live longer in good health and functioning. Although it is true that the oldest segment of the population, those in their 80s and 90s, is now the most rapidly increasing part of the U.S. population, we should be cautious in projecting an extension of this trend. There are lots of centenarians now—compared to what we would have expected from past history of mankind and past figures of life expectancy and longevity—but we cannot assume that this will be true 10 or 20 years from now. There could even be fewer. That is, critical deterioration of the environment and the quality of life as well as drastic cuts in funding for medical care could lead to a declining life expectancy instead of a steadily increasing one.

In this connection, it is often assumed that the presence of more people at ages now associated with higher morbidity means that we would have more decrepit people who would threaten our capacity to care for them. It would seem just as logical, however, that the ones who live to be very old could probably be those who are able to remain in good shape, needing minimal care, for a longer period of time. So I would guess that there would not be an increase in general morbidity, just a shift of onset of disability to later ages. Or there may even be a bimodal curve with a large number of centenarians at one end and few in the next younger decades, as Belle Boone Beard (personal communication, 1971), who was among the first psychologists to study centenarians, believed she was finding. The centenarians she tested, she felt, were superior in many ways to most of the 80-year-olds she tested. She felt they were a genetic strain, marked for longer life and more vigorous at all ages.

One of the chief consequences of an explosion of centenarians in the future could be to diminish their rarity, which could have both positive and negative effects. Because one of the benefits of having old people around should be their expanded memory and wisdom, society as a whole should benefit—although this benefit is greatly undervalued in Western society today. Further, because they would not be as isolated as present-day centenarians, their lives may be more enjoyable. On the other hand, people living beyond 100 would be less precious and perhaps less honored. It is fun to guess about the future, if we keep in mind that multiple and contradictory trajectories are possible.

Acknowledgement

I want to thank both Colleen Johnson and Barbara Barer for their valuable comments and editorial suggestions.

Notes

[1]In fact, few look destined to live to 100. The asymptote for the sample seems closer to 95 than 100. The mean age after the fourth round of interviews was 92, the same mean age as after the third round—14 months earlier.
[2]The questions were, "In what ways have you always been the same?" and "In what ways have you changed over the years?"
[3]This effect was statistically significant for women but not for men.

References

Adams, R. G. & Blieszner, R. (Eds.) (1989). *Older adult friendship: Structure and process*. Newbury Park, CA: Sage.

Atchley, R. C. (1989). A continuity theory of normal aging. *The Gerontologist, 29,* 183–190.

Atchley, R. C. (1991). The influence of aging or frailty on perceptions and expressions of the self: Theoretical and methodological issues. In *The concept and measurement of quality of life in the frail elderly*, (pp. 207–225). New York: Academic Press.

Baltes, P. B. (1993). The aging mind: Potential and limits, *The Gerontologist, 33,* 580–594.

Bengtson, V. L., Reedy, M. N., & Gordon, C. (1985). Aging and self-conceptions: Personality processes and social contexts. In J. E Birren, & K. W Schaie,.(Eds.), *Handbook of the psychology of aging*, (2nd ed., pp. 544–593). New York: Van Nostrand Reinhold.

Browning, R. (1961). Rabbi ben Ezra. In O. Williams (Ed.), *The centennial edition of F. T. Palgreave's The golden treasury of the best songs and lyrical poems*. New York: Mentor. (Original work published 1864)

Hess, B., & Waring, J. (1978). Parent and child in later life: Rethinking the relationship. In R. Lerner, & G. Spanier (Eds.), *Child influences on marital and family interaction*. New York: Academic Press.

James, W. (1892). *Psychology*. New York: Henry Holt.

Johnson, C. L. (Ed.). (in press). Social and cultural diversity of the oldest-old. Special issue, *International Journal of Aging and Human Development*.

Johnson, C. L., & Barer, B. M. (1993). Coping and a sense of control among the oldest-old. *Journal of Aging Studies, 7,* 67-80.

Johnson, C. L., & Catalano, D. J. (1981). Childless elderly and their family supports. *The Gerontologist, 21,* 610-618.

Johnson, C. L., & Troll, L. E. (1994). Family functioning in late late life. *Journal of Gerontology, 47,* S86-S72.

Johnson, C. L., & Troll, L. E. (in press). Constraints and facilitators to friendships in late life. *The Gerontologist, 34* (1), 79-87.

Kahn, R. L., & Antonucci, T. C. (1980). Convoys over the life course: Attachments, roles and social supports. In P. B. Baltes, & O. G. Brim, (Eds.), *Life-span development and behavior*. New York: Academic Press.

Labouvie-Vief, G. (1985). Intelligence and cognition. In J. E. Birren, & K. W. Schaie, (Eds.), *Handbook of the psychology of aging*, (2nd ed., pp. 500-530).

Litwak, E. (1960a). Occupational mobility and extended family cohesion. *American Sociological Review, 25,* 9-21.

Litwak, E. (1960b). Geographic mobility and extended family cohesion. *American Sociological Review, 25,* 385-394.

Mead, G. H. (1934). *Mind, self, & society*. (Edited posthumously by C. W. Morris). Chicago: University of Chicago Press.

Poon, L. W. (1985). Differences in human memory with aging: Nature, causes, and clinical implication. In J. E. Birren, & K. W. Schaie, (Eds.), *Handbook of the psychology of aging*, (pp. 427-462). New York: Van Nostrand Reinhold.

Poon, L. W. (Ed.). (1992). The Georgia centenarian study [Special issue]. *International Journal of Aging and Human Development*.

Reese, H. W., & Rodeheaver, D. (1985). Problem solving and complex decision making. In J. E. Birren, & K. W. Schaie, (Eds.), *Handbook of the psychology of aging*,(pp. 474-499). New York: Van Nostrand Reinhold.

Rose, A. M. (1968). The subculture of the aging: A topic for sociological research. In B. L. Neugarten, (Ed.), *Middle age and aging* (pp. 29–34). Chicago: University of Chicago Press.

Rosenthal, C. J. (1985). Kinkeeping in the familial division of labour. *Journal of Marriage and the Family, 47,* 965–974.

Schaie, K. W. (1965). A general model for the study of developmental problems. *Psychological Bulletin, 64* (2), 92–107.

Seltzer, M. M., & Troll, L. E. (1986). Expected life history: A model in nonlinear time. In J. Hendricks, & M. M. Seltzer (Eds.), Aging and time [Special issue]. *American Behavioral Scientist 29.* 746–764.

Suzman, R. M., Harris, T., Hadley, E. C., Kovar, M. G., & Weindruch, R. (1992). The robust oldest-old: Optimistic perspectives for increasing health life expectancy. In R. M. Suzman, D. P. Willis, & K. G. Manton, (Eds.). *The oldest-old.* (pp. 341–358). New York: University Press.

Tobin, S. (1991). *Personhood in advanced old age.* New York: Springer Publishing Co.

Troll, L. E. (1982). *Continuations: Adult development and aging.* Monterey, CA: Brooks/Cole.

Troll, L. E. (1983). Grandparents: The family watchdogs. In T. Brubaker (Ed.), *Family relationships in later life* (pp. 63–74). Beverly Hills, CA: Sage.

Troll, L. E. (Ed.). (1986). *Family issues in current gerontology.* New York: Springer.

Troll, L. E. (1990, November). *Identity and self–image: Do they change after 85?* Paper presented at meeting of Gerontological Society of America, Boston.

Troll, L. E. (1991, November). *From children to grandchildren.* Paper presented at meeting of Gerontological Society of America, San Francisco.

Troll, L. E. (1994a). Family embedded and family deprived oldest old: A study of contrasts. In C. L. Johnson (Ed.). Social and cultural diversity of the oldest-old [Special issue]. *International Journal of Aging and Human Development.*

Troll, L. E. (1994b). Family connectedness of old women: Attachments in later life. In B. Turner, & L. E. Troll (Eds.), *Women growing older: psychological theories.* Newbury Park, CA: Sage.

Whitbourne, S. K. (1985). The psychological construction of the life span. In J. E. Birren, & K. W. Schaie, (Eds.), *Handbook of the psychology of aging,* (2nd ed., pp. 594–618). New York: Van Nostrand Reinhold.

Chapter 5

Culture as Constraint and Potential for a Long-Lived Society

Dena Shenk and Jennie Keith

Introduction

T his chapter will provide an anthropological perspective on possible implications of an increase of the life expectancy in the United States to 100 years. The characteristic anthropological approach is (a) cross-cultural, (b) holistic, and (c) oriented toward diversity and intracultural variation. To state the focus of anthropology most simplistically, anthropologists study culture. This is the hallmark of anthropology and the work of anthropologists. Ideally, we approach a topic by doing comparative research seeking to comprehend the issue through the eyes of individuals in a range of societies and eventually to distinguish what may be called universal aspects of the topic from features that are culturally shaped and consequently variable.

Indeed, an increase in life expectancy could change the nature and extend the possibilities of anthropological research itself. Anthropological research as we have noted, should be comparative. Typically, however, the long-term and time-intensive nature of anthropological research has allowed most anthropologists to study only one culture in depth. The increase in life expectancy, along with an extended period of healthy old age, would enable anthropologists to complete extensive comparative research in a series of cultures over the course of their careers.

The anthropological paradigm has a dual focus that includes both an internal (*emic*) and an external, comparative orientation (*etic*). The emic perspective seeks to understand the insiders' view of the meaning of certain behaviors as well as their overall view of the world. The etic perspective provides the comparative view which allows us to separate the universal from the particular. For example, Project AGE, of which Jennie Keith was a member, compared the meanings of age and the experiences of older people in seven communities and neighborhoods in Botswana, Ireland, the United States and Hong Kong. The etic framework for the project was provided by a common research design employing concepts such as functionality and well-being and methods such as participant observation, Cantril ladder interviews, a card sort and life story elicitation. The goal of data collection was to gain emic perspectives and included striking differences in perceptions of the life course and of the significance of old age itself. Placing the emic data in the etic framework for comparison revealed the influence on older people of sociocultural features such as residential stability, family organization, and subsistence strategy (Keith, 1994).

In general, the cross-cultural data suggest that the roles and status of older adults in a given society depend to a great extent on the resources that they hold (Sokolovsky, 1990). In societies where the wisdom and experience that are the domain of the elders are valued, the elderly are more likely to be held in high regard and accorded status and power. Similarly, if the elderly are in control of other valued resources, they are more likely to hold positions of power and high status. Related issues include the speed at which cultural change, modernization, and industrialization occur within a particular society. In general, rapid social change undermines the value of experience gained by living many years, so that older adults are more likely to retain positions of power in societies where the rate of social change is slower. Among the sites in Project AGE, for example, social change was by far the most rapid in Hong Kong. The consequence is that members of different generations within the same family have experienced vastly different social circumstances and their associated norms. Older persons who were young in rural China and acquired potent norms of filial piety now share households with children and grandchildren who are members of an intensely competitive urban society and who find pressures toward filial duty a source of anxiety and even hostility. When young and middle-aged Chinese in Hong Kong responded to the request for examples of older persons who were doing well in old age, they described individuals who did not nag, who were tolerant, undemanding and easy to get along with. It came as a surprise to the researchers that the prescription for successful old age in Hong Kong was to stay out of the way of the young!

With its holistic perspective, anthropology recognizes that a cultural system operates as a system. Change in one domain of the system will have an impact which will spread throughout the society. To understand how an increase in the life expectancy to age 100 will affect our society, we must explore the possible implications of this change for other systems of our society. A good example of the interrelatedness between the position of the elderly and other aspects of the cultural system is provided by Charlotte Ikels based on her extensive study of Chinese families and Chinese elderly in three different societies. Her most recent work explores the dynamic interplay between kinship norms, political ideology and economic resources, that determines the particular mix of policies and programs for the elderly developed in each society (Ikels, 1993). Later in this chapter we will explore the case of the Danish system of care as a comparative example that can illuminate the ways in which interaction of various aspects of American culture shape our own provision of care for older persons.

A useful framework for assessing the roles and status of the elderly in a particular society was developed by Marea Teski (1987). Teski's model for the ecology of aging includes five sectors, as outlined in Table 5.1. This model provides the basis for an analysis of the roles and status of the elderly in a particular society.

What do we learn if we use this model to explore the roles and status of the elderly in American society? Generalizing, rather than focusing on regional ecological differences, although the climate and subsistence are not particularly harsh or difficult, older members of our society, as a group, do not make notable contributions to subsistence. In terms of the technological development of society, we are highly modernized, the rate of social change has been and continues to be very rapid, and we are fully incorporated within larger political groups including the global society. Our society is highly stratified in terms of class and sex as well as age. The elderly in American society do not as a group control important resources nor are they accorded great respect or deference. Finally, the ideology and values of American society do not place great value on the elderly or on what they have to offer. In general using this ecological model of aging, we see

TABLE 5.1
The Ecology of Aging

1. The ecology of the group including:
   a. Climate
   b. Subsistence
   c. Difficulty of survival
   d. Contributions which older members made to subsistence

2. The technological development of the society, including:
   a. The social relations of subsistence
   b. Modernization
   c. The rate of social change
   d. Degree of incorporation within larger political groups

3. The stratification of society, in terms of:
   a. Class
   b. Sex
   c. Age

4. Power and decision making which the elderly have in society, especially:
   a. Control of important resources
   b. Respect and deference

5. The ideology and values of the group which have evolved through their history

Adapted from Teski, M. (1987). The evolution of aging, ecology and the elderly in the modern world. In J. Sokolovsky (Ed.), *Growing old in different societies*. (pp. 18–19).

that the elderly as a group do not play important roles or maintain high status in American society.

An understanding of the implications of increased life expectancy in our society must be based on a consideration of the impact of this change on all of the various subsystems and aspects of our culture. The question remains whether the roles and status of the aged would be likely to change in a future with increasing numbers of older adults living longer lives.

An anthropological perspective recognizes intracultural variation and diversity. There is a great deal of variation within the aging experience of older members of our society based on a range of demographic variables including gender, socioeconomic class, rural versus urban environment, educational level, and ethnicity. In fact, intracultural variation and diversity become key issues in our present consideration of the possible implications of increased life expectancy. Specifically, in imagining the ramifications of a drastic increase in life expectancy, the increase can be assumed simply to extend the number of years lived at the end of life. More realistically, however, the extension can be viewed as affecting the entire life course. That is, there would be a greater diversity of roles and experiences for individuals throughout their 20s, 30s, 40s, and so on. Life extension would continue to expand the diversity currently found within the life cycles of various individuals.

There are at least two clear possibilities in this regard, given an increase of life expectancy to age 100. The first is that the increasing diversity which would accompany the increase of life expectancy might undermine the salience of chronological age as a measure, at least within later life. The other distinct possibility is that because of the rapid increase in the numbers of older adults that would accompany the increase in life expectancy, there might be a clearer distinction between subgroups within the older population, like young-old, middle-old, and old-old or healthy aged versus frail elders. In this case, we would see the continuation of age as a grouping with subcategories further dividing the category of old age.

Background Considerations and Points of Departure

There are several background issues to consider before we begin our discussion of the challenges and potentials of increasing the life expectancy to 100 in the United States. First, let us clarify the terms life expectancy and life span. *Life span* (frequently designated the maximum life span potential, or MLP) refers to the outside limit of survival of a particular species. The MLP for humans is approximately 120 years. *Life expectancy* is a projection applied to populations; the number of years actually lived by a specific individual is *performance*. "Life expectancy is computed from life tables that predict the average number of years remaining for a hypothetical group of individuals based on the current set of age-specific rates of dying" (Holmes, 1983, p. 54). So, while we can imagine a continuing increase in life expectancy, the maximum life span potential of 120 for our species can be viewed as the outside limit of this increase. Within any population there is also considerable variation in life expectancy associated with various characteristics including gender, ethnicity, race, and occupation (Holmes, 1983, p. 54).

Life expectancy has, of course, increased dramatically in the United States and continues to increase. Life expectancy tables demonstrate the continuing trend toward an increase in life expectancy of both men and women in this country. Differences in life expectancy in various societies or in various subpopulations within our society can largely be accounted for by differences in environmental hazards such as disease, diet deficiencies, radiation, chemical pollution, accidents, rigors of the physical environment (climate), and mental and physical stress (Holmes, 1983, p. 56).

A global perspective on this issue is relevant because a further increase of life expectancy in the United States is likely to be accompanied by similar increases throughout the world. It is likely that such an increase would begin in the developed nations and be followed by an increase in life expectancy in the developing countries, as has been the case in the current increase of life expectancy. The aged represent a large and expanding proportion of the world's developed societies and their numbers are increasing rapidly in many developing and more traditional societies of the globe (Brody, 1989; Kinsella & Suzman, 1992, as cited in Crews, 1993). Of all persons aged 60 and over, 57% live in developing countries, a figure which is projected to reach 69% by the year 2020 (U.S. Department of Commerce, 1991). The oldest-old segment (80 and over) of the world's elderly population now numbers 50 million, representing one-tenth of all elderly. The oldest-old are the fastest growing portion of the population in many countries worldwide. Unlike the elderly as a whole, the oldest-old today are more likely to reside in developed (54%) than in developing (46%) countries, although the relative balance will shift in favor of developing countries before the turn of the century (U.S. Department of Commerce, 1991).

As Sokolovsky explains, however, this is a complicated issue and the statistics can be misleading (Sokolovsky, 1990). "As of 1988 most Third World nations remain demographically 'young,' with less than 4 percent of their population over sixty-five... or 'youthful,' with 4 to 6 percent over sixty-five" (Kinsella, 1988, as quoted in Sokolovsky, 1990, p. 13). In the near future some Third World countries are even expected to show a slight decline in the percent of the elderly, since improved health care is likely to reduce children's mortality more than adults'. This is in contrast to the "grayer" industrial regions designated as either "mature" (between 7.9% and 9.9% over age 65) or "aged" (10% or more over age 65). Most of the difference between nations with low life expectancy and Western industrial nations can be attributed to the high levels of infant mortality that still persist in the Third World. Once individuals in various societies live into adulthood, the difference in life expectancy between them is slight.

The nonindustrialized nations of the world have contained the majority of the world's elders since a dramatic demographic revolution in the 1980s. These countries will have to contend with an extraordinary increase in actual numbers, going from 200 million to 350 million aged (Sokolovsky, 1990, p. 14). The nature of the adjustments necessary to deal with these rapid increases and demographic changes are similar to those we must imagine based on the hypothetical premise of this volume.

As Crews explains (1993, p. 29): "Such demographic realignments of age cohorts were originally hypothesized to include declines in the status of the elderly, generational competition over scarce resources, and myriad other social phenomena" (see Cowgill, 1974; Cowgill & Holmes, 1972). While the original modernization theory of aging has been greatly modified (Cowgill, 1974, 1986), available research about the effects of industrialization and modernization and various aspects of these social changes can enlighten us about what to expect in terms of future sociocultural developments.

Second, it is essential to recognize that values and cultural norms change very slowly. Changes in values and norms in response to the potential drastic increase in life expectancy will also occur slowly. It is likely, therefore, that there would be a lag between a drastic increase in life expectancy to 100, and the accompanying changes in cultural norms and values (see Riley, Kahn, & Foner, in press, on structural lag). This lag occurrence might lead to increased stresses between the generations, similar to the intergenerational equity arguments of the past decade.

Changes in population age structure imply and often compel changes in the magnitude and nature of social expenditure (U.S. Department of Commerce, 1991). The issue can be examined in terms of the projected changes in social expenditures due to demographic factors and the probable reaction to such changes in our own country. The projected changes in 12 countries included in the Organization for Economic Cooperation and Development (OCED) are summarized in Table 5.2. Although spending on education and family benefits will vary from one country to another, a declining aggregate trend is expected to emerge with a drastic increase in pension expenditures.

Table 5.2
Projected Change in Social Expenditures
Due to Demographic Factors in 12 OECD Countries: 1980–2040.

(in percentages)

100		
80		
60		
40		
20		
0	Health Pensions	Total social expenditures
-20	Education Family benefits	

Note: The 12 countries are Australia, Belgium, Canada, Denmark, France, Germany, Italy, Japan, the Netherlands, Sweden, the United Kingdom, and the United States.

Source: Organization for Economic Cooperation and Development, 1988. *Aging Populations. The Social Policy Implications,* Paris.

Crews suggests that available data can be used to "determine whether sociocultural definitions of 'old age' have lagged behind biomedical changes leading to continued high physiological and mental function during the seventh, eighth, and even ninth decades of life in many societies. These constructs may allow us to answer questions like the following: Have sociocultural definitions of old age changed in response to patterns of health and longevity? What factors have been correlates of current attitudes toward the elderly in various populations? (Crews, 1993, p. 29) Values and cultural norms to consider include family relationships, intergenerational interactions, labor force participation, and retirement.

A third consideration is the characteristic future orientation of our society. Our society is not oriented toward the past or focused on the present but rather toward the future. For instance, as a society we tend to focus on our children as our resources for the future. We do not value what the elderly have to offer, which is typically wisdom and the knowledge gained through a lifetime of experience. We certainly do not emphasize their involvement in the development of our current society through their past work. This is not reason enough for us to provide for their current needs, because instead we are looking to the future. The researchers in Project AGE were impressed by the contrast in views they heard expressed by Herero in Botswana who emphasized care of older people as the focus of family resources and pride. Children were less individualized and more inter-changeable than the elderly, and were in fact often fostered away from their parents to households of older relatives to whom they would be helpful.

Because we are future oriented, past contributions are insufficient rea-son for meeting current needs. Although older American adults are valued within their families and communities, to a great extent they are still not valued as a societal resource. Even within our families, we do not tend to believe that our primary responsibility is towards our parents because of all that they have done in raising us. Instead, our primary responsibility is toward our children within whom we see our hopes for the future.

Another result of our future orientation is our tendency to leave much of the responsibility for the elderly to their families and informal support systems. This is a crucial concern in considering a future which might require a longer period of support for the elderly, and provides one sugges-tion of how we can learn from other societies that have more of an orien-tation toward the present or the past, and therefore are more likely to develop additional support systems for elders.

A fourth preliminary consideration is the fact that our society uses a medical model in our approach to aging. This has led to the development of a paternalistic system of care for older adults. We view old age as an ill-ness or disease, rather than as a natural stage of the life course. For exam-ple, our society's earliest specific response to the needs for care by frail older adults was to develop nursing homes, which often look and feel like hospitals. Nurses and other staff members, often dressed in white uni-forms, provide the care for the residents or patients. Even at lower levels of care our emphasis is often on treating the illness of old age. This orienta-tion has set us up for failure because old age, of course, cannot be cured and, in fact, many of the changes and transitions that come with later life are chronic rather than acute in nature.

Our model of care is based on younger people providing care for the elderly who are perceived as requiring care. The system typically does not allow for a give-and-take, or for exchange between the elders and care-givers. Rather, the elderly are recipients and the care providers are the givers of care, support, and assistance. This is in contrast to the kinds of interaction that occur naturally within families and communities. In these informal interactions each individual is both the recipient and provider of various kinds of support and assistance (e.g., Shenk, 1992). Also, in their own time of need, elders are often able to draw on a lifetime of favors and support provided to others. This kind of exchange, however, is more likely to provide a secure basis for support of elderly individuals in less future-oriented societies. In our society, such reciprocity involving the elderly is more often found in age-homogeneous settings where elderly residents continue to exchange a great deal of mutual support among themselves. Both kinds of informal support are more effective for short-term care than for cases of long-term need for support. More than one society in the Project AGE comparative study illustrated the very different circumstances of the elderly, for example, in settings where either lifelong interdependence makes need for care when elderly a non-issue (as for the !Kung) or dependency of old on young is actually approved and desired by the elders (as for the Chinese in Hong Kong).

In addition, our societal responses to aging tend to relate to the elderly as a unified group. They are not based on a clear understanding of the diversity and variations within the older population. We need greater understanding of subcultural systems and the expectations for aging and old age within these subpopulations. The diversity within the older population would, of course, increase drastically with an increase of life expectancy to age 100.

Societal Challenges and Responses

There are several major problems and challenges in terms of our societal response to a rapid increase in life expectancy. The primary and overriding problem is the lack of a consistent basis for a societal response to the needs of the elderly.

• The Danish Example •

Our society lacks a coherent view of the proper response to the needs of individuals or groups, including the elderly. This deficiency has led to failure to develop a clear and consistent public policy in regard to aging. In comparison, consider the case of Denmark. The system of care in Denmark is based on a firm philosophical base derived from Søren Kierkegaard, the Danish philosopher:

*If real success is to attend the effort to bring a man to a definite position,
one must first of all take pains to find HIM where he is and begin there.
(Bretall, 1951, p. 333)*

Thus, the Danes' approach to service delivery has been built on a strong
philosophical belief in the basic rights of every individual. There is also a
related Danish belief that survival through hard times depends upon cooperation—not competition (Thomas, 1990).

In Denmark, formal services are viewed as a right to be used by any
member of that society who is in need of assistance, premised upon a societal model of mutual self-help. In contrast, in the United States formal services are generally viewed as an approach to be used when one's informal
network is unable to meet one's needs. In meeting the basic needs of
elderly individuals, the Danish system is focused on enabling individuals to
retain control over decisions regarding their care. Based on this social policy of viewing each individual as independent, a policy that was strongly
supported by the economic boom of the 1960s, the elderly came to regard
formal services and not their family or friends as the appropriate way to
meet their basic needs.

The system of formal services and programs to meet the basic needs of
older adults is one component of the larger Danish system of providing for
the basic needs of all citizens. "The Danish tax finance and pay-as-you-go
procedure placed old-age provision within an emerging system of redistribution not only between generations, but between single members of a
given generation. Unmodified this principle has governed Danish pension
policy ever since [the last century]" (Petersen, 1990, p. 73). The system of
health and welfare services is financed essentially by the income taxes paid
by all workers, which begin at 51% of earned income. Services are free of
charge for all residents, except for certain services provided by nursing
homes and social welfare. For those earning more than a basic pension,
there are sliding fee scales for these services. Economic responsibility is
shared by the counties and municipalities, with partial reimbursement by
the national government in the form of lump sum subsidies (Sondergaard
& Krasnik, 1984).

The responsibility of providing for the basic needs of all citizens is
shared between the county and municipal levels of government.
Ownership of hospitals and provision of hospital and medical care services
has been at the county level. The municipalities are responsible for the
range of formal services necessary to meet the needs of elderly people in
their communities. These services include nursing homes, day nursing
homes, home nursing services, home help, meals-on-wheels, day centers,

and sheltered housing. In addition to supplying the services, the decision concerning access to services is made at the municipal level.

The social welfare system in Denmark is based on the concepts of normalization and equalization. The concept of normalization has been described in regard to the mentally retarded as providing the same opportunities and conditions of life to the handicapped as are available to the rest of society and the right to experience and use the environment in a normal way (Bednar, 1974). "For many years, the primary goal of Danish social policies has been social equalization, where few have too much but fewer have too little" (McRae, 1975, p. 28). High priority is placed on providing services that preserve and strengthen the capabilities of the dependent elderly, particularly services that will enable them to remain in their homes as long as possible (Raffel & Raffel, 1987). The basic orientation of this service delivery is toward maintaining the elderly persons' control over choices and enabling them to lead their lives as independently as possible.

Since the reforms of the 1970s, the emphasis has been on community-based care that will enable elders to remain in their own homes rather than force them to move into an institutional setting. There is a commitment to offer the same services to elders remaining in their own homes as are offered nursing home residents (Fejerskov, 1989). Home health care ("home help") and home nursing services have been utilized extensively in all of the Scandinavian countries of Denmark, Finland, Iceland, Norway, and Sweden. Denmark had both the highest volume and intensity of home help service among the Scandinavian countries by the early 1980s (Daatland, 1986). In Denmark not only more clients were being served, but there were also both a broadening and deepening of services, including night and weekend assistance (Daatland, 1986).

The availability of formal services for the elderly in Denmark has changed since the 1970s along with economic changes. The system is a dynamic one and is responsive to changing needs. During the 1970s the system was characterized by the motto "Ask and you will receive," and elders received home help daily. During the 1980s, there was a need for realism, that is, recognition of the fact that services could not be expanded continually. There was an assessment of what the elderly really needed and a concurrent move from "help" to "self-help." In the 1990s there is a strong move to help elders remain in their own homes as long as possible, maintain control of decisions about their environment (normalization), and live as independently as possible.

The commitment to remaining in control of one's own life is now being focused on urging elders to care for themselves and each other. The recent development of formal services for the aged in Denmark has centered around the theme of self-help and has been promoted through the initiation of experimental projects. While these efforts are necessitated by the economic strains that are currently being experienced in Denmark, they are also part of the effort to find positive and creative alternatives that can enable the elderly to remain active and independent. The formal system of service delivery is designed to enable all individuals to live as normal a life as possible, assisted by their choice of services to meet their basic needs.

The Danish view has been that in order to get the necessary social support from family, friends and neighbors, you have to have your basic needs met from somewhere else, that is, through formal services. Changing attitudes are now being encouraged in Denmark due to the economic necessity of cutting back on formal services. The elderly still receive formal services because it is more acceptable. "You can receive formal services without losing face" (K. Christiansen, personal communication, May 19, 1992). The current effort is to get people to care more and to develop the informal system of care through which people help and support each other, as the economic situation worsens.

It is difficult to imagine these efforts being effective in the Danish cultural context, where there is a clear societal expectation that basic needs be met through formal services. It will be difficult to make the present generations reorient their expectations toward the use of formal services and to have them begin expecting more from their informal support systems. In the United States we have the opposite problem of inducing individuals to use formal services effectively to reduce the strain on their informal systems of support. Clearly, the answer for each society must be based on the existing cultural expectations for the way in which the formal and informal systems of care interact in meeting the basic physical and social needs of the elderly (Shenk & Christiansen, 1993a, 1993b). The Danish example demonstrates the advantage of building a service delivery system on a firm and consistent philosophical base providing the basis for shared expectations among members of the society. This philosophically based system of service delivery is also dynamic and particularly responsive to changing needs. These lessons from the dynamic and responsive Danish system are likely to be very valuable ones in a period of change, which would be precipitated by a rapid increase in life expectancy to age 100.

There are potentially positive aspects to the hypothesized increase in life expectancy in our society. The effects of having increasing numbers of elderly in our society and, consequently, more role models for experiencing the aging process will certainly present challenges. Perhaps the increased number of very old could stimulate a more explicit articulation of our philosophy—which we then might debate and possibly modify. The implications depend upon the nature of our societal response to the increasing numbers and needs of older adults.

Possible Societal Adaptations to Increased Life Expectancy

Consideration of possible scenarios for ways a drastic increase in life expectancy is likely to affect American society begins with establishing two possible baselines. There are two vastly different possible effects of increased numbers of older adults on how the elderly are incorporated into our society.

The first possibility is that we will continue to view chronological age as a marker of social differentiation and that old age will continue to be defined as a single, distinct period of life with generalized roles and expectations. In this case, we can anticipate an increase in the diversity in the roles older people play and the ways in which they fill these roles throughout their lives. At the same time, a multiplicity of roles is likely to emerge for older adults as they collect new roles but continue playing out the old ones, over time. The second possibility is that we will see real changes in how age is used as a social marker. Because of the increase in the period of life that would be included in the category of "old age," individuals may be expected to take on successive roles and perhaps drop old ones, as they move through distinct periods *within* their later life. For example, it is likely that the current distinctions of "young-old," "middle-old" and "old-old," or grandparent, great-grandparent, and great-great-grandparent, will become more defined with clearer expectations about the appropriate roles to be played in each of those subcategories. The conception of distinct subcategories within the period defined as old age is called *age grading*. Age grades can be loosely defined as categories that define the social boundaries associated with age in a given society. There are generally well-known norms for the behavior and responsibility assumed to be characteristic and appropriate of a particular grade. In some societies, age grades

are transformed into sharply ascribed age sets, where different spans along the life cycle are sharply set apart by spectacular ritual, distinct dress, specialized tasks, modes of speech, comportment, and deferential gestures. Here persons move through the life cycle collectively and form tightly bound groups performing specific tasks. (Sokolovsky, 1990, p. 84)

It is not anticipated that age sets within our society would become defined to that extent for a number of reasons. There are too many crosscutting variables, including gender and socioeconomic class, that prevent an age cohort from defining themselves as a closely knit group. The concept of age grading, however, is useful in helping to picture how the period of later life might be segmented into subcategories with a range of roles and responsibilities within each distinct period of later life.

In fact, we can conceive of more extreme changes in how age is used as a marker. The category of old age might become meaningless and chronological definitions no longer be used in a future where the possibilities for individuals at any age are vast. In many societies, such as that of the !Kung studied in Project AGE, not chronological but functional definitions of age are used, that is, individuals are defined as "old" or "frail" when they can no longer perform certain roles or activities. Given the powerful salience of chronology in American views of age, a sudden decline in its relevance is unlikely. However, it does seem plausible to us that if chronological age becomes less salient as a basis of differentiation within an extended period of later life, then eventually the chronological boundary of that period itself might be blurred.

To make these two societal adaptations more concrete, let us consider how each of the two most likely implications of the increased numbers of older adults and the extended period of old age, might become incorporated into the realm of kinship. In all societies, the elderly retain a role within the family system and it is within the family that older adults are generally protected and cared for.

The first possibility—old age remaining a marker with generalized expectations for roles and behavior—would translate into older adults playing their family roles over many years. An older woman, for example, might fulfill the role of grandmother to successive generations of offspring within her family. In this case, her behavior as grandmother could be expected to be similar in her relationship with her grandchildren, great-grandchildren, and great-great-grandchildren. This would be a generalized expectation which would probably be interpreted differently within various family systems based on the family situation and personalities of the family members.

The second possibility is even more intriguing to consider. If we anticipate real changes in how age is used as a marker, it is possible that the role definitions and responsibilities will change in successive periods of old age. For example, our imaginary grandmother would fulfill distinct responsibilities in her roles as grandmother, great-grandmother and great-great-grandmother. In fact, then, a woman might fulfill different responsibilities in relation to the various successive generations in her family. These roles are likely to be defined in terms of expectations for particular relationships between the adjacent and alternate generations within the family. Classical research in anthropology suggested that relations between generations are shaped by the allocation of authority. In most societies, adjacent generations are in relationships involving authority, for example, parent and child. Informal, affectionate bonds are therefore most frequent between members of alternate generations, for example, grandparent and grandchild (Apple, 1956).

Against the backdrop of the two baselines we have proposed, we would like to explore possible versions of a future with an increased life expectancy. There are three possible interpretations of what an increase of life expectancy to age 100 might mean. The first interpretation assumes that technology is used effectively to prolong good health, allowing the increased years of life to represent a relatively healthy extension of life. The second interpretation sees the extended period of life as a period of extended frailty. This possibility is unlikely based on the evidence of how medical and technological advances have affected the extension of life to date. We see the extension of life leading instead to prolongation of each phase of the life cycle, rather than lengthening only the end of life. We will not explore the option of an extended period of frailty, apart from one that may be driven by a system of health care rationing based on age. The third interpretation envisions a system where health care rationing is based at least partly on chronological age. These are clearly not completely separate visions of the future; reality would be likely to borrow from each of these somewhat overlapping possibilities. We will now explore the four scenarios derived from envisioning each of the two likely possibilities against the two backdrops we have identified for ways age might define roles and behaviors. The four scenarios are then as follows:

1. a healthy extension of later life with age remaining a generalized marker,
2. a healthy extension of later life with changing role definitions and responsibilities in successive periods of life,
3. health care rationing based at least partly on chronological age with age continuing to serve as a generalized marker, and
4. health care rationing based at least partly on chronological age with changing role definitions and responsibilities in successive periods of life.

• Scenario One •

In our first version of the future, the increase in life expectancy to age 100 would lead to a healthy extension of later life with age remaining a generalized marker and each individual fulfilling a multiplicity of roles. This would be a society in which there would be increasing variability between the life courses of different individuals. Individuals would make choices continually throughout their lives which would affect the multiplicity of roles they would play in later life. For example, an individual might marry in her early 20s and again in her 60s, 70s, 80s, or 90s after outliving her spouse, or she might marry at a late age for the first time. A woman might take a break from her career in her 20s, 30s, or 40s to raise her children and then return to another 40, 50, or 60 years of work.

If a concurrent increased flexibility in the social system develops, individuals would have increased flexibility in making life choices, rather than the limitations imposed by the generally constraining system which now "prefers" that we complete our education, marry and spend the period of time between our 20s and 60s in a career. Recreation and education could instead be integrated more fully into what are now defined as our "work years," with sabbaticals from one's career for raising a family, traveling, or career redirection. Some people might choose to begin a new career in their 70s, 80s, or 90s, whereas others may choose to retire in order to pursue other endeavors.

In the family system we can envision a future where children enjoy the company of not only grandparents and great-grandparents, but even great-great-grandparents. The current, increasing complexity which we are experiencing in family systems today with generations of middle-aged and older children caring for their aging parents and grandparents would be extended to another generation. With the trend toward divorce and remarriage, the possibilities of the number of caregivers and those in need of care by family members are mind-boggling. Imagine the possible call of a 40-year-old working mother to her great-grandmother: "The kids are sick and I have an important appointment. My mother is busy after work and grandmother has a date. Could you possibly take care of the kids for a couple of hours this evening?"

As a society, we would need to make decisions about the relative responsibilities of the informal system of care and the formal system of care in meeting future needs for care of increasing numbers and generations of older adults and their roles and responsibilities. Perhaps the stresses of accommodating vastly increased numbers of older adults would force our society to develop a more comprehensive approach to social policy. Ideally such a policy would be based on a life course perspective.

• Scenario Two •

In our second version of the future, the increase in life expectancy to age 100 would again lead to a healthy extension of later life, but with changing role definitions and responsibilities in successive periods of life. Instead of dividing society only into the categories of youth, middle age and old age, new categories would be added at the end of life. Categories corresponding to the terms young-old, middle-old, and old-old might become institutionalized with specific roles and responsibilities for each. An older friend informed one of the authors that these terms are currently defined jokingly as: the "go-goes," the "slow-goes," and the "no-goes." Each of the categories would be defined with norms and expectations for individuals in each age range, with entry into the next category determined by functional abilities.

We can frame the expectations within the family based on the classical anthropological findings, referred to earlier, that relations between generations are based on the allocation of authority. Relations between grandparents and their grandchildren might become more like those of parents and children if grandparents take on greater responsibility for raising their grandchildren, with great-grandparents taking on the more informal, affectionate bonds and the role of spoiling their great-grandchildren. In the sphere of work, the phenomenon of retirement might be reserved for those in and beyond their 90s. Those in their 70s and 80s might be expected to continue to work, but in more supervisory roles, sharing their knowledge and experience with younger colleagues. The challenges and possibilities are really quite exciting and the realities would be framed by our cultural norms and values.

• Scenario Three •

Our third version of the future envisions a society in which health care rationing is based at least partly on chronological age and age continues to serve as a generalized marker with broad expectations. This would be a society in which, similar to today, the course of one's later life is dependent to a great extent on one's health and socioeconomic situation. As long as individuals remained healthy, they would lead lives in which they chose from the many optional roles in the spheres of family, work, and community. The key difference would be that after a specific age, major illnesses and health problems would no longer be treated aggressively and would represent the beginning of a period of decline leading to death. A major difference in our future society with a life expectancy of 100 is that the chronological age after which aggressive health care is rationed would likely be higher than we now would imagine, perhaps 80 or 90 years of age.

The broad expectations associated with an extended period of later life, we believe, might gradually undermine the use of chronological age as a basis for rationing health care. If chronological age becomes a less constraining basis of role allocation within the period of later life, it may eventually seem less appropriate as a basis for allocation of medical care as well.

• Scenario Four •

In our fourth and final version of the future, health care rationing would again be based, at least partly, on chronological age, but changing role definitions and responsibilities would accompany successive periods of life. This is a future in which, for example, grandparents who are not longer employed might be expected to help raise their grandchildren. If the grandparents are employed, child care/assistance might be provided by great-grandparents.

One can imagine this future by recognizing changes that are already occurring because of the increased life expectancy in our society. The media present reports about the growing numbers of grandparents raising their grandchildren. Middle-aged parents recognize that their views of their parents and grandparents were vastly different from those of their children. For instance, while one of the authors remembers her grandmother in the kitchen and pictures her in housedresses and skirts, her own children see their grandmother in running suits, leading a much more active, leisure lifestyle. Yes, grandmother sometimes cooks, but more often when we visit her we go out to eat.

These dynamic images are representative of the changing ways in which current generations are playing out their roles and they allow us to imagine how these trends might be extended in a society where individuals can regularly be expected to live a healthy 100 years. Age as a basis for rationing health care seems more likely in this scenario, in which society subdivides the extended period of later life into successive stages, each with distinctive role definitions and responsibilities. If these stages are cor-related with chronological age, then age seems more likely to be viewed as a legitimate basis for allocating medical care. A stage in which medical care is rationed would simply be the last one in the progression.

Conclusions

This discussion has been based on an anthropological view of the challenges and possibilities that would face our society if life expectancy were increased to 100. Based on the anthropological perspective, it is possible to envision several divergent views of this future, depending upon how our culture adapts to this challenge. In any case it is safe to assume that this future would be based on our existing cultural norms and expectations taken to the extreme. The cultural perspective is thus a useful framework for envisioning such a future.

References

Apple, D. (1956). The social structure of grandparenthood. *American Anthropologist, 58*, 656–663.

Bednar, M. (1974). *Architecture for the handicapped: Denmark, Sweden and Holland.* Ann Arbor: The University of Michigan.

Bretall, R. (Ed.). (1951). *A Kierkegaard anthology.* Princeton: Princeton University Press.

Brody, J. A. (1989). Toward quantifying the health of the elderly. *American Journal of Public Health, 79*, 685–686.

Cowgill, D. O. (1974). Aging and modernization: A revision of theory. In J. Gubrium (Ed.), *Late life: Communities and environment policy.* Springfield, IL: Charles C. Thomas.

Cowgill, D. O. (1986). *Aging around the world.* Belmont, CA: Wadsworth.

Cowgill, D. O. and Holmes, L. D. (Eds.). (1972). *Aging and Modernization.* New York: Appleton-Century-Crofts.

Crews, D. E. (1993). Cultural lags in social perceptions of the aged. *Generations, 17* (2), 29–33.

Daatland, S. O. (1986, Spring). Nordic countries emphasize community care. *Aging International,* 13–14.

Fejerskov, R. (1989). Danish old-age policy. In *The elderly in Denmark* (pp. 5–10). Copenhagen: The Danish Cultural Institute.

Holmes, L. (1983). *Other cultures, elder years: An introduction to cultural gerontology.* Minneapolis, MN: Burgess.

Ikels, C. (1993). Chinese kinship and the state: Shaping of policy for the elderly. In Maddox, G. & M. P. Lawton (Eds.), Focus on kinship, aging, and social change, *Annual Review of Gerontology and Geriatrics, 13,* pp. 123-146. New York: Springer Publishing Co..

Keith, J., (1994) *Age and culture.* Beverly Hills: Sage.

Kinsella, K. (1988). *Aging in the third world.* Washington, DC: Center for International Research, U.S. Bureau of the Census.

Kinsella, K., & Suzman, R. (1992). Demographic dimensions of population aging in developing countries. *American Journal of Human Biology, 4,* 3-8.

McRae, J. (1975). *Elderly in the environment: Northern Europe.* Gainesville, FL: College of Architecture and Center for Gerontological Studies and Programs.

Peterson, J. (1990, January). The Danish 1891 Act on Old Age Relief: A response to agrarian demand and pressure. *Journal of Social Policy, 19,* 69-91.

Raffel, M. & Raffel, N. (1987). Elderly care: similarities and solutions in Denmark and the United States. *Public Health Reports, 102,* 494-500.

Riley, M., R. Kahn. & A. Foner (Eds.). (in press). *Age and structural lag: essays on changing work, retirement and other structures.* New York: Wiley.

Shenk, D. (1992). Someone to lend a helping hand: Older rural women as recipients and providers of care. *Journal of Aging Studies, 5,* 347-358.

Shenk, D., & Christiansen, K. (1993a). The dynamic system of care for the aged in Denmark. In S.A. Bass & R. Morris (Eds.), *International perspectives on state and family support for the elderly,* pp. 169-186. New York: Haworth.

Shenk, D., & Christiansen, K. (1993b). The dynamic system of care for the aged in Denmark. In *Journal of Aging and Social Policy, 5,* (1, 2), 169-186.

Sokolovsky, J. (Ed.). (1990). *The cultural context of aging—Worldwide perspectives.* New York: Bergin and Garvey.

Sondergaard, W., & Krasnik, A. (1984). Health services in Denmark. In M. Raffel (Ed.), *Comparative health systems: Descriptive analyses of fourteen national health systems.* University Park: Pennsylvania State University Press.

Teski, M. (1987). The evolution of aging, ecology, and the elderly in the modern world. In J. Sokolovsky (Ed.), *Growing old in different societies: Cross-cultural perspectives.* Acton, MA: Copley.

Thomas, F. (1990). *Americans in Denmark: Comparisons of the two cultures by writers, artists and teachers.* Carbondale: Southern Illinois Press.

U.S. Department of Commerce, Economics and Statistics Administration, Bureau of the Census. (1991, September), *Global aging: Comparative indicators and future trends.* Washington, DC: Author.

Chapter 6

Political Implications of an Extended Life Span

Robert B. Hudson

As in other social sectors, the political consequences of an extension of the ordinary life span by one-third would be of seismic proportions. Yet, if living to 100 is—to extend the metaphor—"the big one," minor tremors are already occurring which give us some inkling of what may lie ahead. Images and realities of aging that date to the beginning of this century have undergone significant alteration during recent decades. The absolute and relative size of the older population, its internal diversity, its similarity to the remainder of the population, and its sense of self are all different than was long the case. Today, "the aging" no longer passes as an adequate population referent, and, should the aging live to 100, its meaning becomes yet further lost in a host of demographic, economic, and political crosscurrents.

The heightened heterogeneity associated with an extension of the life span would necessitate reconceptualizing and reworking age-related public policy. It would first be necessary to reassess for policy purposes when "old" begins. Today, the ages of 60, 62, 65, and 70 are each thresholds for different provisions of the Social Security Act. The age of 65 as the eligibility age for normal retirement is already scheduled to be pushed back to 66 and then to 67 early in the next century. A normal life expectancy of 100 might easily lead to unprecedented further delays in chronologically based benchmarks. More fundamental than these recalculations would be reinvestigation of chronological age as an eligibility criterion. As specific future scenarios later in this chapter will show, advanced age may well bring with it a host of problems, but heightened heterogeneity among the future old (and young) will subject age-based criteria to unprecedented pressures. One intriguing, if remote, policy possibility finds a notable shift in the balance of support toward older Americans being charged with contributing to the support of younger Americans.

Toward both understanding and anticipating a range of situations involving an extremely old population, this chapter first reviews the politically relevant shift already underway centered on who constitutes the old and how they are understood. More than of just historical interest, an understanding of this first transition phase holds lessons regarding what might be expected by more dramatic reductions in mortality. The chapter next posits a series of political and policy scenarios that might unfold based on divergent projections of morbidity rates, population growth, and economic expansion. The chapter concludes by briefly arguing that a risk-based policy methodology for making determinations about who should be in receipt of public benefits and under what circumstances represents a means for reinventing social welfare eligibility and benefit determination. The logic of this approach puts less of a premium on chronological age, a shift that the lengthened years and growing diversity accompanying the rise of a very old population would require. Advanced age will still correlate with well-known contingent conditions, but the stretching of life may well have the effect of rendering any given chronological marker an increasingly poor proxy.

Aging and the Fall of Homogeneity

In imagery, in theory, in politics, and in policy, presumptions about the singularity of the old have increasingly come under attack. An encompassing image of older persons as being senescent, weak, short-tempered, and unattractive has been joined—and occasionally supplanted—by a contrasting image of older persons as well-off, involved in leisure-time activities, politically active, and capable of giving to society as well as receiving from it (Binstock, 1983; Wetle, 1991). Theories promoting massive disengagement of the old and/or prescribing age-specific activity sets for them have given way to ones emphasizing the differential class (Olson, 1982), gender (Gonyea, 1991), and ethnic composition (Burton, Dilworth-Anderson, & Bengtson, 1992) of the older population and ones emphasizing variations among different generations of elders. Contemporary changes in understanding of who the old are makes longstanding dichotomous references, such as "the aging and society," increasingly suspect in both theory and practice.

• Political Reemergence of the Old •

Policy understandings of the old have followed a path parallel to these larger developments. Early policies directed toward the old were fully consistent with ideas of disengagement. Whether understood as a deserving population that needed assistance (Schlesinger, 1958), a worn out group of workers who had earned a retirement wage (Rimlinger, 1971), or a category of employees who cost too much or worked too slow (Graebner, 1980), the old were the recipient of policy benefits that got them—collectively—out of the way.

Politically as well, the old were long a passive force—organized rather than organizing. The Townsend movement of the Depression Era rested on the activity and appeal of its leader and a desire—emphasized by Townsend himself—to get older people out of the work force (in exchange for $200 per month and a promise to spend it rather rather than save it). With the passage of the Social Security Act and the lack of any organized infrastructure, the movement disappeared by the early 1940s. Little else organizationally was done by or for the aged during the 1940s and 1950s (Pratt, 1976). The 1950s did see liberalization in Social Security benefits, but, again, these were more "for the elderly" than "by the elderly."

Organized political involvement of the old picks up circa 1960. Growth in the population brought aging-related problems increasingly to the fore—most notably in the area of health care—and the aged began organizing on their own behalf. Aging-based organizations emerged (e.g., Senior Citizens for Kennedy; later the National Council of Senior Citizens, which grew out of Senior Citizens for Kennedy) or assumed more of a political posture (e.g., the National Association of Retired Federal Employees and the National Retired Teachers Association/American Association of Retired Persons).

This increasing organizational activity midway through a 20-year period of extraordinary economic growth brought new political recognition and policy benefits to the old. The period 1965-1974 saw the enactment of Medicare,

Medicaid, the Older Americans Act, the Age Discrimination in Employment Act, an overall 35% increase in Social Security benefits, the tying of future Social Security benefit increases to the cost of living, enactment of Supplemental Security Income, and creation of a state and substate network of aging-based social service delivery agencies. Both symbolically and fiscally, these were important enactments. No longer could advocates maintain, as had been the tenor of White House Conferences on Aging held in 1961 and 1971, that problems of the elderly were being ignored. As well, the aged were becoming politically engaged, with images of power beginning to complement images of passivity.

• Economic and Political Transformation •

By the late 1970s, financing pressures were building on Social Security requiring responsible, that is to say, painful choices. New taxes and/or benefit cuts replaced the earlier politics of extending benefits to the apparent detriment of no one. In 1977, Social Security taxes were sharply raised at a time when wage growth had begun slowing, and unemployment and inflation rates were rising. Especially sensitive politically was a leveling-off in median family income, which had doubled between 1947 and 1972 (Marmor, Mashaw, & Harvey, 1990). These aggregate pressures on Social Security proved fertile ground to neo-conservative analysts, who undertook an assault on so-called "uncontrolled entitlement spending." Much of the attack was aimed at the old (Samuelson, 1978; Longman, 1985). As a result of these developments, Social Security—and, inferentially, politics for the old—went from being "distributive" to "dedistributive" (Light, 1985).

A second factor transforming the politics of aging during this period was growing concern about identifiable populations of elders who continued to be in dire straits. Ironically, the enduring and special problems facing older women, older minority group members, and older low-income workers were highlighted by very different sets of reform interests. Liberal advocates for these populations called for new and extended benefits to be made available to these groups, most notably factoring in "family time" to the retirement benefits of women (Quadagno & Meyer, 1990). Conservatives, as well, expressed interest in providing greater assistance to these selected disadvantaged groups. However, the strict targeting called for in their plans meant that benefits would have to be formally means-tested and that significant numbers of persons currently receiving benefits would lose them while smaller numbers of demonstrably needy would be assisted.

The proposed schemes represent two very different philosophies of aiding the disadvantaged. The first is based firmly in a social insurance tradition of inclusive and progressive benefit provision, and the latter comes out of a "residualist" tradition wherein the government provides benefits only when market and family sources have failed. However, the renewed concern of both camps to questions of adequacy acknowledges that, just as many elders were moving ahead economically, many others were being left behind.

• Two Telling Cases •

That forces on both the right and the left now focused their attention on certain subsets of the old represented a sharp break with much of aging-related policy making up to that time. In the 1980s, the presumptive homogeneity of the aged began giving way to understandings and options that recognized differential levels of well-being among the old. Two major legislative episodes of the 1980s speak directly to this new approach. The emerging diversity of the old was first officially recognized in the actions of a bipartisan commission created in the early 1980s to buttress the Social Security trust funds. One provision—and one that was politically unthinkable 10 years earlier—imposed taxation on half of the benefits of Social Security recipients whose incomes exceeded $25,000 for individuals and $32,000 for couples. This provision acknowledged that not all elders were poor and, for some, Social Security income was not all they had to stave off severe deprivation. The commission also recommended (and Congress enacted) the phased-in increase in the retirement age for receipt of full Social Security benefits. For policy purposes, age 65 would no longer be officially "old."

A more extreme example of differentiating the needs and abilities of the old came with the Medicare Catastrophic Coverage Act of 1988 (MCCA). President Reagan said he would support selected catastrophic care for the old but only in a manner that "would not penalize one generation for the sake of another" (Quadagno, 1989). The benefits included in the final bill (extended hospitalization, prescription drugs, and spousal protection) exceeded what could realistically be covered through the only financing feature in Medicare restricted to the aging, the flat-rate Part B premium. Therefore, an income tax surcharge was included, aimed at middle and upper income elders. Although defensible as a progressive financing feature, it encountered a firestorm of opposition from the affected elders. Two years later, Congress was ignominiously forced to repeal virtually the entire law. The two-part lesson to be drawn from the MCCA debacle was, first, that within the older population, there are well-off elders little in need of new public provisions and less well-off elders who very much need such added protection, and, second, that the first group has little interest in supporting the second.

By the late 1980s, public policy increasingly recognized that there was a growing *diversity* within the older population—structured by class, race, gender, and age—and that eligibility criteria, benefit formulas, and financing mechanisms would need to recognize those differences. Paraphrasing Nelson (1982), among the old are included the rich and poor, the healthy and ill, the vigorous and frail, the integrated and isolated.

The Alternative Worlds of an Extended Life Span

Stunning as the prospect of Americans routinely living to age 100 may be, the discussion to this point should underscore how little that fact alone tells us about the well-being of long-lived persons. The composition of this extended population might vary widely by race, class, and gender. Its relative size would be an unknown function of future fertility and immigration rates. Its well-being would be affected by future economic growth, and, as Fries (1989) describes, its "life-curve" might be "squared" (viz., quality of life enhanced) through biomedical advances and improved lifestyle behaviors. Outcomes in each of these areas would differentially affect the politics surrounding a new extremely old population, most notably how much need be done on their behalf, on what basis, and by whom.

• The Factors •

The range and quality of possibilities of living to 100 can be concretized by simply dichotomizing possible futures along critical dimensions. Of the myriad relevant factors, three stand out as most central: (a) the status of the economy (growth vs. stagnation), (b) advances in biomedical research/health behaviors (major breakthroughs/changes vs. no advance), and (c) demographic trends (considerable vs. negligible population growth). Different outcomes along these lines—there are eight possibilities in all—have very different consequences for the roles and responsibilities for both those who might live to 100 and for younger members of society.

As already suggested, changes in these areas can be both extensive and unpredictable. Two such historical situations stand out in economics and aging of the twentieth century. The Great Depression caught financiers, officials, and the public at large totally by surprise, and its consequences were unprecedented. More subtle and extended has been the contrast in economic performance of the United States and other industrial nations between the century's third and fourth quarters. The post-World War Two period was marked by unprecedented economic growth, whereas the post-1975 period saw both slower growth, more skewed distribution of wealth, and a stubborn inability to generate resources to cope with looming social problems.

Population growth—of both old and young—is equally hard to anticipate. The assigned premise of the present volume eliminates one source of uncertainty by positing the extended life expectancy. Yet, unknowable future fertility and immigration rates will determine the size of the remainder of the population, and possible biomedical and disease prevention activities will determine the well-being of those living to very advanced ages. Arguments and data pointing to a squaring of the life curve (Fries, 1989) and of improving morbidity trends (Manton, Corder, & Stallard, 1993) are countered by less encouraging findings (Katz et al., 1983). Recent research increasingly points to improved health behaviors of Americans, but the ultimate effects of these lifestyle changes on mortality and morbidity rates remain unknown (Singer & Manton, 1993).

• Living to 100: The Possibilities •

Schematically, the dichotomized possibilities of marked improvements or declines in each of the three areas critical to the volume and distribution of well-being in the future are shown in Table 6.1.

TABLE 6.1
A Framework for Anticipating Well-Being in Old Age

Scenario:	1	2	3	4	5	6	7	8
Economic growth	+	+	+	−	+	−	−	−
Biomedical advances	+	+	−	+	−	−	+	−
Population growth	+	−	+	+	−	+	−	−

The politics of living to 100 also unfold very differently in the eight scenarios. The increasingly textured politics of aging set forth above would become yet more complex. The political meaning of age, the bases for benefits, and the locus of social responsibility—already undergoing significant transformation—could move far from what we are only now adjusting to in light of recent developments. Here, we set out the range of possibilities and in the concluding section review the kind of approach that might be useful for adapting to different—and always significantly unknowable—futures. In the discussion that follows, E=economic growth, B=biomedical advances/health promotion behaviors, and P=population growth. (See Table 6.2)

• Scenario One: Positive Future for All (E=+ B=+ P=+) •

This combination portrays a vigorous future for the very old and everyone else. A strong economy provides broad-based opportunities. Biomedical advances and efficacious health promotion behaviors make it possible for the newly emergent "very, very old" population to participate in remunerative, voluntary or leisure-time activities. The vigor of this population brings the added advantage of reduced strains on both family caregivers and government programs. Population growth in conjunction with a strong economy suggests jobs and purchasing power for younger Americans and, inferentially, an environment in which intergenerational tensions would be minimal.

The world of politics and policy would also be pleasantly manageable under such circumstances. The combination of economic growth and elder well-being would place minimal new pressures on government programs. There would be little tension in the politics of aging under this rosy scenario: Overall physical and economic well-being would make restrictions in aging-related benefits less onerous than under other circumstances, but, in fact, there would be few pressures to move in that direction. In short, in a world of economic and physical harmony, social and political pressures would be at a minimum.

• Scenario Two:
Needed: New Roles for the Old (E=+ B=+ P= −) •

Under this set of circumstances, the very old emerge as both a vigorous and courted population. Not only have years been added to life, but life has been added to these new years. Short-term prospects look good under these conditions, but economists point to longer term destabilizing factors. Although opportunities for older workers now abound, they demand high wages and benefits in exchange for working and possibly having to defer retirement and pension benefits. Resentment grows against elders, who are increasingly seen by some younger critics as engaging in a form of demographic blackmail by maintaining their labor force participation. Under these circumstances, America comes to replace France as "the old man" of the industrial world, and politicians push for pronatalist policies, including progressive family allowances, extended maternity and paternity leave policies, and affordable housing policies for young families. The welfare state, which had "aged" along with populations during the latter two-thirds of the 20th century (Thomson, 1989), now turns its attention increasingly to the needs of younger Americans. The old can and do produce and, ironically, find themselves in the unprecedented position of becoming providers as well as recipients where welfare state benefits are concerned.

• Scenario Three: Resources for the Frail Old (E=+ B= − P=+) •

Talk of the burden of an aging population—dating back to the late 1970s—continues as the additional years are not leading to the hoped for improvements in well-being among the very old. Hopes that the traditional nursing home might have a reduced place in health care provision fade as these facilities and chronic care hospitals continue to require greater health and social care expenditures. Population growth eases some of these pressures, but middle-aged and young-old family members demand that facilities be in place to meet the needs of their mothers and now their grandmothers.

Policymakers reluctantly ride with this tide of need and expectations. However, pressure continues to mount for more stringent means-testing of beneficiaries as do ever more stringent proposals to limit intergenerational transfers and to "tax back" the estates of very old decedents, through increased estate taxes. Criticism mounts as well of the scientific research community, which has made only modest strides in addressing the enormous rise of degenerative afflictions of both mind and body among the very old population.

• Scenario Four: Generational Tensions (E= − B=+ P=+) •

Demography, narrowly construed, does not emerge as a prominent problem, as the growth of an increasingly vigorous older population is matched by population growth among younger Americans. The issue here centers on economic stagnation, with both wages and benefits under pressure. This combination of events suggests, however, disturbing trends among younger cohorts. The inability of the economy to grow, despite the strength of the old and the numbers of the young, points to the persistence of education and employment issues emerging in much of the work force. The growing number of younger Americans without employable skills leads to major underemployment problems and a commensurate slackening in economic demand. Secretary of Labor, Robert Reich, renews his call for training American workers for the expanding high-technology global economy. Again, pressures grow for new benefits for younger workers, and demands are made on middle- and upper-class individuals of all ages. Need for new supports for the very old are few, but concern about the future leads here to a shift in emphasis in welfare state spending in the direction of younger and less skilled people.

• Scenario Five: Who Will Care? (E=+ B= − P= −) •

To many, demographic trends have begun assuming alarming proportions. Population aging continues at unprecedented rates, and the growing interests and abilities of persons well into their 80s are more than offset by the heightened volume and severity of problems of persons now ranging from their 90s to over 110. It is, in fact, this "demographic cold front" within the traditional older population that is causing growing alarm. The middle-aged and elderly daughters and granddaughters of these centenarians have made it clear—with their thoughts and their votes—that they are not going to assume seemingly endless responsibility for their remarkably aged—but often infirm— relatives.

This is leading to a "skip-generation" distribution of policy preferences not previously documented in aging politics—though it has been discussed in the broader family psychology literature (Troll, Chapter 4, in this volume). The grandchildren and great-grandchildren of the very old are finding growing opportunities for themselves in a strong economy and see a minimal role for themselves in caring for their aged relatives, whom they tend to love from a distance. In any event, they are under increasingly intense role-strain pressures. In light of stagnant population growth, industry and government are demanding substantial labor force participation. In addition, recently enacted family allowance provisions—scaled by income—are explicitly designed to promote parenthood among these same individuals. Younger women in particular are experiencing enormous pressures—to work, to raise families, to see to the needs of their growing lineal families. The tensions between daughters and granddaughters around these issues are receiving growing attention in social and political psychology and are, indirectly, generating great pressures for increased governmental programmatic support to support the large numbers of very old survivors.

• Scenario Six: Ethnic Tensions (E= − B= − P=+) •

Simultaneous growth in populations of color and of the frail old has been a growing concern among gerontologists and other social observers. In the case of Social Security, the concern has been that the former populations have had higher mortality rates and, therefore, received benefits for fewer years than have their white counterparts. In the case of long-term care, the concern has been that women of color constitute overwhelmingly the cadre of formal caregivers to the frail old, who are disproportionately white and often of higher income. Confronted with population aging and a stagnant economy, pressures and inequities of this kind are easily exacerbated. In bad economic times, marginal and unskilled workers are most adversely affected, and the growing frail older population represents a proportionally greater employment source than under other circumstances. The fact that there is, as well, a growing pool of surplus labor bodes poorly for the wages and working conditions to be faced by the growing number of caregivers to the frail old.

• Scenario Seven: New Opportunities for a New Population (E= − B=+ P= −) •

The importance of biomedical breakthroughs becomes clear in a future marked by such advances in combination with slow population and economic growth. The importance of improved morbidity figures associated with living to 100 emerges most clearly under this scenario. Slow population growth, in the near term at least, leads to neither a shortage of workers nor a shortage of care providers. Under these circumstances, economic difficulties are likely to be population-wide: the aged are presenting no special problems.

More positively, new opportunities for the old unfold. In the absence of pressures to reamin in the labor market and with the blessings of health and independence bestowed by science, elements of "productive aging" (Morris & Bass, 1988) and "the third age" (Laslett, 1987) take root here. The activities of the elderly include work, education, service, and leisure. Elders here serve as a reserve army of the employable for such time as the economy picks up but population growth does not. Until such time—and presuming economic stagnation had not been long lasting—circumstances possibly of concern to others redound to the advantage of the new old.

• Scenario Eight: A Troubled Future (E= − B= − P= −) •

This combination produces the most troubling consequences associated with an aging society. Growth in the older population continues with a linear progression toward heightened levels of frailty among the very old. The ratio of dependent retirees to workers becomes increasingly unfavorable. The economy is stagnant and perceived to be excessively burdened by an unrelenting growth among the frail aged. It is to this scenario that those citing growing intergenerational inequity point with alarm—an economy and younger population burdened by the needs and demands of an "army" of the retired.

Under these conditions, the politics of aging are steeped in allocational and ethical dilemmas. The increasing need for care by the very old populations places pressures on all social sectors: public and private, formal and informal. Elders and families demand public resources, younger Americans and the private sectors cite further damage to a weak economy, and a debate about rationing overwhelms quality of life considerations for a growing cohort of incapacitated centenarians. The absence of biomedical breakthroughs completes a circle in which the potential burdens of an aging society are realized in their starkest form. Even allowing for the growth of an "able-old" population enjoying "a third age" cannot offset new population burdens. It is the stark logic of this confluence of negative events that currently and increasingly is leading to new efforts to add "life to years" and "new roles for older persons."

• A Host of Futures •

As these blurbs suggest, different assumptions yield widely divergent patterns of well-being and tension. Most easily understood are the extreme cases (Scenarios 1 and 8), where the future bodes very well or very badly. Comparing the six remaining mixed scenarios shows more clearly how inextricably the economy, health and medicine, and population growth are linked in assessing futures. Table 6.2 reveals how pairing scenarios for which two of the three variables are the same shows that one of the pair leads to an optimistic prediction and the other leads to a pessimistic one.

An extended life expectancy can bring with it very different futures. These futures can be roughly divided into more or less desirable, but none of the positive values—strong economy, biomedical/health breakthroughs, and population growth—necessarily brings with it unbridled good news. Scenario 4 is the most startling in this regard, associating well-being among the very old with social problems. In fact, the difficulties presented here are quite familiar in today's economies—too many able-bodied workers in slow growth economies. The paradigmatic shift required by Scenario 4, however, is in emphasis: "Older workers" are now more "workers" than they are "older."

The possibilities laid out in Scenarios 5 and 6 are more likely to arise than those in Scenario 4, and they are more complex. In these we see the generational and ethnic tensions that have marked much recent aging-related commentary. Scenario 5 finds fewer persons available to care for a growing frail population in a growing economy, and Scenario 6 charts a growing younger population forced into low-paying caregiving jobs in a slow growth economy.

On the positive side, the strong economy and biomedical/health promotion advances offset slow population growth in Scenario 2 and, in fact, create great demand for older workers. In Scenario 3, strong economic and demographic conditions ease the burden of a very old very frail population. And, in Scenario 7, biomedical/health promotion advances create new opportunities for the old because a weak economy does not require their presence and their own well-being eases pressures on a stagnant younger population. Again, one is struck by the shifting dynamics among these three sets of factors and, by the point that pluses as well as minuses can contribute to troublesome futures.

TABLE 6.2
Contrasting Futures of Paired Scenarios

Optimistic	Pessimistic
Scenario 1 Good Future for All E=+ B=+ P=+ A future with few near-term worries as older population and economy fare well and population growth continues	*Scenario 8* A Troubled Future E=- B=- P=- A dire situation in which a slow-growth economy and stagnant population growth have grave difficulty in aiding very frail, very old population
Scenario 2 New Roles for the Old E =+ B=+ P=- Strong economy and biomedical/health advances offset flat population growth	*Scenario 5* Who Will Care? E=+ B=- P=- Role strains and pressures on public programs are created by strong economy, large, frail old population and flat overall population growth
Scenario 3 Resources for the Frail E=+ B=- P=+ Economic and population growth ease pressures generated by growing numbers of old and frail	*Scenario 6* Ethnic Tensions E=- B=- P=+ Growth of younger population in slow-growth economy with frail, very old population creates ethnic and generational tension
Scenario 7 New Opportunities E=- B=+ P=- Biomedical/health advances offset pressures on stable younger population in slow-growth economy	*Scenario 4* Generational Tensions E=- B=+ P=+ Abilities of very old in conjunction with population growth create situation where gains to either party bring corresponding losses for the other

Politics, Policy, and an Extended Life Span

Without other stipulations, positing a normal life expectancy of 100 years can lead to very different futures for the old and for everyone else as well. Isolating and then combining only three dimensions along which change can be projected leads to massive variation. Political futures are equally diverse. Each of the scenarios has vastly different consequences for the key political questions one asks about any population: Which populations require benefits? What benefits do they require? Who should be responsible for making them available? and From whom are resources generated for various benefit packages?

The chapter's first section charted what the course of American policy has been to the early 1990s. A population once viewed as homogeneous is today increasingly noted for its diversity; a politics that once was expansive has become contentious and more restrictive; intergenerational understandings that were once taken for granted are now challenged or, at least, uneasy insofar as public transfers are concerned. None of this is to say that new initiatives for the old will not surface, nor do I mean to suggest that expenditures for the old cannot be expected to grow. But *known* changes of this kind have already been seen in aging politics and policy.

The high political standing of the old and the large proportion of public benefits they receive are well-known realities in the American welfare state. The political and allocational questions that have been raised during the past decade will be far more wide ranging should the normal life span extend to 100. If chronological age is still to be used as a great gatekeeper to eligibility, that age clearly will not be 65 in these futures. If the new old are frail, affordability will be the issue; if the new old are healthy, questions of relative need and interpopulation equity will be raised.

On the assumption that age-based criteria will not be eliminated altogether, there will nonetheless be need for additional eligibility tests for such a large population. Certainly, if morbidity remains fairly stable, costs associated with long-term care will increase enormously. Only under Scenarios 1 and 4 could this development be readily handled; under all other circumstances new resources would be needed and hard to come by. These scenarios also point out that the heavy weighting of social welfare expenditures toward the old will become increasingly hard to justify. It is already the case that younger Americans require protections they do not have, and under various forecasts here—most notably Scenarios 4, 5, and 6—such need will increase.

In order to accommodate high levels of uncertainty and unknown patterns of need, policy makers will need to develop some type of risk-analysis or contingency plan. Weightings must be assigned to different contingent situations population members may encounter, and assessments must be made of where responsibility should lie, whether it be with the individual him- or herself, the private sector, government, or some combination of all three. Although these questions draw widely divergent responses across the political spectrum, it is nonetheless possible to develop objective criteria for assessing and assigning different risks. Three such efforts are Barr's (1992) discussion of where government welfare state efforts are especially appropriate, Holden and Smeeding's (1990) review of risk situations faced by contemporary elders, and Hudson's (1993) attempt to weigh response patterns by the severity, insurability, and assessibility of different negative events.

Government's collective and coercive features make conceivable—although often controversial—interventions beyond those possible for individuals and the private sector. Only government can compel the creation of large risk pools and, thereby, address adverse selection problems that mar private insurance efforts. Where the old are concerned, acute and long-term care insurance are critical areas of application. Yet few today question the need for such protection among younger populations as well; certain events, should they occur, will outstrip the resources of all but the very rich.

There may be areas where protection is also needed but where individual or private sector activity can suffice to a greater degree than in the instances above. Saving for retirement is one area where an expanded role for individual and private sector activity is being hotly debated (Ferrara, 1983; Schulz, 1993). The need for retirement income is unquestioned, but it is a known and generally predictable event about which assumptions can be made long in advance.

Risk analysis would be a useful way to help anticipate the vagaries of a population routinely living to 100. Yet the status of the economy, net immigration, and non-age-based welfare policies will always provide the broader context in which such analysis must be set. Those anticipating a life of 100 years should keep these fundamentals very much in mind.

References

Barr, N. (1992). Economic theory and the welfare state. *Journal of Economic Literature, 30*, 741–803.

Binstock, R. H. 1983. The aged as scapegoat. *Gerontologist, 23,* 136–143.

Burton, L., Dilworth-Anderson, P., & Bengtson, V., (1992). Creating culturally relevant ways to think about diversity. *Generations, 15*, (4), 67-72.

Ferrera, P. (1983). The prospect of real reform. *Cato Journal, 3*, (2), 430-444.

Fries, J. F. (1989). The compression of morbidity: Near or far? *Milbank Quarterly, 67*, 208-232.

Gonyea, J. G. (1991, November). The paradox of the advantaged elder and the feminization of poverty. Paper presented to the Annual Meeting of the Gerontological Society of America, San Francisco.

Graebner, W. (1980). *A history of retirement*. New Haven: Yale University Press.

Holden, K. C., & Smeeding, T. M. (1990). The poor, the rich, and the insecure elderly caught in between. *Milbank Quarterly, 68*, 191-220.

Hudson, R. B. (1993). Social contingencies, the aged, and public policy. *Milbank Quarterly, 71*, 253-277.

Katz, S., Branch, L. G., Branson, M. H., Papsidero, J. A., Beck, J. C., & Greer, D. S. (1983). Active life expectancy. *New England Journal of Medicine, 309*, 1218-1223.

Laslett, P. (1987). The emergence of the third age. *Ageing and Society, 7*, 133-160.

Light, P. (1985). *Artful work: The politics of social security reform*. New York: Random House.

Longman, P. 1985. Justice between generations. *Atlantic Monthly*, June, pp. 73-81.

Manton, K. G., Corder, L. S., & Stallard, E. (1993). Estimates of change in chronic disability and institutional incidence and prevalence rates in the U.S. elderly population from the 1982, 1984, and 1989 National Long Term Care Survey. *Journal of Gerontology: Social Sciences, 48*, (4), S153-S166.

Marmor, T. R., Mashaw, J., & Harvey, P. (1990). *America's misunderstood welfare state*. New York: Basic Books.

Morris, R., & Bass, S. (1988). Toward a new paradigm about work and age. In R. Morris & S. Bass (Eds.). *Retirement reconsidered*. (pp. 3-14). New York: Springer.

Nelson, D. (1982). Alternative images of old age as the bases for policy. In B. Neugarten, (Ed.). *Age or Need?* (pp. 131-170). Beverly Hills: Sage.

Olson, L. K. (1982). *The political economy of aging*. New York: Columbia University Press.

Pratt, H. (1976). *The gray lobby*. Chicago: University of Chicago Press.

Quadagno, J. (1989). Generational equity and the politics of the welfare state. *Politics and Society, 17,* 353–376.

Quadagno, J., & Meyer, M. H. (1990). Gender and public policy. *Generations, 14,* (3), 64–66.

Rimlinger, G. (1971). *Welfare policy and Industrialization in Europe, America, and Russia.* New York: Wiley.

Samuelson, R.T. (1978). Aging America: Who will shoulder the growing burden? *National Journal, 10,* 1712–1717.

Schlesinger, A. (1958). *The politics of upheaval.* Boston: Houghton Mifflin.

Schulz, J. S. (1993, July). Economic support and old age: The role of social insurance in developing countries. Paper presented to the Fifteenth Congress of the International Association of Gerontology, Budapest, Hungary.

Singer, B. H., & Manton, K. G. (1993). How many elderly in the next generation? *Focus, 15,* (2), 1–10.

Thomson, D. (1989). The welfare state and generation conflict. In P. Johnson, C. Conrad, and D. Thomson, (Eds.), *Workers and Pensioners* (pp. 33–56). New York. St. Martin's.

Wetle, T. (1991). Successful aging: New hope for optimizing mental and physical well being. *Journal of Geriatric Psychiatry, 24,* 1–12.

PART III

From Theory
to Practice

Introduction to Part III

Regardless of basic assumptions accounting for the increase in life expectancy to 100 and regardless of the nature of the social system, the odds are that the three professions represented in this section of the book would be the ones most affected by that increase. Social work, medicine, and long-term care services would continue to be necessary components of any human services programs. All three discuss staffing issues for the anticipated programs for old people. The authors of the following chapters assume that we would experience long healthy lives followed by a terminal collapse and fairly immediate death; even so, there still remains the need to care for the "immediately dying." The questions that arise, then, are, For whom will services be needed? and, How will these needs be met? These questions are not unique to service providers; they were raised earlier in chapters found in Part 2. There appears to be a basic assumption that there will always be people in need of some kind of help.

As have others in this book, the authors in this section call attention to the increasing diversity of the entire population and, specifically, of the older population. Friedsam and Dunkle and Lynch comment on how this diversity would affect the labor force, particularly with reference to human service workers. Friedsam stresses the changing nature of work itself, shifting increasingly in the direction of services. If a major sector of the labor force is engaged in caring for people, then, as Dunkle and Lynch point out, many of the "hands on" jobs will be filled by young Hispanics and members of other ethnic and minority categories—although increasingly it seems inappropriate to use the label "minority" to describe what constitutes numerical majorities in some areas of the nation. Ethnic differences, added to the chronological ones, between formal caregivers and care recipients can be a source of strain and discomfort unless we begin to accept the diversity of our society as a permanent fixture. Friedsam, on the other hand, suggests that some of the jobs will be filled by middle-aged and young-old workers, reflecting the existence of a smaller labor force and different definitions of age categories, and putting a focus on ageism. McRae, on the other hand, suggests that services could be provided by means of electronic monitoring or paying informal caregivers.

Like Troll, earlier in this book, McRae draws on both research and his own personal experiences to describe a potential future reality. He points out that his efforts at describing medical care and research are complicated by the fact that the nature of medical care itself is currently undergoing change or, at least, attempts at change. McRae describes a health care system in which Medicare no longer exists; rather there will be a universal health insurance program. Because it will be driven by the stress of cost containment, there will be more emphasis on preventive medicine.

Both Friedsam and McRae discuss issues relating to death. The latter points out that the real issue is whether care shortens an individual's life or the individual's dying. Friedsam raises the specter of cost when he asks "... how much will society be willing to pay for death with dignity and solace for survivors?"

Undergirding the three papers are issues of cost—primarily financial cost and secondarily emotional cost. Another issue that comes up, particularly in the McRae and Friedsam chapters, is the struggle for control of the health and long-term care systems. There may be turf battles to be waged and the authors speculate on how they will be settled. Indeed, as several of the authors have pointed out, "it boggles the mind" to consider the complexities of a society of centenarians.

Chapter 7

Social Work: More of the Same or Something New?

Ruth E. Dunkle and Susan Lynch

For the profession of social work, the prospect of the average life expectancy increasing to 100 years raises many questions about the impact of such an increase on the social functioning of individuals, families, communities, and even society itself. The question of how this increase will affect the physical, mental, and social functioning of individuals must be examined in light of the fact that an increased life expectancy does not preclude the existence of mental and physical impairments. Indeed, an expanded life expectancy would probably result in more people living longer with varying degrees of disability. In addition to the impact on individuals, how would this increased life expectancy affect family functioning? Families already struggle with the needs of aging members. If people lived to be 100, many families would be faced with meeting the needs of, and making hard choices for, not one but perhaps two or more aging generations. Further, on a societal level, how would the demands of more people living longer lives affect entitlement programs such as Social Security and Medicare? Would the increased numbers drawing benefits lead to the collapse of an already overtaxed system? How would this affect not only program beneficiaries, but also younger members of the work force? Finally, how would an increase in life expectancy be affected by such factors as race, gender, and socioeconomic status? Currently, these variables figure prominently in expected life expectancy calculations. Would the increase in life expectancy cross racial, gender, and socioeconomic divisions, and if it did, what types of individual, family, and societal changes might result?

This chapter will explore these and other issues from a social work perspective. First, we present a review of professional social work practice with the elderly that includes a description of the purpose, values, knowledge base, and methods of direct practice with the individuals, families, groups, and communities. Next there is an overview of the expected demographic and societal changes in the coming decades. The chapter considers the effects on each of these potential client populations should life expectancy be increased to 100 years. Finally, there will be a discussion of how the profession of social work might respond to individual, family, community, and societal needs.

The Profession of Social Work

The profession of social work is unique among the social sciences due to the fact that its practical knowledge base is concerned with the ability of individuals to function within their social environments (Hepworth & Larsen, 1993). Social work practice can target one of three levels for intervention: micro, mezzo, and macro. Micro-level intervention is commonly referred to as direct or clinical practice and is targeted to a specific individual client or client group (e.g., an elderly person, a family, residents at a nursing home). An example of social work intervention at this level would be working with an individual elderly client during the beginning of retirement, widowhood, or recent surgery. It can also consist of family intervention, such as working with an elderly person and the family to help resolve issues around shared living arrangements or the diminishing physical and mental capacities of an elderly client. Within an agency or institutional setting, micro-level practice may also include group work, such as leading a support group for caretakers of Alzheimer patients or a group for elderly heart patients.

Mezzo-level practice, on the other hand, is focused on the systems within which micro-level interventions occur. Commonly referred to as indirect practice, mezzo-level interventions include working with the administrative systems that set policy, design programs, allocate funds and resources, and/or manage internal and interorganizational operations, all of which are activities that affect client services. Social work interventions with elderly clients at this level might include advocating for changes in the policies of a nursing home to allow residents to have more autonomy, or lobbying a legislative body to provide funds for needed elderly services.

Finally, interventions that occur at the societal or macro-level include both social action and community organization activities. Macro-level social work practice with the elderly is generally concerned with developing and working with community groups or organizations to plan, develop and implement programs, as well as set policy. Once a problem area is identified, for example, social workers may try to influence policy makers by researching different designs and implementation strategies or by helping identify ways to reach targeted groups.

• Social Work Values and Professional Purpose •

Professional social work values prescribe a commitment to enhancing the social functioning of individuals, families, and groups while also working to make society and social institutions more responsive to human needs (Hepworth & Larsen, 1993). In 1981, the National Association of Social Workers (NASW) published a working paper that states, in part, "the purpose of social work is to promote or restore a mutually beneficial interaction between individuals and society" (NASW, 1981, p. 6). This statement further outlines certain beliefs held by the social worker profession. These include: (a) that people should be treated with humanity and justice; (b) that ample resources and opportunities for achievement should be provided by social, physical, and/or organizational environments; and, (c) that interactions between individuals and people in their environment should enhance the dignity, self-determination, and individuality of all participants.

Therefore, key to the purpose of social work is the focus on the interaction between the person and the person's social environment. In working with elderly clients, this focus on the person-in-the-environment is particularly important given the heterogeneity of this population. The elderly, as a demographic group, exhibit a large amount of diversity in regard to health, race, socioeconomic status, and even age (Beaver & Miller, 1992). It is obvious that attention must be paid to each client's unique situation and that the ways in which they fit into their social and physical world can be improved. With some elderly clients, this may involve working individually on such issues as depression or adjustment to loss, while for others, intervention may focus on changing social policies that impede the ability of clients to live independently. When working with elderly (and other) client populations, social work practice tries to accomplish three broad purposes: the enhancement of social functioning, the remediation of personal dysfunction, and the promotion of social justice (Hepworth & Larsen, 1993). Thus, as social workers see elderly clients across the wide variety of settings that address the myriad of problems afflicting this group, they focus on improving both individual functioning and the ability of the social environment to meet individual needs.

• Prevention, Restoration, and Remediation •

The focus of social work practice on the individual's ability to function within her or his social environment necessitates an assessment of a problem in terms of both personal impairment, which might limit the client's ability to utilize resources available in the environment, and environmental deprivation, which might limit the availability or accessibility of resources in the environment. For this reason, social work practice interventions aimed at enhancing social functioning include three types of services: preventive, restorative, and remediative. All three types of services can be targeted to micro-level, mezzo-level, and/or macro-level problems. Preventive services are aimed at bolstering the coping abilities of elderly clients and attempting to avert problems before they occur. Micro-level preventive services may include exercise and nutrition programs to improve physical health and delay the onset of health problems, self-help and social groups that offer support and socializing activities, and classes that increase clients' awareness of such problems as overuse of medication, substance abuse, and how to avoid accidents (Beaver & Miller, 1992). Preventive services that target mezzo-level problems, however, may entail advocating for clients to become more involved in the administration of their own programs and services. For example, within a retirement community, a social worker may advocate for clients to be included on decision making boards, or to coordinate their own self-help groups.

When providing preventive services, social workers are active in a variety of roles. For example, they may act as consultant/educators when increasing clients' awareness of health risks, or giving information about nutrition, or may take on a clinical role by leading a support group.

Similarly, a social worker may be a consultant for a client self-help group, or an advocate for an exercise group for the elderly at a local health club.

Interventions intended to rehabilitate client functioning impaired by mental or physical problems, called restorative services, generally occur at a micro-level, although they can occur on mezzo- and macro- levels as well. They focus on providing elderly clients with the means to function to the best of their ability in their social environment. Often, services are also needed by the client's family and may necessitate acquiring aid from several different sources. In these situations, the roles social workers play may include a clinical role, when working directly with the client and the family; a broker role, when accessing different service systems; and/or advocate, when needed services are not readily available.

Finally, social workers provide remediative services that focus on eliminating existing problems. On a micro-level, social workers may work with elderly clients and their families to alleviate stress caused by shared living conditions. Mezzo-level interventions, however, may focus on eliminating institutional problems that impede communication between nursing home residents and staff. On a macro-level, remediative services would target larger systems in an attempt to change policy, or develop a program that could eradicate an existing problem, such as elder abuse.

These three service areas highlight the objectives social workers attempt to meet with clients. One objective is to increase the competence of individuals and to enhance their coping and problem-solving abilities (Hepworth & Larsen, 1993). As the physical or mental functioning of elderly clients becomes impaired, many find it difficult to live independently and still attend to important activities of daily living. Social work strives to increase environmental supports to enhance both competence and coping ability. In this way, they try to insure that elderly clients can remain independent or semiindependent as long as possible. Social workers also help elderly clients obtain needed resources, such as health care, financial assistance, and nutritional support. A third social work objective is to facilitate the elderly clients' interactions with the social environment. This includes not only increasing the fit between the client and the environment, but also insuring that needed resources exist within this environment.

At mezzo- and macro-levels of intervention, social workers try to influence interactions that occur between organizations and institutions that serve elderly clients. This may include acting as a liaison between a group, such as the American Association of Retired Persons (AARP), and agencies that provide elderly services, such as the Area Agency on Aging (AAA) to improve communication and enhance cooperation. Two other objectives at this level are to influence policy on both social and environmental issues and to increase organizational responsiveness to elderly needs. Both of these objectives may call for social workers to lobby legislators in an effort to increase services, influence policy, and enhance awareness of the needs of older adults.

• Social Work Knowledge Base •

Toward the accomplishment of these objectives, social work utilizes a knowledge base that integrates theoretical frameworks drawn from other social sciences with concepts deemed essential by the profession. These concepts emphasize human behavior in the social environment, and an understanding of the developmental tasks faced by individuals throughout the life span. Unfortunately, many theoretical schemata have focused extensively on early developmental stages, especially the years from birth to early adulthood, while paying scant attention to later stages, especially those of old age. Although the profession of social work has, in the past decade, made significant contributions to theoretical knowledge about the developmental stages of later life, the lack of attention this area has received may have ramifications for the ability of social work, and other social sciences, to adequately address the needs of a population whose members live to be 100 years of age.

• Practice Methods •

The practice methods of social work, while informed by theory drawn from other social sciences, are anchored in an ecological system framework (Germain, 1979; Hepworth & Larsen, 1993). Due to the focus on the interaction between the identified client and the client's social environment, during the course of an intervention the target of change may shift from the client to others in the client's environment, including organizations, and the level of intervention may range from a micro- to a macro-perspective, that is, from a focus on individual or family change to a focus on change on a societal level.

Because an ecological system framework highlights the need to assess all or at least most of the systems of which the client is a part, social workers providing services to elderly clients explore family and friend relationships as well as organizations in which the client participates and agencies from which the client receives services. It is particularly important with elderly clients to assess the interaction between medical systems, informal support systems, and formal support systems. For example, do the client's informal support systems enhance or hinder the client's use of health services? If the client has little family support, how helpful are friends and can they facilitate the client's use of formal sources of support?

• Social Policy •

Social work practice is also unique due to its emphasis on social policy. Not only are professional social workers charged with knowing how current social policy affects their elderly clients, there is also the expectation that they will actively work to enact policy that advances the rights of these clients. Furthermore, social worker practitioners are expected to advocate for clients by working to change policy that conflicts with their right to self-determination and well-being (Hepworth & Larsen, 1993). Thus, social work professionals need to be knowledgeable regarding the inequities that exist in the systems affecting elderly clients and the ways in which the inequities can be addressed or the systems changed.

Finally, social workers need to be knowledgeable about practice methods and skills that will enable them to increase the ability of older individuals to utilize resources available in the environment while decreasing behaviors that are dysfunctional or counterproductive. In order to do this, practitioners must learn the skills and methods that are appropriate for interventions with the elderly.

Demographic and Societal Issues

Social workers are currently faced with a myriad of client needs that have resulted from the increasing longevity of Americans combined with other demographic and societal changes. These needs will be further exaggerated if people live, on average, to 100. Of growing concern is whether people are living longer but less healthy lives. One rather optimistic scenario suggests that the human life expectancy is fixed at about 85 years or so, and that increasingly, modern societies will be able to postpone the onset of disease and disability until relatively late in the life course (Fries, 1980).

Others argue, however, that the human life expectancy may not be fixed, that life expectancy may extend well beyond the average of 85 years at a faster pace than disease and disability can be postponed (Schneider & Brody, 1983; Verbrugge, 1984). An increase in longevity may result in added years during which people are sick and disabled and in greater need of formal and informal health care resources.

Whether or not the compression of morbidity is currently taking place or will ever take place remains to be seen. However, we do know that increasingly large numbers of older people will advance into the next century, many of them with chronic illness and disabilities. Increased need for long-term care is perhaps one of the more obvious problems that could result. Current estimates place the number of elderly people needing long-term care at 9 million in the year 2000 and 19 million by 2040 (Rice & Feldman, 1983). Furthermore, there is evidence that as many as 10% of the 27.9 million older people living in the community may be as functionally impaired as older people living in institutions (Callahan, Diamond, Giele, & Morris, 1980).

Thus, it seems clear that caregiving is one area of need that will expand as the number of older people increases. Unfortunately, many long-term care recipients are people whose functional capacities are chronically impaired. They require services on a sustained basis to enable them to be maintained at their maximal levels of psychological, physical, and social well-being (Kane & Kane, 1987). Regardless of whether these services are provided in the community or in an institution, families are often highly involved in providing care to their elderly members. Indeed, more than 80% of care provided to older persons is provided by family (Brody, 1985).

If an increase in longevity did, in fact, result in people living longer lives with more severe illness and disabilities, how would this effect family members who are called upon to provide care? The ability of families to meet the needs of elderly members is already hindered by a scarcity of resources. It is probable that an increase in life expectancy would only exacerbate other factors that currently jeopardize the ability of families to remain a central feature in the care of older people (Brody, 1985). The growing numbers of single parent households that have resulted from high rates of divorce and childbirth to unmarried persons will be subjected to even greater burdens. The increase in such households, generally headed by women, combined with the increased participation of women in the labor force, has substantially decreased the availability of an important source of elder care: adult daughters and daughters-in-law. As these women experience more environmental and emotional stress caused by the lack of financial resources, strained emotional energy, and/or conflicting demands on their time, they will be less able to meet the long-term needs of older family members.

The ability of family to care for aging members is also compromised by the growing preference for smaller families, which results in fewer children to share caregiving, and by the increasing numbers of families who choose to remain childless. Given the current importance of adult children in the provision of informal elder care, these trends suggest that elderly people in the coming decades will become more dependent on formal sources of care. This could result in more institutionalization unless resources to support older people in their communities are provided. However, there is already a growing need for a better financed and better organized system of community care services. Despite the growth in community care with respect to funding and scope of care and services, many older people currently do not receive needed services and their numbers are expected to grow. Defining, measuring, and assuring quality care within community settings continue to be areas of paramount importance (Applebaum, 1990). A significant problem is the need for more home care workers, particularly paraprofessional home care workers who provide the bulk of care to older disabled people living in the community.

With the changing demographic picture of the population in the United States, numerous problems could emerge if longevity were to increase to 100 years of age. Growing disparities in socioeconomic status, and the consequences associated with low economic status are both problems that will require greater attention in the future. Despite the often claimed leveling of economic disparities in old age, analysis of recent census data suggests that economic inequality continues into old age, particularly for women, minorities, and the physically impaired (Crystal & Shea, 1990). Even though average life expectancy has increased, socioeconomic differences in mortality and health persist, and in some cases have increased (Kitigawa & Hauser, 1973; Williams, 1990). Moreover, individuals of lower socioeconomic status are at a disadvantage when it comes to many of the psychosocial and environmental risk factors associated with the etiology and course of disease and functional limitations (e.g., health behaviors, acute and chronic stress, sense of self-efficacy and control, social relations and supports, and work-related hazards). These factors may have additive and cumulative negative effects on health and physical functioning over the life course (House et al., 1990). It may be the case that social policies and programs will increasingly need to focus not on age per se, but on problems or life conditions that call for intervention (Neugarten, 1982).

The Future Political Climate Affecting Social Service Need

The main political and social challenge in the coming decade is acceptance of a multiracial and multi-generational society. There is no doubt that cultural pluralism is a force that will affect the future of the United States. Growing numbers of ethnic and minority populations have, in fact, become the majority in various sections of the country (Torres-Gil, 1986).

Hispanics, apart from the other national minority groups of Asians, African Americans, Pacific Islanders, and Native Americans, are the largest minority in the country. While minority groups in general are underrepresented in the older age groups, their presence affects the aging society. Hispanics are the only group that has had to assimilate in large numbers into the American culture while the society is aging and, therefore, pulling resources away from education, health care, and jobs. A life expectancy extended to 100 years would reduce the political power of younger Hispanics even further. Present inequality between young Hispanic and older white voters is due to the size of the Hispanic community in combination with its lower registration and voting rates. Further, the greater likelihood of Hispanics to be poor—they are twice as likely to be poor as the general population (Torres-Gil, 1986)—increases their need of employment and eduction, two critial features in the ongoing struggle for funds.

Even for the minority groups over age 65 that are increasing faster than whites in the same age group (for example, blacks), their absolute numbers are smaller than the number of whites (Johnson, Gibson & Luckey, 1990). It is predicted, therefore, that whites will fare better in the competition for services. Other factors further complicate service availability for minority populations. For example, statistics show that older blacks are at greater risk than whites for morbidity and mortality (Reed, 1990) and, therefore, are physically less able than whites to participate in programs and services outside the home. Additionally, while many black elderly are in need of home services before they reach age 65 (Johnson, et al., 1990), nonwhites generally receive less needed care than do whites (Aday & Andersen, 1975; Health Resources Administration, 1977).

The entire population of the United States will need to prepare for an aging society, and nonwhites are a critical ingredient in that adjustment. When the baby boom generation ages, younger black and Hispanic minorities will be the mainstay in the labor force as well as the military (Torres-Gil, 1986). Thus, these young men and women will be increasingly called upon to support a predominantly white elderly population. In order for this to happen, it is crucial that young minority men and women are trained in high-skill, high-wage occupations. Therefore, educational support for these minority groups will be necessary. Unfortunately, the provision of such support will be primarily determined by white voters who may or may not see the connection to their own well-being.

If our society were to experience an increase in longevity, the sheer numbers of people, alone, warrants special planning efforts. Of particular concern will be the needs of minority subgroups within our society and in the elderly subpopulation. However, these groups' use of services is not always consistent with what we would expect given their numbers, health status, and economic need (Leutz, Capitman, MacAdam, & Abrahans, 1992). Based on current trends and future projections, many of the elderly who will need care in the future will be quite old (85+), female, and of low economic status. Additionally, many will have few or inadequate social resources, that is, family, friends, and/or organizational affiliations. Whether their needs are met will be determined by policy decisions. Diversity, longevity, and political and social generational claims (Torres-Gil, 1992) will all come into play in determining whether the needs of older people are met.

Social Welfare Trends in Recent Years and Future Projections

Since 1980 there has been a marked shift in social welfare expenditures, programs, and goals, and a dramatic shift toward private provision of services (Sarri, 1988). The reduction in social welfare expenditures has meant that far fewer individuals have been raised out of poverty by federal and state programs (Greenstein, 1987; U.S. House of Representatives Committee on Ways and Means, 1987). Programs and policies such as deinstitutionalization have never been fully funded and therefore have not been fully implemented. One result is the presence on our streets of a large group of homeless, chronically mentally ill persons. Patients were released from the institutions without provision of adequate services.

Whereas social work was once viewed optimistically, since the 1980s the profession has been viewed with hostility (Murray, 1984). The profession has been placed in further jeopardy by major socioeconomic changes in the United States and the world that have significance for the profession of social work ("Change in America," 1986; Wetzel, 1987). A few of these have particular importance for older people (Sarri, 1988):

1. The need for caregiving at many points across the life expectancy is growing. Increasingly, elderly people (especially those over the age of 80) require care. At the same time, increasing numbers of infants and young children are at risk because of poverty, racism, and single parent households where the parent must be fully employed. This issue has not been examined as closely in the United States as it has been in other industrial and postindustrial countries (Finch & Groves, 1983; Kinnear & Graycar, 1982; Rossiter & Graycar, 1984), but could have major consequences for the ability of families to provide care to aging members.

2. More children as well as more adults will be undereducated and functionally illiterate. It is obvious that without adequate education, children cannot get jobs in high-skill occupations, and, thus, cannot provide the needed financial base required to meet the needs of elderly people.

3. There will be further decline in the postsecondary education of minorities, leaving whites more likely to remain in control of service delivery decisions (Thomas, 1986). Again, this defacto discrimination could have serious repercussions, especially given that the labor force will be predominantly composed of minority group members.

4. The proportion of the population aged 15–24 will decline. Currently it is 30% of the population and is expected to drop to 16% in the year 2000 resulting in greater competition for jobs among older age groups. Moreover, 29% of the growth in the young labor force will be minority group members. Unfortunately, these youth will remain unemployed unless their educational level increases ("Change in America," 1986).

5. Currently, one in six Americans lacks access to health care thorough health insurance. This situation primarily affects minority children, their parents, and single young adults (Johnson, 1985). Although older people have health coverage through Medicare, coverage is becoming problematic as the co-pay requirements and other insurance programs increase.

These trends will affect social work practice patterns for social work educators, administrators, policy makers, and community and direct service practitioners (Patti, 1984; Gummer, 1984). Existing social service delivery patterns tend to relate to past situations and are weak in anticipating future need (Sarri, Vinter, & Steketee, 1988). The positioning of social workers in areas that will influence the developments in social welfare policies and programs is less likely as social workers occupy fewer positions of influence in administration and policy than they have in the past.

The 21st century poses new problems for social workers. Meeting the needs of people in underdeveloped countries will be a real challenge. Only 20% of the world's population lives in developed countries where professional social work focuses most of its attention. This minority has as many resources as the remaining 80%. Further, 12% of the population of the developed countries is over the age of 65, whereas for developing countries, the figure on average is 4% (Population Reference Bureau, 1990). The percentage of older people is expected to increase all over the world.

• Necessary Changes in the Social Work Profession •

Prevention makes service delivery more cost effective as well as more humanistic (Allen-Mears, 1993). It is anticipated that two models of social work will emerge in greater force to meet the challenges of large scale institutional and social changes facing our society: private practice and resource mobilization. Within the private practice model, independent practitioners offer their services to individuals, groups, and families. The resource mobilization model means that the worker is employed by an agency or advocacy group that develops programs that prevent or remediate specific problems.

It is anticipated that the need for social workers will continue to increase from 335,000 jobs in 1984 to 640,000 in the year 2020 (National Institutes of Health [NIH], 1988). A greter proportion will need training to work with older people. At present only 20% of NASW members serve people over the age of 65. To date, the large majority of workers in nursing homes have not had any professional training in social work. In addition, most professionally trained social workers who work with older people have not had any professional training in geriatric or gerontological social work. Less than 10% of the full-time faculty in schools of social work have any formal training in aging issues. More social workers will need education and training in the special conditions and needs of older persons and their families in order to meet the needs that will exist.

The personnel needs for social workers in the future will be in areas such as homemaking and home health programs, day programs, family service associations, community mental health centers, senior centers, respite programs, hospice programs, care management activities, information and referral programs, advocacy and legal services programs, protective social services, nutrition programs, nursing homes and homes for the aged, acute care and mental hospitals, discharge planning activities, and state and local surveillance and licensure programs (NIH, 1988).

Conclusion

Social workers provide and will increasingly provide a wide range of services to older people and their families. They may be individual practitioners or members of multidisciplinary teams or organizations. High-risk groups of elders that have special social service needs will be focal points for future service delivery. These groups include the frail elderly, the mentally ill or retarded, and low income persons, as well as minority elders. Two groups that are particularly vulnerable are elders living alone as well as older people who live with an older spouse or other older relatives who require support.

It is clear that the need for social workers to work with older people is going to continue in the future. Needs currently met through informal and formal service delivery networks will in all likelihood go unmet in the future. Two major reasons for this are the thinning of the social support networks as more generations are alive simultaneously (certainly the case if older people live to 100 years) and the expected changes in social service delivery trends. It is anticipated that social workers will be providing services to older people through private practice as well as through agencies that mobilize resources. In both cases the successful delivery of service will be tied to the client's ability to pay. Although some elders and their families will be able to use Medicaid funds, a greater majority will need to pay out of their own financial resources or enroll on a waiting list until limited subsidies become available.

With the economic inequality anticipated for minorities and women, these particular groups will have unmet needs. The current situation in which older blacks are at risk for greater morbidity and mortality than are whites and are less able to seek service outside the home because of poorer functional ability than whites, will become more exaggerated.

The general racial and ethnic composition of the population of the United States will no doubt affect the social service delivery system. With the anticipated racial and ethnic composition and a need for educational resources to facilitate the assimilation of groups into the American culture and economy, money could be siphoned from social services to older people.

The social work profession will need to explore new service delivery models in order to provide the needed services for elders, especially if life expectancy reaches 100 years. Simply training more social workers to work with the elderly will not solve the problem. Peer counselors as well as neighbors and volunteers will become more important participants in the service delivery system. Qualified administrators who embrace innovative service strategies will help. Lastly, social policy that supports service delivery to the nonpoor will be an important piece of undergirding for the entire delivery structure serving older people.

References

Aday, L., & Anderson, R. (1975). *Development of indices of access to medical care.* Ann Arbor, MI: Health Administration Press.

Allen-Mears, P. (1993). State of the School Address and A Personal Statement on Goals. School of Social Work, Ann Arbor, MI. August 24, 1993.

Applebaum, R. (1990). Social supports and social relationships. In R. Binstock & L. George, (Eds.), *The handbook of aging and social sciences* pp. (205–226). New York: Academic Press.

Beaver, M. L., & Miller, D. S. (1992). Clinical social work practice with the elderly: Primary, secondary, and tertiary intervention. Belmont, CA: Wadsworth.

Brody, E. (1985). Parent care as a normative family stress. *The Gerontologist, 25,* 19–25.

Callahan, J. J., Diamond, L., Giele, J., & Morris, R. (1980). Responsibility of families caring for their severely disabled elderly. *Health Care Financing Review, 1,* 29–48.

Crystal, S., & Shea, D. (1990). Cumulative advantage, cumulative disadvantage, and inequality among elderly people. *The Gerontologist, 30,* 437–443.

Finch, J., & Groves, D. (1983). A labor of love: Women, work, and caring. Boston: Routledge and Kegan Paul.

Fries, J. F. (1980). Aging, natural death, and the compression of morbidity. *New England Journal of Medicine, 330,* 130–135.

Germain, C. B. (1979). Social work Practical People and environment. New York: Columbia University Press.

Greenstein, R. (1987, September). Impact of government benefit programs declines, add to number of poor families. Washington, DC: Center on Budget and Policy Priorities.

Gummer, B. (1984). The changing context of social administration: Tight money, loose organization, and uppity workers. *Administration in Social Work, 8* (3), 5–16.

Health Resources Administration. (1977). *Health of the disadvantaged* [chartbook]. (DHEW Publication No. HRA 77–628). Washington, DC: U.S. Department of Health, Education and Welfare, Public Health Service, Office of Health Resources Opportunity.

Hepworth, D. H., & Larsen, J.A. (1993). Direct social work practice: Theory and skills (4th ed.), Belmont, CA: Wadsworth.

House, J. S., Kessler, R. C., Herzog, R.A., Miro, R. P., Kinney, A. M., & Breslow, M. J. (1990). Age, socioeconomic status and health. *Milbank Memorial Quarterly/Health and Society, 68*, 383-411.

Johnson, H., Gibson, R., & Luckey, I. (1990). Health and social characteristics: Implications for services. In Z. Harel, E. McKinney, & M. Williams (Eds.), *Black aged: Understanding diversity and service needs* (pp. 69-81). Newbury Park: Sage.

Johnson, R. (1985). Foundation report on health care in the U.S. Chicago

Kane, R., & Kane, R. (1987). *Long term care: Principles, programs, and policies*. New York: Springer.

Kinnear, D., & Graycar, A. (1982). *Family care of elderly people: Australian perspectives*. Sydney, NSW.: Social Welfare Research Centre.

Kitigawa, E. M., & Hauser, P. M. (1973). *Differential mortality in the United States: A study of socioeconomic epidemiology.* Cambridge: Harvard University Press.

Leutz, W.N., Capitman, J.A., MacAdam, M., & Abrahans, R., (1992). *Care for frail elders: Developing community solutions.* Connecticut: Auburn Horse.

Murray, C. (1984). Losing ground. New York: Basic Books.

National Association of Social Workers. (1981). Working statement on the purpose of social work. *Social Work. 26*(1), 6.

Neugarten, B. (1982). *Age or need? Public policies for older people.* Beverly Hills: Sage.

Patti, R. (1984). Who leads the human services? The prospects for social-work leadership in an age of political conservatism. *Administration in Social Work, 8* (1), 17-30.

Population Reference Bureau. (1990). America in the 21st century: Social and economic support systems. Washington, DC: Population Reference Bureau.

Reed, W. (1990). Health care needs and services. In Z. Harel, E. McKinney, & M. Williams (Eds.), *Black aged: Understanding diversity and service needs.* (pp. 183-204). Newbury Park: Sage.

Rice, D., & Feldman, J. (1983). Living longer in the United States: Demographic changes and health needs of the elderly. *Milbank Quarterly/Health and Society, 61*, 362-397.

Rossiter, G., & Graycar, A. (1984). *Survey of family care of the elderly.* Sydney, NSW: Social Welfare Research Centre.

Sarri, R., Vinter, R., & Steketee, M. (1988). *The future of social work and social work education: Final report of the interdisciplinary seminar.* Report.

Schneider, E. L., & Brody, J.A. (1983). Aging, natural death, and the compression of morbidity: Another view. *New England Journal of Medicine, 309*, 854-856.

Staff. (1986, September). Change in America. *Chronicle of Higher Education*, p. 1.

Thomas, F. (1986). *The new demographics.* New York: Ford Foundation.

Torres-Gil, F. (1986). The Latinization of a multigenerational population: Hispanics in an aging society. *Daedalus, 115* (1), pp. 325-348.

Torres-Gil, F. (1992). *The new aging: Politics and change in America.* New York: Auburn House.

U. S. House of Representatives, Committee on Ways and Means (1987). Subcommittee on Public Assistance: Programs within the purview of the committee. Washington, DC: GPO, March.

Verbrugge, L. (1984). "Longer life but worsening health." Trends in health and mortality of middle aged and older persons. *Milbank Quarterly/Health and Society, 62* (3), 475.

Wetzel, J. (1987). *American youth: A statistical profile.* New York: W.T. Grant Foundation.

Williams, D. R. (1990). Socioeconomic differentials in health: A review and redirection. *Social Psychology Quarterly, 53* (2), pp. 81-99.

Chapter 8

"But Doctor, My Left Knee is Also 100"

Thomas D. McRae

The title of this chapter stems from an anecdote with which many readers will be familiar. Its origins are apocryphal, but I first heard it over 15 years ago from Dr. Robert Butler when I was a medical student and he was addressing a convention of the American Medical Students' Association. For those who have not heard the story, as he told it, it goes like this:

> *A 95-year-old man visited his doctor complaining of a pain in his right knee. His doctor took a look at him and said, "What do you expect? You're 95!" To which the patient replied, "But, doctor, my left knee is also 95 and it feels just fine!"*

At the time I heard this story, it had the desired effect—it impressed indelibly on my thinking the dangers of ageism in medical care. In fact, it was so powerful that in teaching medical students and house staff in the years since, I have often employed it (usually with proper attribution). Thus this parable seemed an appropriate meditation on which to begin this chapter that will explore the effects on medical care and medical research should I and a lot of other people live to be 100 or more.

The first thought that this prompts in my mind is an optimistic one. If large numbers of people live to be older than 100, there may be less ageism in medical care because elderly people will be so common, and 65-, 75-, even 85-year-olds will seem young by comparison. On the other hand, the problem could get worse for the oldest group because the gap in life experience between young doctors in their 20s and 30s, or even in their 40s and 50s, and patients over 100 would be so great that it almost boggles the mind and surely would create barriers to optimal medical care.

Because of the speculative nature of our entire discussion, this dichotomy between an improvement in some problems doctors and older patients currently face and a worsening of others will be unavoidable unless we make certain assumptions about what our population of centenarians will be like. We could be totally idealistic and assume that all will remain cognitively intact and physically vigorous until the very end when they all will die peacefully in their sleep. Or we could be totally nihilistic and assume that the final years for all will be marked by cognitive decline and extreme physical frailty. Choosing one of these assumptions would perhaps make this discussion easier, but my desire is, rather, to make this discussion as realistic as possible. In an attempt to do so, I turned to the current literature on centenarians for a description of the population that now exists. Although not many studies of this increasing population have been published, I was able to turn up a handful of papers.

Centenarians: Basing Projections on What We Now Know

• Autopsy Studies •

It was somewhat disquieting, though probably not surprising, that the majority of reports that I did find were of autopsy studies. In the earliest, from 1978, Ishii and Sternby (1978a, 1978b, 1978c) reported the results of all autopsies done on centenarians at Malmö General Hospital in Sweden between 1966 and 1975. Their cases totaled 7 men and 16 women ranging in age from 100 to 104. For comparison, the total number of deaths of centenarians in all of Sweden during this time frame was 947 (275 men and 672 women; age range 100 to 110). Regrettably, this series of three articles focuses primarily on descriptive changes in the major organ systems, telling us nothing about premorbid conditions or final hospital course. Even the causes of death are less than clearly stated. What we do learn is that atrophy characterized these individuals, whether looking at their height and weight or at specific organs. In addition, virtually all of the patients had moderate to severe atherosclerosis. Nearly two-thirds had some form of pneumonia. A similar number had osteoporosis. Just over one-third had a pulmonary embolism. Roughly one quarter had malignant neoplasms, but in only two of these six was it considered the primary cause of death.

In the second autopsy study, Klatt and Meyer (1987) report on 32 centenarian autopsies done at Los Angeles County-University of Southern California Medical Center between 1921 and 1983. This study is atypical in that men outnumbered women; numbers were 20 and 12, respectively. The authors note, however, that this reflects the demographics of the hospital's admissions over this period. The same was true for the racial mixture—16 whites, 8 Hispanics, 7 blacks, and 1 Native American. The age range was from 100 to 115, though the authors do not report how these ages were verified. Body height and weight as well as organ weights were similar to the Swedish group. Unlike the Swedish group, only 78% of this group had generalized atherosclerosis, only 47% had pneumonia, only 12.5% had pulmonary emboli, and only 10%, markedly less than the Swedish group, had osteoporosis. (This is explained in part by the predominance of males in this group; it also likely reflects autopsy methodology and reporting.) Malignant neoplasms were found in 40% of these American centenarians, somewhat more than for the Swedish group, and they were considered the primary cause of death in 8 of the 13 subjects. Of particular interest in this study is the report that the majority of patients (21 of 32) died within 3 days of hospital admission. The average length of stay was 6 days, and the range was 1 to 72 days.

In the third autopsy study that I was able to find, Mizutani & Shimada (1992) report primarily on brain findings in 27 Japanese centenarians autopsied between 1975 and 1991. As in the two previous studies, these authors also found that pneumonia was the most common cause of death (11 of 27 cases). As in the Swedish study, cancer was less common (7 cases) and was the cause of death in only 2 cases. These authors also found the number of cardiovascular deaths (5 of 27) similar to the Swedish group. This study is particularly useful to us because it reports directly, although not in clear or standard detail, on the functional level of the centenarians involved. Of these subjects, 11 of 27 were cognitively normal and had active daily lives. Another 9 had "slight cognitive dysfunction and disturbance of daily activities before the final admission" (p. 169). In addition, 4 patients were definitely demented—one due solely to a subdural hematoma and one exacerbated by a subdural—and 4 were hemiparetic secondary to strokes. (One of these was in the definitely demented group.)

None of these patients had definite Alzheimer's disease. Many of them had neuritic plaques and/or neurofibrillary tangles, but not as many as seen in Alzheimer's disease. This leads the authors to conclude that their data support the generally held contention that Alzheimer's disease is, in fact, a disease and not merely a consequence of aging.

• Living Centenarian Studies •

The only study of living centenarians clearly describing functional status that I was able to find was published by Karasawa, Kawashima, and Kasahara in 1979. In this work, the authors surveyed 115 Japanese centenarians living in Tokyo (about one-third of Japan's total population of centenarians at the time). The study participants ranged in age from 100 to 105. There were 95 women and 20 men (slightly higher than the national female-to-male ratio of 4.2 to 1 for Japanese centenarians at that time). For our purposes, the most useful aspects of this study were a simple mental status test and a descriptive evaluation of activities of daily living (ADL). On all measures, the centenarians as a group did worse than a group of nonagenarians surveyed for comparison. On the mental status test, almost 75% of the centenarians scored in the range of moderate to marked mental decline. About 22% were in the mild mental decline range, and only 3% were in the normal range. Regrettably, the authors did not correlate these scores with the educational levels of the centenarians, which are likely to be low given the preponderance of women. The authors do show a significant relationship between education and these mental status scores in the nonagenarian group. The daily activities are described in six categories: "constantly bedridden" (22.6%), "occasionally bedridden" (24.3%), "least active—out of bed but hardly move" (20.0%), "less active—take care of themselves but poor in movement" (16.5%), "active—move normally in their homes, go out around the house" (16.5%), and "very active—more active, go out steadily, get on the bus or train, even alone" (0%). Unfortunately, there are no descriptions of medical conditions that might have had an impact on the functional status of this group.

The only other study that I have been able to find that has a bearing on helping to define our projected population of centenarians was published recently by Manton, Stallard, and Liu (1993). In this work, the authors construct models of active life expectancy based on data from the National Long Term Care Surveys of 1982, 1984, and 1989. They use this data to create disability distribution curves for both men and women. These curves suggest that for men over 100 years of age, approximately 52% will be fully active, while for women the number is about 47%. In addition, there are six categories of decline and approximate projected distributions for men and women: mild cognitive impairment (men, 18%; women, 13%), moderate instrumental activities of daily living (IADL) function (men 1%; women, 2%), physical impairment (men 5%; women, 4%), frailty (men, 19%; women, 5%), high degrees of frailty (men, 4%; women, 7%), and institutionalization (men, 10%; women, 22%). It is notable that these data suggest somewhat more frailty and dependence for women who survive past 100. Not surprisingly, the most marked increase in these more dependent groups begins about age 85.

• Personal Experiences •

My other source for help in defining this speculative group of centenarians is my own personal experience in caring for them. This experience is limited to two patients. The first was a woman that I agreed to care for precisely because I wanted the experience of caring for someone over 100. She had become homebound by her frailty, and I agreed to make home visits. She was blind and nearly deaf and had suffered a stroke which left her bedridden, hemiplegic, and contracted. Because of her sensory deprivation, she often suffered hallucinations. Nonetheless she was in her own home, where she very much wanted to be, and was cared for by two very good home attendants. She had two children, both in their 70s, who lived 1 to 2 hours away and visited regularly. Communicating with her was not easy because of her hearing impairment, but I managed with the aid of an assistive listening device. On our first visit, I was struck by what she said when I asked her about her age. "Why am I still here? I had my 100th birthday last November. It was a lovely party. The family was here, and there was a card from the President, and I thought that after that it would all be over." She was in my care for about 6 months when she stopped eating. It was clear what her wishes were, and her family concurred that no aggressive measures should be taken. In a few days she died peacefully at home, just short of her 101st birthday.

My second centenarian patient is another woman for whom I have cared for the past six years. She turned 100 this year, though initially she did not want to admit it. She is not quite as frail as the first woman, but over the time I have known her she has declined substantially. She, too, is severely hearing-impaired. She is now no longer able to walk because of severe arthritis, but is able to come to my office in a wheelchair. Cognitively she has also declined, apparently due to multiple little cerebral infarcts and possibly also due to Alzheimer's disease. This patient is also a widow cared for by two good home attendants, but unlike the first, she has no children, only an elderly nephew and his family. Her nephew would like very much to see her placed in a nursing home, but her strongest wish is to remain in her own apartment, and I will do my best to honor that wish.

I have indirect experience of one other centenarian, a colleague at the medical center who lived to be nearly 103. In his final year, he suffered a series of strokes which led to his death. But up until he was 102 or so, he remained intellectually and physically active, coming into his lab every day. I did not know him personally, but I would often see him in the faculty dining room, and when I did see him, I was always a little bit awed and inspired.

So, based on the little I have been able to glean from the literature and on my own limited experience, I will make the following assumptions about our speculative population of centenarians: Women will outnumber men at least two or three to one. A spectrum of vigor will exist from the fully physically and cognitively intact to the extremely frail with both physical and mental impairment. About half of the population will be fully active, while the other half will have at least mild physical and/or mental impairment. Of this latter group with impairments, some 30% to 40% will require institutionalization, representing 15% to 20% of the whole population. Few will simply die in their sleep. For most, the final months up to the last year of their lives will be marked by increased morbidity leading to death.

It is on this set of assumptions that I will base the remainder of my discussion. As I noted at the outset, the effort to establish these assumptions was made in order to give the discussion at least some grounding in possible future reality. I realize that this is probably just as arbitrary as choosing either idealist or nihilist scenarios would have been; however, I hope that, regardless of my approach, the reader will find some value in the ensuing discussion.

Medical Care in an Era of Centenarians

At this juncture, having defined the assumptions about the population on which this discussion is to be based, I would like to begin to discuss what medical care and research will be like in this age of centenarians; however, I am immediately faced with another dilemma—the unknown of just what medical care itself will be like 40 to 60 years from now. (I choose this time frame as the rough amount of time that it will take most of the current authors to reach 100—another arbitrary attempt at realism.) As this is written, a major attempt at restructuring the American health care system is underway. The great likelihood is that even when this book is published, the nation will be no closer to a final version of the health care system of the future. Even if the government has succeeded in passing a health care reform plan, chances are its provisions for the elderly will be murky. If the current public discourse is any indication, provisions for the future, when the tidal wave of babyboomers rolls past the age of 65, will be slim to none.

The reason that so little is being said about the demographic imperative is that the natural first impulse of just about any policy planner is to recoil in horror when speculating about the impact of this population on the medical care of the future. Currently people over the age of 65 number about 12% of the United States population, but they consume 30% to 50% of the health care resources. Current projections of the population for 40 to 60 years from now are that those over 65 years of age will number 20% of the total American population, and their utilization of the health care system will likely increase proportionately. Already, most writers who have speculated about the medical care of the elderly in the future have worried that resources will not be adequate. If we add to this an even larger number of centenarians than currently predicted, the percentage of the total population who are elderly will be even greater than 20% (because fewer will have died), and the strain on resources will be greater still.

So, faced with yet another inherent uncertainty in this discussion, let me plunge into prognostication: In our future society of centenarians, Medicare will no longer exist. It will be replaced by a form of universal health insurance which will be provided mainly by employers and which will pay for basic coverage. For most this will mean membership in a health maintenance organization (HMO). Some employers will provide continued payment for this coverage as part of retirement benefits. Many employers will not be able to do so; thus, many elderly will be forced to maintain some form of employment well beyond the traditional retirement age (which will certainly have increased from 65, anyway). For those who cannot work, the government will pay a portion of the HMO coverage, with the individual paying the rest; the actual proportions will depend on the individual's resources. A small percentage of the elderly population will refuse to participate in this system and instead will pay for a comprehensive insurance package that will cover a full spectrum of care and allow choice of physicians and institutions (as long as they participate by accepting the insurance coverage, which, of course, they will be forced to do). Needless to say, this coverage will be very expensive and only affordable by the very well off, which will be ironic, because they will need it least, given the positive correlation between health and socio-economic status.

The driving force behind care anywhere in the health care system, but particularly in the HMOs, will be cost containment. Thus, there will be an emphasis on preventive medicine—especially primary prevention such as vaccinations. Medications will be paid for, but only if they are prescribed from the HMO's formulary, which will be restricted to low-cost generic drugs as much as possible. Prescriptions of expensive, newer drugs and of experimental drugs will be restricted to selected specialists in the HMO to whom access will be tightly controlled. This emphasis on cost containment in the pharmaceutical industry will result in decreased spending on advertising, leading, in turn, to the demise of "throwaway" journals and a marked rise in subscription fees to the standard journals. There will also be fewer sales representatives pitching drugs to individual doctors, and there will no longer be any need for companies to support continuing medical education. Instead, companies will need only a relatively few sales people to win contracts with the HMOs. (The potential for bribery and other forms of corruption in order to win these contracts will be great and will need to be monitored closely, presumably by federal oversight.) The competition will force companies to stop developing "copycat" drugs in the same class as their competitors. It may also force them to stop efforts at developing truly new drugs, unless they have some guarantee of recouping their investment and subsequently making a profit. Such reduced incentive may force the government or the HMOs, into subsidizing new drug research and development.

Hospitalization, invasive procedures, and nursing home care will all be discouraged because of their cost to the HMO system. Advances in technology will allow most surgeries to be performed as outpatient day surgeries anyway, but access to even these will be tightly controlled. As much care as possible will be provided at home. As already noted, as much as 20% of our centenarian population will need institutional care. Coupled with the frail elderly in the 85- to 100-year-old group, this will put a great strain on existing institutions and will likely result in creating more nursing home beds. Staffing for these beds will be less of a problem than it is today because acute care staffs will be reduced as demands for acute inpatient services are met in other ways. Most long-term care beds will be under the control of the HMOs, which will tightly restrict access. Thus, most beds will truly be a last resort: some beds in HMO nursing homes, however, will function as short-term rehabilitation beds because of the increased demand to keep people in the community. The need for these short-term rehab beds will be great, and so they will also likely exist in acute care hospitals (an opportunity to utilize closed wards) and perhaps even in freestanding facilities constructed by the HMOs.

As noted, home care will receive increasing emphasis. Families will be encouraged to do more for patients. Because our centenarians' children will be elderly themselves, burdens may need to be shifted to grandchildren or even great-grandchildren. Financial incentive for this care may be provided to the family caregivers by the HMOs in the form of reduced premiums or perhaps increased service packages or even credits for future long-term care for the family caregivers. (By this time, health care will have become a form of currency.) Home care will no longer be provided by independent agencies as it usually is today but rather by agencies under direct HMO control. There will also be a greater acceptance of risk in keeping the centenarians at home than there is today; 24-hour home attendants will rarely be allowed because of their expense. Instead, we might see some form of electronic monitoring with a central dispatcher able to respond to needs as they arise. Already there are various emergency notification devices. In the future, when the "information superhighway" has reached into most homes, both active and interactive monitoring should be feasible. If our centenarian has no family to provide support, which will certainly be the case for some—either by choice or by circumstance of their longevity—paid caregivers will be required. These may be trained individuals, provided by and salaried by the HMO. Another option, however, may be more informal caregivers chosen by the patient from among friends and neighbors, who again may be reimbursed by the HMO through some form of health care credits.

• The Doctor–Patient Relationship •

As alluded to at the outset of this chapter, the relationships between doctors and patients in the age of centenarians hold a wealth of possibilities. Some patients will be fortunate to age in place with their doctors. Even in the world of relatively quick visits mandated by the HMOs, 40 or more years of such a professional relationship will result in a knowledge and understanding of the patient by the doctor almost unheard of in today's climate. This kind of long-term relationship also has the potential to foster an increased sense of self-responsibility for health on the part of the patient, so that decisions about health care can be truly mutual rather than dictated solely by the physician. For centenarians who do not have the good fortune to have a long relationship with their physician, there still may be an assertiveness in decision making based on a sense of survivorship. Of course, numerous negative possibilities exist as well. Younger physicians may shun working with centenarians, or if they do work with them, they may be nihilistic in their approach. Still others may be overly aggressive or totally paternalistic.

• Medical Ethics •

Certainly an area of tremendous importance to this scenario will be the field of medical ethics. Using our assumption of increased morbidity in the final years of advanced old age, will our society have come to terms with protocols for death? Will efforts be made to intervene in acute potentially life-ending illnesses or will therapeutic nihilism rule the day? Will the patient's wishes still be paramount or will society have decided that resources are too scarce to be expended on anyone who has lived to 100? Will there be increased physician-assisted suicide? Will it logically fall to physicians who have, themselves, reached 100 to help their peers through the final exit?

In my mind, the ethical principles that guide us today will still hold in the future, and I believe that patient autonomy will be the overriding principle. The key to maintaining autonomy will be determining and recording what it is that the patient actually wants while the patient is still capable of making that determination. Perhaps in addition to a card from the President on their 100th birthdays, everyone should also be sent a living will or health care proxy and required to return it to where it could be recorded in a national database, accessible to doctors' offices, emergency rooms, hospitals, and nursing homes. Then, when illness strikes, as it will in most cases, the patient's guidance will be readily available to his or her doctors. Even if this or something similar is accomplished, however, two problems will remain. The first could occur in the instance that the patient chooses to limit interventions and wants only comfort care to allow a dignified death. Efforts will need to be made to ensure that choice has not been coerced, either directly or subtly, by the attitudes and demands of the patient's family or society. Most older patients, in my experience, do not want to be a burden and they do not want to lose their independence. Without adequate reassurances regarding these issues, they will readily choose to limit intervention, even though the acute problem may be completely treatable. Depending on their knowledge of the patient and their experience, physicians could all too easily acquiesce to these wishes; they may even be pressured to do so by resource considerations.

The second potential problem is really the flip side of the first. It could occur in the instance that the patient chooses to demand that everything possible be done. In this case, the physician is faced with issues of medical futility as well as resource considerations. It would indeed be ironic if the demands and expenditures of centenarians result in the limitation of resources available to younger elderly. (It is not too difficult to imagine, however, a centenarian-dominated society confronted by the attitude: "We are the survivors. We deserve the resources. If you younger elderly cannot survive without them, you shouldn't survive.")

The solutions to both these problems consist of the patients making truly informed choices and of the doctors really knowing the patients and having enough experience with centenarian care to be able to predict patient outcomes with reasonable reliability. In my mind, the question to be answered when making a decision to actively intervene or a decision to withdraw or to withhold treatment is fairly straightforward: "Does this action prolong the patient's life, or does it prolong the patient's death?" The physician's ability to answer this question comes only with experience and then only if the physician is trained to take the responsibility. The experience may come as physicians age with their patients. The training to take the responsibility will have to be mandated by society.

An intimately related and even more difficult aspect of the ethical issues that will be brought into focus in our age of the centenarians is the question of physician-assisted suicide. This is truly a thorny issue. By the time we have reached this speculative time, laws may have been passed regulating such practices. So far, of course, American society has been reluctant to condone such practices, rightly, in my opinion, fearing the slippery slope. Nonetheless, following our assumptions about the centenarian population, there will likely be a group for whom this is an issue. Even today, the highest suicide rate in the country is among white males over the age of 75, and I know of more than one elderly person who has hoarded sleeping pills in case they feel the need to use them. Ultimately the issue boils down to individual autonomy—the ability to control one's own end, to limit suffering, to relieve burdens. Certainly Judeo-Christian religious doctrine teaches that this ultimate control is not ours to hold. The development of such teaching, however, has not encompassed the technological advances of modern medicine. In the past, death was a matter of fate or "when God said it was time." Today, certainly in the acute care setting, there is at least the appearance of being able to control when death occurs. Although this may, ultimately, be an illusion, it is one that is likely to become even more convincing in the future. Thus, many reject the traditional religious teachings and argue not only for their right to decide but also to receive help in carrying out their decisions thoroughly and painlessly. It is interesting that in a recent survey of physicians regarding this issue (Watts, Howell, & Priefer, 1992), the majority of respondents wanted to preserve the right to choose suicide for themselves, but a similar majority did not want to be required to assist in suicide.

Obviously, there are no easy answers to this question. In my opinion, the crux of the matter is the same as in medical treatment decisions—does this act shorten life or does it shorten dying? Take as an example, one of the first cases of Dr. Jack Kevorkian, a woman in the early stages of Alzheimer's disease. While I certainly believe that Alzheimer's disease is a terminal illness, this woman was clearly not in the terminal stage of the disease, and while no one can say for certain just what her course would have been, she probably had several years before she would have reached the final stage. I have no doubt that this was a case of shortening a life rather than shortening a death, and I think it is truly tragic that this woman did not have the resources to face the challenge of her decline. Furthermore, I believe that in this case in particular, Dr. Kevorkian not only violated the Hippocratic oath, he desecrated the sacred trust that forms the bond between patient and physician. Now, I suppose that he would say that he was honoring the patient's wishes, but I find it deeply troubling that her major stated reason for choosing to end her life when she did was that she did not want to become a significant burden for her family. Though Dr. Kevorkian deserves credit for forcing society to consider this issue, in this case he was terribly wrong. He was not simply starting down the slippery slope; he was rushing headlong towards the nadir of a civilization that can no longer lift up its burdens but chooses instead to eliminate them. This is surely a cautionary tale for our age of centenarians, wherein for many the burdens will be great; even greater will be the temptation to eliminate these burdens in the name of life having reached an acceptable maximum time span rather than to lift them up in the name of allowing life to be fully lived.

• Medical Education •

The final topic that I will discuss briefly in this consideration of what medical care will be like in the age of centenarians is medical education. I think it is obvious how crucial this is to determining just what medical care for our centenarians will be like. I think most readers are probably also aware that unless things get rapidly better, our century survivors are going to be in big trouble. A recent survey that I conducted with the Association for Gerontology in Higher Education and the American Geriatrics Society revealed that at present, less than 20% of all medical students in this country are getting what can be considered adequate exposure to geriatrics and gerontology. On top of that, the number of students entering primary care still appears to be declining, and geriatrics fellowships, like most noninvasive, not highly reimbursed areas of medicine, are significantly undersubscribed. Efforts are again underway to address these problems, but they stand only a slight chance of addressing our real projected needs, much less those of a large number of centenarians. Nonetheless, in the spirit of the discussion, I will offer two thoughts, neither of which is original, except as applied to this scenario. I have already hinted at the first—namely, that centenarian (or at least post-85-year-old) physicians may be the solution to providing good care to this population, especially if at around the age of 70 all specialist physicians were required to cross train to become generalists. This would make more room for upcoming young specialists, and meet a significant need with individuals experienced enough to do the job well. My second thought is that centenarian physicians be required to serve in medical schools as docents and role models. Based on my own student experience, I still believe that this practice will go a long way toward generating the necessary interest among students—that and paying twice as much as dermatologists and radiologists.

Medical Research in the Centenarian Future

It is now my task to turn to medical research in our society of centenarians. Again, myriad possibilities abound. For the sake of some sort of order, however, I will consider the possibilities in two groups: the conventional and the totally speculative. I will further attempt to consider both research in my own area of expertise, Alzheimer's disease, as well as medical research in general.

To begin with Alzheimer's disease, I am hopeful that by the time we have reached this future age, we will have discovered the basic pathogenesis of the disease as well as treatments that offer significant amelioration. In addition, definitive antemortem diagnostic tests will have been found. If this is the case, work will then be focused on prevention and on outright cures. It seems clear now that malfunction at the molecular level in brain cells is what leads to their demise in this disease. In many, if not most, this capacity for molecular function to go awry is inherited. The keys to preventing the disease will be twofold: identifying carriers of the genetic capacity for the disease and discovering the factor or factors that trigger the molecular malfunction. Regarding the former, the gene or genes involved will no doubt have been identified, and genetic screening via blood sampling should not be difficult. The difficulty will lie in what to do with the knowledge. Appropriate genetic counseling and strict confidentiality will be essential. Regarding the latter, longitudinal cohort studies will be needed. Factors to be examined will include nutrition, environmental exposures, stress, and neurohormones. Most researchers agree that the prevalence of Alzheimer's disease increases markedly with age. If the autopsy research discussed earlier is an accurate indication, centenarians as a group have very little Alzheimer's disease. Thus, a large population of centenarians will be invaluable controls for the cohort studies. Of course, one could argue that those who survive to pass the century mark simply did not inherit the genetic capacity for the disease, but we have assumed that a genetic screen will be used to define these cohorts. Mizutani and Shimada's (1992) autopsy studies did show neuritic plaques and neurofibrillary tangles in centenarian brains, just at much lower levels than in the full-blown disease. Thus, successful centenarians might have avoided the triggering factors which well-designed cohort studies could reveal. It is also possible that these individuals have active mechanisms for suppressing the spread of such pathology. Cross-sectional case control studies may be able to identify these mechanisms.

The above are some of the more conventional sorts of research on Alzheimer's disease that I can readily envision. Thinking of research on an outright cure for the disease moves me more into the realm of the totally speculative. Two such possibilities that are already mentioned today but are very, very far from realization are replacing brain cells destroyed by the disease with fetal tissue transplants and regenerating affected cells through nerve growth factors. Tremendous difficulties exist with either of these strategies, not the least of which is how to deliver either to the areas of the brain where it is needed and will be effective. Nonetheless, fledgling research is being conducted in both areas, and eventually, one or both may succeed. An even more distant possibility would be some sort of molecular engineering that could correct the malfunction that leads to the disease. The Human Genome Project ought to have been completed by our centenarian age, and knowledge that it generates could contribute to this strategy. Certainly, early efforts in this regard are already being made with diseases like cystic fibrosis.

If my optimism about progress in Alzheimer's research is well founded, by the time I reach 100, I will have to focus on another area of interest. I don't think this will be difficult because there will still be tremendous amounts to learn and understand about how the brain works. How does thought occur? How are memories formed and stored? What is the nature of emotion or of complex constructs like aggressive behavior or gender identity? What is the basis for all of the other mental and neurodegenerative diseases? Because I am what I term a structuralist, I believe that progress in molecular biology will ultimately lead to the answers to these questions. I also believe that the presence of a large centenarian population will facilitate these studies, as they will have done for Alzheimer's disease. In recent years, through my work with Alzheimer's disease, I have become a junior molecular biologist. I hope that in the next 60 years I will become an accomplished one still able to come into my lab to pursue these questions.

Turning now to other areas of medical research, on the conventional side, there will be vast amounts to be done in a society of centenarians. Society must, of course, continue to support research with this group. An aging society, however, should have its own interest at heart, so I am reasonably optimistic that research support will continue. At any rate, assuming the funding is provided, I predict that several diseases will be major focuses with efforts to fully understand their pathogenesis, as well as to develop both preventive and curative strategies. These diseases will include atherosclerosis, cancer, osteoporosis, and degenerative joint diseases. Of course, these diseases are already more or less major focuses of medical research—it doesn't take a wizard to predict that given their prevalence in centenarians, the interest will continue. It may be that one or more of these medical puzzles, such as osteoporosis, will have been completely solved. I am confident, however, that at least some work will remain to be done.

Pneumonia, as already noted, is probably the leading killer of centenarians. New causative organisms will continue to evolve, and new antibiotics will continue to be developed. With a large centenarian population, though, the focus of research in this area would become the immune system. Having functioned so well for so long, why does it fail when it does? What factors lead to the susceptibility to the infection in the first place? Why is the infection so often fatal once it does get started? Can new preventive vaccines be developed? These are questions that will be of prime importance in the age of centenarians, and answers to them may well come from techniques developed by another 40 years of AIDS research. A medical truism describes pneumonia as the "old man's friend". If these questions are successfully answered, as I believe they will be, there will then remain a much more difficult question: "Who will be the old man's friend now?"

Other conventional areas of research will be aimed at restoring various disabilities. Efforts at cochlear implants and joint replacement already exist, some more successful than others. Likewise, cataract removal and intraocular lens implants are now easily done and are largely successful. In the age of centenarians, these procedures will become more refined and, depending on resources, more widely utilized so that serious deficiencies of vision, hearing and joint function will become relatively rare (Yes, I did watch "The Six Million Dollar Man" when I was a kid.) Efforts at restoring muscle function and vigor through exercise, nutrition, hormone replacement, and growth factors are another logical area for restorative research that have all had their beginnings today and could have wide applications both cross-sectionally and longitudinally with a large centenarian population. And I mustn't leave out health services research. One would think that we might have learned how to provide adequate and responsive services by then, but a big burst of 100-year-olds could be just enough to upset the apple cart.

In the realm of the totally speculative, I see research projects on the nature of longevity and, inevitably, life extension. Some of this work will be generated by the Human Genome Project. Some will come from AIDS work and our better understanding of the immune system. Cures for the diseases discussed above will lead to other work. Eventually, we may really understand the keys to successfully living more than a century. Expanding the maximum human life span beyond 110 to 120 years will then become the next frontier. By then we may be able to answer whether we would want to do so.

Summary

In closing, I would hope that I have provided the reader with some stimulating food for thought. I set out to do so by trying to define the population for discussion as realistically as possible, based on what we now know. Then I proceeded to make my best guess about the future systems that would serve them—not a pretty picture, but not horrendous, either. Exploring this system, I presented my views on several issues of medical ethics that I believe will be critical in the future, whether we see this centenarian age or not. I then tried to raise the banner of medical education, which I also believe to be critical. Finally, I shared some of my ideas about future medical research, both conventional and totally speculative, in Alzheimer's disease, my area of expertise, and in general. If I have stimulated the reader to think more deeply or creatively about the medical care and problems of the oldest-old, then I have accomplished my goal.

References

Ishii, T., & Sternby, N. (1982) Pathology of centenarians. I. The cardiovascular system and lungs. *Journal of the American Geriatrics Society, 26,* 108–115.

Ishii, T., & Sternby, N. (1978) Pathology of centenarians. II. Urogenital and digestive systems. *Journal of the American Geriatrics Society, 26,* 391–396.

Ishii, T., & Sternby, N. (1978) Pathology of centenarians. III. Osseous system, malignant lesions, and causes of death. *Journal of the American Geriatrics Society, 26,* 529–533.

Klatt, E., & Meyer, P. (1987) Geriatric autopsy pathology in centenarians. *Archives of Pathology and Laboratory Medicine,* 111, 367–369.

Karasawa, A., Kawashima, K., & H. Kasahara. (1979) Mental aging and its medico-psycho-social background in the very old Japanese. *Journal of Gerontology, 34,* 680–686.

Manton, K., Stallard, E., & Liu, K. (1992). Forecasts of active life expectancy: policy and fiscal implications. *Journal of Gerontology 48:*(special issue):11–26.

Mizutani, T., & Shimada, H. (1992) Neuropathological background of twenty-seven centenarian brains. *The Journal of Neurological Sciences, 108:*168–177.

Watts, D., Howell, T., & Priefer, B. (1992). Geriatricians attitudes toward assisting suicide of dementia patients. *Journal of the American Geriatrics Society, 40:*878–885.

Chapter 9

Long-Term Care in the Very Long Term

Hiram J. Friedsam

THE FUTURE AIN'T WHAT IT USED TO BE.
-attributed to Arthur C. Clarke

The potential impact of life extension on long-term care has been a basic concern of many gerontologists for more than three decades. It has been a concern resting on a substructure of fear—fear that the predictable increase in the proportion of the oldest old will ultimately result in hundreds of thousands of frail, disabled, and dependent persons whose care will overwhelm informal caregivers and strain the resources of this and any other society that has undergone the (still ongoing) demographic revolution.

In a paper originally presented at the Ninth International Congress of Gerontology, Neugarten (1972), stated the issue succinctly: "Is it merely wishful thinking that an increased lifespan can be achieved without keeping marginally functioning individuals alive for extended periods? Or is it more likely that as the numbers of old people increase the numbers also increase of those who are physically or psychologically impaired?" (pp. 438-439). She posed questions that we still cannot answer: Could even affluent societies support the new numbers of the old? Could the situation of the old become worse than it is now? What would be the deleterious and the beneficial effects on the rest of society?

The author wishes to thank Cora Martin, Herbert Shore, and Thomas Fairchild for their assistance during the preparation of this chapter.

Before and during the 1970s other articles and books called attention to the virtual certainty of increased life extension and posed similar questions. These contributions were necessarily speculative and usually addressed an amorphous 21st century although some authors looked to the year 2000 as a convenient intermediate target. Like Neugarten, they were convinced that social and biological scientists had given insufficient attention to the implications of an extended life expectancy. Like her, they sought to bring life extension and its possible consequences into prominence in the study of aging and to increase public awareness of the issues involved.

Reaching a One-Hundred-Year Life Expectancy

In his essay on the societal implications of increased life expectancy, Kalish (1974) wrote that "we can be fairly certain that it [the increase] will occur—we are only uncertain as to when" (p. 135). If we are concerned with a future in which life expectancy has reached or at least approaches 100, "when" becomes a function of "how." A repeated theme in discussions of the likelihood of life extension of that magnitude is that the "how" will involve the postponement of mortality by improved prevention and advances in the treatment of disease, particularly those responsible for high mortality rates in middle and late adulthood and that it will also involve learning how to slow the rate of aging.

Recent Census Bureau projections (U.S. Bureau of the Census, 1989) offer one picture of the future age distribution and life expectancy of the United States population to the year 2080. They place special emphasis on the population aged 85 and over, an emphasis that is widely reflected in discussions of chronic illness and disability, where age 85 is rapidly taking on the aura that once attached to age 65 in discussions of retirement. Like that marker it can be both useful and misleading: useful in ordering age data, misleading if reified.

Based upon the assumption that persons 85 and above will benefit more than the young-old from future improvement in mortality, as they have in recent past, the census projections indicate that the rate of increase of the very old will continue to be well above that for the total population 65 and above. The Census Bureau's middle series mortality assumptions result in a projected 85-plus population of approximately 17 million persons in 2080, but the highest series (lowest mortality) assumptions result in a projected very old population of almost 34 million, of which approximately 6 million would be centenarians. Even so, the centenarians would account for only a fraction over 1% of the total United States population.

Although such numbers are necessary for a picture of future age distribution, projected life expectancies based on the underlying mortality assumptions are a much better index of how near (or how far) we may be from achieving a life expectancy of 100. Thus under the middle mortality assumption, between 1987 and 2080 life expectancy at birth for females would increase by slightly more than 6 years, to 84.7. For males the increase would be comparable but life expectancy would be 74.7 years. But since a life expectancy of 100 can only be achieved with very sharply reduced mortality, the low mortality assumption, which doubles the assumed decline for the middle series, is more important. Under it, female life expectancy at birth will have reached 91 years, and male life expectancy will have come close to 85 years.

Given the assumption that future improvement in mortality will have its greatest impact on older persons, projections of life expectancy at age 65 are especially significant. The projected life expectancy for females of that age under the low mortality assumption is 29.5 years and for males 24.5 years. Clearly, in 2080 many 65 year old women and a smaller number of men of that age could expect to celebrate their 100th birthday. In fact, depending upon which series of projections is used, the number could range from 5.3 to 6.8 million.

The census predictions indicate that gender differences will still exist and may even increase, although other sources have suggested that the gap is narrowing and may eventually disappear (Fries, 1989). The predictions also include a simplifying and hopeful assumption that black and white differences in mortality will have disappeared by 2080 and that male and female life expectancies at birth and at age 65 for both racial groups will be identical. One can speculate on the changes that would have to occur in our society, especially in access to health care, in order to realize that prediction.

We must of course maintain a healthy skepticism about all projections and especially those for a remote future. The Census Bureau report not only discusses possible sources of error but also includes the author's understated observation that "unforeseen events can rapidly modify the demographic environment" (p. 14).

Nevertheless the projections offer a base from which to discuss the real time possibility of a 100-year life expectancy. They tell us that we can anticipate significant life extension in the more or less foreseeable future. The number of people who will live to 100 will increase dramatically, but on the average most of us will still die considerably short of that age. The projections rest upon what Cain (1968) has described as "the relative security of probability theory." To bring a 100-year life expectancy into that more or less foreseeable future will require that we move to what he refers to as "possibility theory" (p. 251). In the context of possible life extension that means depending on biologists' learning to slow the rate of aging and thereby extending the human life span.

Life Extension as Probability

Brody (1987) borrows Dickens' phrase, "the best of times, the worst of times," to capture the promise and threat of life extension. Family relationships, economic security, living arrangements and housing design, the possibility of working or enjoying leisure, and the need for social and health care services will ultimately turn on whether increased life expectancy results in a sharp increase in the number of ill and disabled persons or whether most of the added years can be lived without the disabilities that plague so many in today's oldest cohorts. In terms of Laslett's (1991) description of stages of the life course, how will the added years be divided between the "third age" of personal achievement and fulfillment and the "fourth age" of dependence and decrepitude?

In this context Cain's probability is reflected in assessments of the potential for prevention or postponement of chronic disease and disability in terms of lifestyle changes, medical interventions, and public health measures. Increasingly the discussion of this issue focuses on the compression of morbidity hypothesis and the resulting rectangular survival curve, that is, reducing the time spent in the fourth age and presumably in long-term care.

The contributions of lifestyle changes (e.g., exercise, diet, or cessation of smoking) to a lengthened and healthier life expectancy are now the stuff of health promotion efforts directed toward both younger and older adults. If only because of the rebuttals it has provoked, probably the best known formal statement of the potential of lifestyle changes to reduce morbidity is in the work of Fries (Fries, 1980; Fries & Crapo, 1981). Briefly stated, the thesis states that there is evidence that chronic disease and disability are being postponed and can be much further postponed in large part by personal decisions and personal choice. The postponement will ultimately press against a fixed average human life span (arguably, 85 years of age) with the consequence that the period of illness and disability will be greatly foreshortened and death will occur as a terminal collapse.

Criticisms of the compression-of-morbidity hypothesis have been many and varied but generally speaking they rely on three arguments: 1. The available evidence does not support the hypothesis as stated by Fries. 2. The emphasis on personal life-style changes as preventive measures tends to minimize the significance of genetic, environmental, and occupational factors. 3. Based on present knowledge, the limits of life expectancy are unknown; they remain, in Laslett's phrase, "an ultimate uncertainty." Recently, a fourth objection has been added: The unforeseen emergence of a disease such as AIDS can have a significant impact on disability and mortality.

The potential benefits of lifestyle changes among older persons go beyond life extension. By definition, the earlier and more consistently that a preventive lifestyle is lived, the greater its impact is likely to be. Similarly, despite the role that medical interventions have played in extending life expectancy at older ages, the common criticism has been that too little attention has been given to preventive measures. Furthermore, the most appropriate use of specific preventive measures, such as cholesterol screening and mammography, which are already widely advised and used, is still a matter of debate among physicians. Similar questions are frequently raised about other preventive measures.

Despite the emphasis and attention given to prevention, Hickey and Stillwell (1991) point out that all is not well. A basic problem, they argue, is that our knowledge of preventive medicine for older persons is limited. In some cases research findings, particularly with respect to the effect of lifestyle changes (other than cessation of smoking) and even with respect to some widely recommended medical interventions, are inconsistent and often based upon samples that have not included sufficient numbers of older persons.

Although we have long recognized the contribution of public health services to past increases in life expectancy, especially in such areas as the reduction of infant and child mortality, we find it difficult to take action with respect to what many have described as a "toxic society." Hickey and Stillwell speak of the "abrogation of governmental responsibility for public health" (1991, p. 828), but the abrogation grows out of a structured inability to reconcile competing interests. Even when we occasionally succeed in legislating "clean air" or cleaning up the worst cases of industrial pollution, the implementation is agonizingly slow. We refuse to accept the idea that homicide or the disability resulting from attempted homicide can be regarded as public health problems.

The role of prevention in life extension can undoubtedly be enhanced by more research focused on, or at least including, older persons, by improved patient and provider education, by the inevitable development of new and better screening techniques, and by research that leads to new and better interventions. Whether or not black-white mortality differentials will have disappeared by 2080, it is obvious that even now overall average life expectancy could be increased simply by extending what is known about prevention to economically disadvantaged persons and by improving their access to health care and to improved living conditions regardless of racial and ethnic background. It seems doubtful, however, that foreseeable changes in social structure including real-income distribution (or redistribution) and attitudes toward the poor will be sufficient to ensure equal access to health care or even to a clean environment.

"Probability theory," to invoke Cain's phrase again, assumes that the human life span is fixed within fairly narrow limits, although there is considerable argument as to where those limits are chronologically. Educated guesses tend to fall within a range of 85 and 115 years of age, but there is widespread acknowledgment that we do not know where the upper limit is. Wherever it is, the critical question is how close we will come to it, with or without disease and disability. Many observers have taken a pessimistic view of the assertion that prevention and postponement of disease and disability will move ahead rapidly enough to reduce their prevalence among the rapidly increasing oldest old. In this context fear of the costs of long-term care (financial and also psychological) become very real. But even the postponement of disease and disability may not allay that fear. As Soldo and Manton (1985) have noted, "By postponing age at death, we may also be postponing the period of intense service need until even later in the life cycle when fewer financial and/or family resources may be available to ameliorate the public costs of long-term care" (p. 314).

The elders who will have those intense service needs will include large numbers of the oldest old, but the definition of that term will ultimately change. If we assume that the upper limit of the life span is on the order of 115 years, postponement of disability and death must sooner or later create a "new" generation of elders. The age category for the oldest-old will be shifted upward to encompass those who are aged 100 and above.

How increased life expectancy will be divided between Laslett's (1991) third age and fourth age has had a direct impact upon one aspect of long-term care research. Emphasis is increasingly placed upon the interrelationships of morbidity, disability, and mortality, and active life expectancy (ALE) or a closely related concept has been consistently introduced into analyses of existing and projected survival curves during the past decade.

Two consequences of these developments are especially important. First, what has emerged is a general framework into which all discussion of the sources of life extension and its demographic/epidemiological consequences can be fitted (Manton & Soldo, 1985; Manton, 1989). Second, the definition and measurement of active life becomes critical because the residual (i.e., the difference between total life expectancy and active life expectancy) largely defines the need for long-term care. Although assessment instruments abound for a variety of clinical and research purposes in gerontology and geriatrics, studies of active life expectancy tend to utilize fairly simple scales of activities of daily living (ADL) and/or instrumental activities of daily living (IADL). Given the databases typically used or created for such studies, existing social and cultural patterns in areas such as family relations, housing, communications, mobility, self-help, and technology become implicit assumptions with respect to the meaning of disability. We are still in the realm of probability rather than possibility.

• Life Extension as Possibility •

Possibility lies in the potential of biochemistry to discover how to slow the rate of aging, that is, to increase life expectancy by moving the barrier of an uncertain human life span forward by an uncertain number of years or, in that most threatening of all scenarios, removing it altogether. The possibility and hypothetical means of altering the life span have been discussed for several decades, and in the 1960s and 1970s many scientists believed that the basic discoveries and their application would not be long delayed. Segerberg (1974) describes a study conducted in 1964 in which experts were asked when "chemical control of the aging process, permitting extension of life span by 50 years" would occur. The range of replies was from 1992 to 2065 with 2023 as the midpoint. He also describes a similar study that resulted in a consensus that significant extension of the life span due to control of aging would occur by 1993.

Scientific optimism about control of the aging process has proved to be conservative when played against the claims of the "immortalists." A title like *No More Dying* (Kurtzman & Gordon, 1976) suggests the flavor of these claims, and a very astute futurist has predicted that immortality will be achieved by the end of the 21st century (Clarke, 1967). Responding to similar claims, Strehler (1970), who was among the scientific optimists, listed the idea of man having the power to become physically immortal as the first of ten myths about aging.

Comfort (1978), also an optimist, dismissed as "wild" estimates of life extension of 200 to 300 years and suggested that we are on the threshold of an increase on the order of 10% to 20% beyond the years prevention or postponement of the causes of premature death alone can bring. The means, he argued, will be simple and cheap; their use and acceptance will be similar to the spread of antibiotics. Existing medical services and governments will elect to apply them or at least will be unable to prevent their application.

A contrary speculation held that a breakthrough in control of the rate of aging might not result in rapid societal movement to life span extension (Zeckhauser, 1974). Its introduction might be piecemeal and its high costs could restrict distribution initially to those who could afford it. The question of public support would inevitably arise, however, and in the long run, if the cost were reduced, it might become (in today's terms) an entitlement.

A third position has held that lifespan extension is not likely to occur, at least not within the relatively short time span that many have envisaged (Smith, 1993). Even though its possibility is not denied, the discovery of the scientific basis for life span extension has thus far proved to be an intractable problem. The plethora of theories of biological aging has yet to produce a solution.

Possibly because it borders on science fiction, which, to paraphrase Boulding, one must read to keep up with the news, surprisingly little has been written in scientific or academic literature about the societal implications of life span extension. Its obvious impact on population growth is duly noted, sometimes accompanied by an assertion that the growth will lead to the imposition of a severe restriction of births. In one of the few essays that go further, Boulding (1974) speculated on the impact of extreme life extension on a social structure built upon age-specific roles that are adapted to "pre-scientific mortality tables" (p. 267). His speculations ranged across virtually all major social institutions from the family to the economy with sharp thrusts at academia and academic roles (e.g., impact on time in academic rank, the potential for intellectual obsolescence).

Writing in a similar vein, Wheeler (1970) offered a challenging political scenario. Based on the assumption that the means of extension will be a scarce resource, he paints a (hopefully, tongue in cheek) picture of a gerontocratic society in which the means have become the focus of intense intergenerational and class conflict. The postulated treatments and the aging medications will be under rigid governmental control and a black market will emerge. The means will be available to children of the favored and powerful while "underprivileged youth...will employ every possible ruse" to gain access to them (p. 43). Indeed, the only function of the young will be to become old.

Generally speaking, life span extension has not been seen as a panacea for frailty and disability at the end of the life course. The immortalists apart, it would not cure the infirmities of old age; presumably it would move old age and its frailties ahead by 10 or more years. Strehler (1970), for example, has argued that the additional years will be added to the healthy, productive period of the life course and therefore will not create an economic burden. In the long run, slowing the aging process will result in a population in which the proportion "in all states of disrepair" will not have changed (p. 47). If this proves to be correct, those in need of long-term care will simply be older and more numerous.

Long-Term Care in the Fourth Age

The discussion of life extension leads us to three different but interrelated paths to the age of dependence and decrepitude. In one, healthy lifestyles and innovations in health care continue to postpone chronic diseases and their concomitant disabilities until the period of intense service need is reached. In the second, which builds upon the first, we will be free of chronic disease and "will die of relatively minor stress in old age after a long and healthy life, and the maximum lifespan will not be much increased" (Duncan, 1968, p. 82). This is, of course, essentially the concept of terminal collapse and natural death that Fries advanced later. The third path extends the time of onset of the fourth age but offers no alternative to its end.

It can be argued that the emphasis of each of these perspectives is on how we reach the terminal phase of the life course and that what awaits us is left unexamined. The significance of all these paths lies precisely in the fact that they redefine or even abolish the problem of long-term care. In Robert Heinlein's *Methuselah's Children* (1958), a science fiction novel, one of the long-lived characters describes the end of the life course in terms not very different from some of the professional life extension literature: "Senility is simply postponed...and shortened. About ninety days from the first clear warning—then death from old age" (p. 18).

Whether the period after the "clear warning," whatever that proves to be, is a few months, a few weeks, or a few days at the end of 85 or 100 or 115 years is relatively unimportant because its onset has been defined as imminent, inevitable, and irreversible. In this scenario long-term care is replaced with the equivalent of Huxley's (1992) Park Lane Hospital for the Dying, where "wholesome death conditioning" (p. 212) is carried on in brightly painted wards, with continuous music and television (possibly replaced by some future development of virtual reality), and automatic change of scents in the wards each quarter of an hour. Or one can imagine Megalopolis with dozens upon dozens of small neighborhood institutions linked by the latest communications technology. Because rehabilitation and, perhaps, even activities are meaningless concepts in either milieu, they could be staffed primarily by Huxleyan Deltas. Rationing is no longer an issue because the terminal phase is rationing.

In terms less laden with hyperbole, hospice may be the only care system required in the period of intense service need. Institutions will survive as hospices with walls, and home care programs will survive as hospices without walls. Writing before the spread of hospices based on home care, Anderson (1976) saw even the institutional hospice as an antidote to an increase in "store houses" for the sick aged. It would be "a place where dying will be institutionalized and presumably dignified" and where qualified personnel and other "comforters" would help the dying patient and his or her sorrowing relatives (p. 94). Since these ideas are today's common parlance, why bring them up? The answer is that they cannot be taken for granted in a future in which the numbers of the dying are greatly increased. The critical question is, how much will society be willing to pay for death with dignity and solace for survivors? If the numbers are large and the resources limited, the answer may be "Not much."

Anderson also foresaw the probable weakening of the taboo on choosing one's own death. Now, at a time when that concept and physician-assisted suicide to relieve pain and suffering have entered public discourse and when an expected-suicide model is offered as an ethical alternative to rationing by denial-of-treatment (Battin, 1987), the likelihood of high rates of suicide among the future oldest-old cannot be ignored. Those who suffer from chronic disease and perceive their futures in terms of ever increasing debility, decrepitude, and dependency may, like the Struldbrugs in Luggnagg, condemned to immortality, wish for the surcease of death. Many of the oldest-old may interpret a physical collapse as the "clear warning" of their expected demise and turn to suicide rather than wait for the inevitable. Although we live now in a society that has erected a moral barrier to suicide, the very existence of the public debate that Dr. Kervorkian's activities have generated suggests that the barrier may ultimately be breached for the elderly by a value change brought about by the perception of the burden arising from vast future numbers of infirm aged. We can, as Battin writes, "foresee the newly advertised and accepted view of suicide: 'It's what you do when you get too old'" (p. 172).

• One Call Does All: Integrated Long-Term Care? •

We still have a long road to travel before reaching a time when long-term care may have shrunk to a brief period of palliative care immediately prior to certain death. In the short run we are likely to continue to respond to the need for care with a strong dependence on informal care combined with a haphazard system of formal services. We will continue to decry the fragmentation of services, call for the coordination of community-based continuity of care, and support limited projects that presumably demonstrate how that goal can be achieved.

The reasons the goal has not been achieved are well known. Among the most important have been the differing streams of payment or the absence of a single source of payment for different and sometimes for the same service, even when the ultimate source for much of the payment is the federal government; a bias toward institutions over home care in long-term care policy; competition among agencies and professions determined to get a piece of (or control) the action; the service delivery tradition of a large number of small, independent, local agencies, each devoted to a narrow client need or set of needs or set of clients; and the crosscutting bureaucratic tendency to protect one's turf. Case management has long been advocated and occasionally demonstrated on a small scale as a solution to fragmentation of services, but too often it is overlaid on resource and structural problems that it cannot resolve. Judged against the claims made for it, case management, which has segued into managed care, has thus far not been successful (Estes, 1993).

But managed care may have a brighter future. As this is written, the issue of a national, "universal" health insurance plan dominates health policy discussions. One area of consensus among the proponents of various plans that have been advanced is that the emphasis in subacute (including long-term) care should be placed on home care. Even with the restrictions that inevitably will be placed upon it, the prospects for the expansion of the "home care industry" have never been better. If, as some studies suggest, reductions in cost of care prove to be chimerical, we may still be willing to pay for the satisfaction that home care offers to the ill elderly and their caregivers (Weissert, Cready, & Pawelak, 1988), assuming of course that future kinship structures will provide the caregivers.

The assurance of a profitable level of reimbursement for home care is likely to set in motion a struggle for the possession of the infirm aged. It is easy to conjecture that many hospitals, for example, that heretofore have avoided home care will develop programs. Small local home care organizations and chains of home health agencies will be encouraged to expand as will health maintenance organizations [HMOs] social health maintenance organizations [SHMOs], and other types of coordinating agencies. Leaders in the nonprofit field and others have argued that institutions should provide services to persons in the community (Shore, 1974; American Association of Homes for the Aging, 1981; Mason, 1986). Many already do, and others will be encouraged to try. Similarly, an enhanced role in service delivery through elderly housing has been advocated (Fairchild, Dunkelman, & Folts, 1989).

What may well happen in the long run, however, is simply the inclusion of any type of reimbursed long-term care among the services offered by what Starr (1982) predicted will be an industry dominated by huge health care conglomerates, a prediction that is reinforced almost daily by business news. To date the trend toward horizontal integration of acute care hospitals and other medical services has been matched by the largely separate trend toward the horizontal integration of nursing homes and, more recently, home health care (Estes, Swan, & Associates, 1993). Vertical integration, which is developing rapidly, is simply the next step.

Vertical integration has taken place thus far through emerging patterns of relationships between acute care hospitals, ambulatory clinics, nursing homes, and some specialized types of home health care. Although close students of the future need for long-term care have observed that further vertical integration of health services seems inevitable (Soldo & Manton, 1985), their concern has not been with how it will be organized. On the other hand, Mason (1986), who is an advocate of vertical integration sees the development as one that could lead to a corporate entity that owns all of the types of resources needed for formal care.

With enough mergers, buyouts, and subsidiaries that entity might well be a corporation with numerous "profit centers" ranging from elderly housing to cemeteries and crematoria (an area in which horizontal integration is also expanding). With the inclusion of attention to the long-term care needs of younger groups such as the profoundly retarded, the mentally ill, the neurologically damaged, and AIDS patients, and with an assured source of payment, there should no longer be a structural barrier to offering long-term care services from the cradle to the grave. And because structural barriers have been removed, managed care should work—but to whose advantage?

It is probable that some nonprofit organizations, particularly those with strong religious and ethnic bases, and some local organizations with strong philanthropic support will survive the coming of the corporation, but recent experience demonstrates that even they will be under great competitive pressures (AAHA, 1981; Estes et al., 1993). The emphasis on marketing which only recently has become a staple of their programs, is not likely to diminish.

The linchpin of this scenario is the assumption that the level of payment for services is sufficient to continue and to expand the privatization of formal long-term care services. Starr argues that the transformation of health care began when public financing made it attractive to investors and led to large-scale corporate enterprises. If one turns this argument on its head, levels of payment that are unprofitable could reverse the process. In the worst case scenario one can envision the success of a future generational equity movement emerging from the exhaustion of resources, a failed economy, political power explicitly based on age discrimination, or some combination of these and similar factors. A picture of long-term care would then be one of limited access based largely on personal or family resources, the growth of institutional warehousing and the expansion of personal care homes, voluntary organizations engaged in "creaming" the easy cases, and families unable to cope with the illnesses of their elderly members. In other words, the picture would resemble the past of long-term care and might be worse because of the sheer numbers involved.

An alternative scenario strongly advocated by Estes and her associates is one achieved through empowerment of the elderly. Ultimately, they propose a system from which profit in health care has been removed as a matter of public policy, in which long-term care is assured through public provision of insurance, and in which health and social services are nationalized under local community control (Estes et al. 1993). Such a scenario obviously assumes a sea change in our value system, but before it is dismissed out of hand, we should remember that we are already facing a change in demographic structure whose consequences we cannot clearly foresee.

More Tech: High and Low

The role of the corporation has been enhanced by its ability to attract the funds essential for investment in a health care system built in large part on an ever changing high technology. Not surprisingly, discussions of technological change have come to play an increasingly central role in discussions of aging and long-term care (Charness, 1993; Haber, 1986; U. S. Congress, Office of Technology Assessment, 1984). Improvements in medical technologies are seen on the one hand as the major extenders of life expectancy and therefore as the prime mover in the creation of the problems of long-term care; on the other hand the development of both medical and nonmedical technologies are seen as ameliorating problems for elderly persons and for caregivers, both formal and informal. Whatever the future of long-term care, we can be certain that both low-tech and high-tech will have an expanding role.

Many low-tech devices (e.g., grab bars, color coding, ramps, and walkers) are closely associated with housing. They improve the capacity of older persons, including the mildly disabled, to continue to function adequately in their own homes with limited or no support services. Under the leadership of gerontologists such as Howell, Lawton, and Pastalan, and an increasing number of architects and designers, low-tech has also become an integral part of the routine recommendations for construction of specially designed housing for the elderly, including nursing homes. It is obvious that we will have to utilize much more special housing in the future, and there is no dearth of literature that describes the existing knowledge base and future research and policy needs (AARP & Stein Gerontological Institute, 1993; Tilson, 1989). What is problematic is how soon (or if) the increased number of the very old will result in a housing policy that encourages development of a variety of types of housing that responds to their diverse needs. Undoubtedly, future housing will incorporate both low- and high-tech and attack the problem of "retrofitting" existing residences, but cost will limit how much is done and for whom.

The use of low-tech equipment by disabled older persons has increased during the past decade (Manton, Corder, & Stallard, 1993). Even though that trend may continue, the future lies with high-tech. The possible applications of computers, telecommunications, interactive TV, and robotics are being widely discussed. Illustrations gleaned from a variety of recent publications include remote monitoring of patients, assistance to elderly persons and their caregivers by computer or interactive TV, voice-activated telephones, automatic alarm devices, computers activated by voice or by head movement as writing aids, "speechware," devices to overcome severe sight and hearing deficits, the Dick Tracy (wristwatch) computer, inflatable and robotic lifters, intelligent walkers, sensors for wheelchairs, fetch-and-carry robots, computer-controlled prosthetic limbs, and beyond these the "wild cards" that the surprise factor will almost certainly produce.

Two aspects of the high-tech inventory deserve special emphasis. One is that several of the items listed are either currently available although not widely distributed or are being used in demonstration programs. The second is that much of the developmental work for such devices goes on in the context of rehabilitation of younger persons, which is an important factor in the continuing calls for rapprochement between the gerontological and (younger) rehabilitation communities (Galvin & LaBuda 1991; Simon-Rusinowitz & Hofland, 1993).

Despite its apparent inevitability, a number of reservations have been voiced about the use of high-tech of one kind or another in long-term care. The possible resistance of elderly persons to its use may be the least important because future generations will have lived from childhood on in a high tech society. Another response could be the Luddite reaction: resistance by staff who fear that job security will be threatened directly by labor-saving devices or indirectly by the higher levels of skill their work may require. If the dominance of the corporation suggested earlier proves to be accurate, the fears of some staff will undoubtedly prove to be well grounded.

Probably the most comprehensive assessment of the potential drawbacks of high-tech utilization was offered by Morris (1984) at a conference on communications technology. He described a worst case scenario in which advanced technology leads to a relatively small number of the more competent handicapped elderly being served at higher costs. A part of the scenario is a service system in which there is more specialization and less care as new professions and occupations and their attendant organizations emerge in response to new technologies. At a time when health care rationing is being seriously considered, his comments on possible value and funding biases in utilization are especially pertinent.

At the same conference Bengston (1984) offered a much more sanguine view. Although observing that technological innovation is usually produced by and for elites, a point substantially in agreement with one implied by Morris, he argued that over time the benefits will trickle down to more and more persons and enable us to create a client-centered service system in which users will be able to exercise greater and more individualized control.

In that system the traditional superordinate/subordinate relationship of client and professional will be modified to the benefit of both.

Such speculations offer gerontologists perspectives that have yet to be fully incorporated into teaching and research about the future of long-term care. Indeed, they have been largely ignored in discussions of informal caregiving, community-based care, and institutional care in which the primary emphasis has been on the sociopsychological dimensions of care. Fortunately, an increasing number of articles in gerontology periodicals, a specialized journal devoted to technology and aging, and an occasional (thus far) book indicate that at least the problem is no longer one of resources. Today's teachers must keep in mind that many of their students will be engaged in practice until well into the 21st century and will wisely ask how practice may change in the course of their careers.

Changing Clients, Changing Caregivers

We have already mentioned the common observation that medical advances (including an ever increasing flow of pharmaceuticals) based on high-tech have been and will continue to be a major factor in increased life expectancy. What is less commonly noted is that although continued overall progress in prevention, care, and treatment of chronic disease and disability can be expected, there is no reason to assume that the rate of progress will be equal for all diseases and disabilities. For example, as gene modification develops, the specific diseases affected will be critical. Bioengineering could have an impact on sensory deficits and the development of new and more efficient prosthetics before much progress has been made at the genetic level. Progress in overcoming vision and hearing deficits could occur at different rates. New techniques for the diagnosis and treatment of one type of cancer may precede (or lag) or prove more effective than those for other types. New drugs will undoubtedly be developed but which diseases will be cured or controlled first? Furthermore, serendipity will play an important role.

An even more important example of the relationship between research and caregiving is suggested by studies indicating that the cognitive and physical sources of disability can occur independently and give rise to differing service needs; for example, younger, physically disabled persons may need special equipment while older cognitively impaired persons may require more personal assistance (Manton & Soldo, 1985). The rapid growth of special facilities and programs for Alzheimer's patients adds a significant dimension to this contention (Sloane & Mathew, 1991). A future in which significant progress has been achieved in the postponement of physical disability but little or no progress has been made in postponing or eliminating cognitive disability would obviously require fundamental changes in long-term care planning and practice.

Nor can we ignore the consequences that would arise from an explicit policy of rationing. A policy based on cost and prognosis might be applied to specific conditions such as end stage renal disease (Ingman, Gill, & Campbell, 1987) or, as noted above, it might be applied generally if long-term care and hospice become synonymous. Short of an explicit policy, we could have a continuation of institutionalized rationing as the result of lack of access to health care based on economic status or such practices as the failure to give adequate attention to diseases that are gender or ethnically-related or the failure to include women, minorities, and the elderly in research samples.

Cultural factors will also play their part in defining the at-risk population. The increasing ethnic and racial diversity of the United States population will ultimately be reflected among those who are very old. That diversity poses questions about how cultural behaviors and attitudes that may persist in a rapidly cooling melting pot will affect long-term care in terms of both the recipients and suppliers of long-term care services. The myth that families "take care of their own" in immigrant or minority groups has been shattered, but historically the emergence of nonprofit nursing homes and homes for the aged was in large part ethnically and culturally based. The pattern could be repeated in the future, even though systems of care of the aged in the 21st century will differ radically from those in the 19th century.

In another example of possible change, narrowing the mortality and morbidity gaps between males and females might be expected to increase the proportion of males among recipients of formal services and might also modify the usual spousal relationship in caregiving. The point of these examples is that although we can be certain that long-term care will be needed, we cannot be certain of how the characteristics of those who will be in need will affect how their needs are met.

We can, however, raise some questions and hazard some guesses about future caregivers. We have just noted that narrowing the mortality and morbidity gap could modify spousal patterns of caregiving, but in a society in which life expectancy is 100, it might also increase greatly the number of households in which both husband and wife are disabled. Similarly, the role of daughters as informal caregivers is well known, but what expectations can we have when the parent or parents are 100 or 105 and the daughter (or son) is 75 or 80? Apart from the possibility that future fertility rates could severely limit the number of potential caregivers in four- and five- generation families, can we anticipate that a sense of family solidarity and obligation will extend to grandchildren, great-grandchildren, or great-great-grandchildren wherever they may be and whatever they may be doing? Can we predict how divorce and alternative lifestyles in any generation will affect a sense of family obligation? Such questions assume that we will continue to shift as much of the cost and burden of care as possible to families. But what are we to make of the increasing body of research that indicates that family care may not be the preference of the elderly (Estes, 1993)? Will a diffuse, multigenerational family in which the traditional caregivers are themselves very old reinforce this attitude?

Even without narrowing the gender gap in mortality, further changes in gender role expectations could increase the proportion of men among both informal and formal caregivers. As in the past, role changes will be strongly influenced by the changing nature of work. One futurist (Williams, 1983) has argued that the denigration of the "ordinary nurture and care of people" will end because capitalism will prove to be "overmanned" as various skills become redundant (p. 89) The area of work that will not be made redundant, he argues, is the nurture and lifelong care of people. If his argument proves to be correct, the proportion of men in formal caregiving roles could increase sharply.

An alternative but not necessarily contradictory point of view is that the current three-tiered structure of service providers will persist with professionals and executives at the top, supervisors and skilled service providers in the middle, and at the bottom workers with low skill levels who do most of the hands-on work and virtually all of the really dirty work. The "clean hands" providers have been fortunate in having a large pool of economically disadvantaged people willing if not always happy to work at or near the minimum wage. Because that pool has been fed by tides of migration, ethnic and racial diversity has had and will continue to have a major impact on the provider side of care.

We can expect that demographic trends will produce an older work force in long-term care and might increase employment opportunities for middle-aged and young-old persons, although the extensive use of new tides of young immigrants could pose a countertrend. Expanded utilization of high technology might have an even greater impact. At a minimum new skills will be required. The nature of the innovation will determine whether its acquisition is seen as a prerogative of the clean hands providers or as a means of upgrading hands-on workers' jobs or at least making their tasks less burdensome. If new professions and new occupations emerge, as Morris has suggested might happen, most likely they will recruit young clean hands workers from "outside."

Growing Very Old in Dystopia

It is not much of an exaggeration to say that social gerontology is a by-product of population aging. That favorite phrase, "an aging society," summarizes the theme of the impact of the increased proportion of older people in the population on social institutions, on the field's research agenda, and on definitions of societal problems, opportunities, and policies. Even though aging in the 21st century has attracted some speculation in the final decades of the 20th, the issues addressed have generally been within the impact-of-aging-on-society paradigm: the effect of early retirement practices, the search for meaningful roles, the realization of lifelong education, adaptations in housing to the needs of the elderly, the cost and burden of long-term care, and other topics. Too often the future is simply an extrapolation from the present (Binstock, 1985); too often the mode of discussion tends to be advocacy.

Issues that address the impact of society on aging are less frequently discussed. Among the most familiar examples are those that assert the effect of ageism and a youth-oriented society or the "roleless role" on growing old. Overt and covert discrimination in employment and social participation, exploitation of an elderly market, and the service delivery consequences of fiscal constraints are other examples. Here, too, the mode of discussion tends to be advocacy and the future has been implied by the expectation (or hope) for an attitude or policy change in the short run.

Against that background, research that examines the past and potential impact of health care innovations or applications of future technology to aging represents a major advance, but even carefully conducted studies tell us little about the long-run direction of social change in the larger society. Apart from more and older old people, the implied future of American society in gerontology is business as usual. That phrase carries several meanings, but the most important is that with few exceptions we do not foresee or do not concern ourselves with fundamental structural changes that may be required by life extension. We seem to believe that our institutions will adapt readily; or, at worst, we will muddle through with a little tinkering around the edges. Of course, that tinkering could involve such policies as raising the age of eligibility for full social security benefits to age 75 or later, penalizing early retirement while employers use early retirement to downsize their work forces, substituting means testing for age entitlements, steadily increasing out-of-pocket costs for health care, and rationing by denial of care.

In one sense, business as usual is a continuation of the belief that ultimately science and technology will supply answers to the problems that are only in part the consequences of science and technology. Because that belief permits us to assume the stability of our institutions and the adequacy of resources in the future, it allows us to ignore dystopian futures or to treat them as fiction. They are fictions, but that is the point of all alternative futures.

Probably the most disturbing dystopias for gerontology are those built upon assumptions of the exhaustion of resources, exemplified in the Club of Rome's *The Limits of Growth* (Meadows, Randers, & Bahrens, 1972). Although the thesis that a drastic reduction in economic growth in the next century is inevitable has been soundly criticized, Wallimann (1994), a Swiss social scientist, has made it the centerpiece of an apocalyptic future in which the continued growth of the world's population leads to severely diminished land and energy resources and to environmental degradation. It is a future in which "the distribution of scarcity" is accomplished through conflict and the political control of markets.

Although Wallimann does not spell out the probable implications of that future for the elderly, they are explored in *The Children of Men*, a recent novel by P. D. James (1993). Marrying the theme of exhausted resources to dehumanization and authoritarianism, two other recurrent themes of dystopias, she paints a grim picture of the elderly as losers in generational conflict who are faced with deprivation, maltreatment, and, finally, ceremonial euthanasia.

If we are to avoid that fate, we need to recall de Jouvenal's dictum that knowledge of the future is a contradiction in terms (1972). The future, he adds, is the domain that can receive what is elsewhere false as "possibles" beckoning us to make them real.

In the 1972 paper cited at the outset of this chapter, Neugarten called on gerontologists to take the lead in opening to public discussion the issues involved in life extension. Whether we have done so is debatable, but events have rapidly pushed those issues into a central role in gerontology. In no little part, the push has come from the subset of issues that surround long-term care. We are threatened by scenarios in which care of large numbers of very old disabled persons may require an increasing proportion of available resources. We are even more threatened by scenarios in which resources are denied to the very old. From among the "possibles" we must create and ultimately make real an alternative scenario that will permit us to say with Mrs. Lutestring (Shaw, 1922, p. 121), "Long life is complicated, and even terrible; but it is glorious all the same."

References

American Association of Homes for the Aging (1981). *The report of the committee on the future.* Washington, DC: Author.

American Association of Retired Persons & Stein Gerontological Institute (1993). *Life span design of residential environments for an aging population.* Washington, DC: American Association of Retired Persons.

Anderson, O. W. (1976). Reflections on the sick aged and helping systems. In B. L. Neugarten & R. J. Havighurst (Eds.), *Social policy, social ethics, and the aging society.* Washington, DC: U.S. Government Printing Office.

Battin, M. P. (1987). Choosing the time to die: The ethics and economics of suicide in old age. In S. F. Spicker, S. R. Ingman, & I. R. Lawson (Eds.), *Ethical dimensions of geriatric care: Value conflicts for the 21st century.* Dordrecht, Holland: D. Reidel.

Bengston, V. L. (1984). Competence, aging, and social support systems: Implications of the telecommunications technology. In R. E. Dunkle, M. R. Haug, & M. Rosenberg (Eds.), *Communications technology and the elderly.* New York: Springer.

Binstock, R. (1985). "The oldest old: A fresh perspective or compassionate ageism revisited." *Milbank Quarterly, 63*:420–451.

Boulding, K. E. (1974). The Menace of Methusaleh: Possible consequences of increased life expectancy. In L. D. Singell (Ed.), Kenneth E. Boulding: *Collected Papers*, (Vol. 4.), Boulder, CO: Associated University Press.

Brody, J. A. (1987). The best of times/the worst of times: Aging dependency in the 21st century. In S. F. Spicker, S. R. Ingman, & I. R. Lawson (Eds.), *Ethical dimensions of geriatric care: Value conflicts for the 21st century.* Dordrecht, Holland: D. Reidel.

Cain, L. D. Jr. (1968). Aging and the character of our times. *The Gerontologist, 8*, 250–258.

Charness, N. H. (1993, April). Whither technology and aging? *Gerontology News*, pp. 2, 10.

Clarke, A. C. (1967). *Profiles of the future.* New York: Harper & Row. (Bantam Science and Mathematics edition).

Comfort, A. (1978). A biologist laments and exhorts. In L. F. Jarvik (Ed.), *Aging into the 21st century: Middle agers today.* New York: Gardner.

de Jouvenal, B. (1972). On the nature of the future. In A. Toffler (Ed.), *The futurists.* New York: Random House.

Duncan, L. E., Jr. (1968). Ecology and aging. *The Gerontologist, 8,* 80–83.

Estes, C. L. (1993). The aging enterprise revisited. *The Gerontologist, 33,* 292–298.

Estes, C. L., Swan, J. H., & Associates (1993). *The long-term care crisis: Elders trapped in the no-care zone.* Newbury Park, CA: Sage.

Fairchild, T., Dunkelman, D., & Folts, E. (1989). The forces of change: Elderly housing in the 21st century. *Retirement Housing Report, 4*(1), 11–12.

Fries, J. (1980). Aging, natural death, and the compression of morbidity. *The New England Journal of Medicine, 303,* 130–135.

Fries, J. F. (1989). The compression of morbidity: Near or far. *Milbank Quarterly, 67,* 208–232.

Fries, J. F., & Crapo, L. M. (1981). *Vitality and aging: Implications of the rectangular curve.* San Francisco: W. H. Freeman.

Galvin, J. C., & Labuda, D. R. (1991). United States health policy into the next century. *International Journal of Technology and Aging, 4,* 115–126.

Haber, P. (1986). Technology in aging. *The Gerontologist, 26,* 350–356.

Heinlein, R. (1958) *Methusaleh's children.* New York: Street & Smith, New American Library edition. (Original published 1941).

Hickey, T., & Stillwell, D. L. (1991). Health promotion for older people: All is not well. *The Gerontologist, 31,* 822–829.

Huxley, A. (1992). *Brave New World.* New York: Harper Collins, Harper Perennial edition. (Original published 1932).

Ingman, S. R., Gill, D., & Campbell, J. (1987). ESRD and the elderly: Cross-national perspective on distributive justice. In S. F. Spicker, S. R. Ingman, & I. R. Lawson (Eds.), *Ethical dimensions of geriatric care: Value conflicts for the 21st century.* Dordrecht, Holland: D. Reidel.

James, P. D. (1993). *The children of men.* New York: Alfred A. Knopf.

Kalish, R. A. (1974). Four score and ten. *The Gerontologist, 14,* 129–135.

Kurtzman, J., & Gordon, P. (1976). *No more dying: The conquest of aging and the extension of human life.* Los Angeles: J. P. Tarcher.

Laslett, P. (1991). *A fresh map of life: The emergence of the third age.* Cambridge, MA: Harvard University Press.

Manton, K. G. (1989). Epidemiological, demographic, and social correlates of disability among the elderly. *Milbank Quarterly, 67*, 13–58.

Manton, K. G., Corder, L., & Stallard, E. (1993). Changes in use of personal assistance and special equipment from 1982 to 1989: Results from the 1982 and 1989 NLTCS. *The Gerontologist, 33*, 168–176.

Manton, K. G., & Soldo, B. J. (1985). Dynamics of health changes in the oldest old: New perspectives and evidence. *Milbank Quarterly, 63*, 206–285.

Mason, S. A. (1986). Vertical integration in the health care industry: Where do services to the elderly fit? In M. B. Kapp, H. E. Pies, & A. E. Doudera (Eds), *Legal and ethical aspects of health care for the elderly*. Ann Arbor, MI: Health Administration Press.

Meadows, D. H., Meadows, D. L., Randers, J., & Behrens, W. W., III. (1972). *The limits to growth*. New York: Universe Books.

Morris, R. (1984). The impact of technology on service delivery systems and manpower. In R. E. Dunkle, M. R. Haug, & M. Rosenberg (Eds.), *Communications technology and the elderly: Issues and forecasts*. New York: Springer.

Neugarten, B. L. (1972). Social implications of a prolonged life span. *The Gerontologist, 12*, 323, 438–440.

Segerberg, O. (1974). *The immortality factor*. New York: E. P. Dutton.

Shaw, G. B. (1922). *Back to Methusaleh: A metabiological pentateuch*. London: Constable.

Shore, H. (1974). What's new about alternatives. *The Gerontologist, 14*, 6–11.

Simon-Rusinowitz, L., & Hofland, B. F. (1993). Adopting a disability approach to home care services for older adults. *The Gerontologist, 33*, 159–167.

Sloane, P. D., & Mathew, L. J. (Eds.). (1991). *Dementia units in long-term care*. Baltimore: Johns Hopkins University Press.

Smith, D. (1993). *Human Longevity*. New York: Oxford University Press.

Soldo, B. J., & Manton, K. G. (1985). Changes in the health status and service needs of the oldest old: Current patterns and future trends. *Milbank Quarterly, 63*, 286–319.

Starr, P. (1982). *The social transformation of American medicine*. New York: Basic Books.

Strehler, B. (1970, July/August). Ten myths about aging. *Center Magazine*, pp. 41–48.

Tilson, D. (Ed.). (1989). *Aging in place: Supporting the frail elderly in residential environments*. Glenview, IL: Scott, Foresman.

U.S. Bureau of the Census (1989). *Projections of the population of the United States, by age, sex, and race: 1988 to 2080* (Current population reports. P-25, No. 1018). Washington, DC: U.S. Government Printing Office.

U.S. Congress, Office of Technology Assessment (1984). *Technology and aging in America: Summary*. Washington, DC: Author.

Wallimann, I. (1994). Can the world industrialization project be sustained? *Monthly Labor Review, 45,* 41-51.

Weissert, W. G., Cready, C. M., & Pawelak, J.E. (1988). The past and future of home and community-based long-term care. *Milbank Quarterly, 66,* 309-388.

Wheeler, H. (1970, December). The rise of the elders. *Saturday Review*, pp. 14-15.

Williams, R. (1983). *The year 2000.* New York: Pantheon.

Zeckhauser, R. (1974). The welfare implications of the extension of life. *The Gerontologist, 14,* 2-3, 93, 95.

PART IV

The Meaning of Age

Introduction to Part IV

T his concluding section of the book contains two chapters: one by Charles Longino and John Murphy and a concluding one by the volume editor. Longino and Murphy approach the issue of increased life expectancy in a somewhat different fashion than do the previous authors. Although the other authors touch on the subject, possible ideological shifts are the sole focus of Longino and Murphy's chapter. They examine the interrelationships of population dynamics and medical ideology. They note the inconsistencies between the traditional medical view and the realities of an aging population. They further note that the core of the biomedical model is dualism, that is, an either-or approach. This dualism is further evidenced in the mind-body distinction, objectivity and subjectivity, rationality as epitomized by scientific thought, and irrationality as embodied in nonscientific thinking. Disease and health are treated as objective data, not experiential phenomena. The doctor is the expert, the patient is the object of expertise.

This model, however, is changing. Longino and Murphy point to current philosophical, scientific, and literary trends that attack the premises and approach of conventional medicine. Critics suggest that the patient may be more important than the symptom; that their experiences and opinions may be more valid than physicians' versions of their conditions. This represents a change in the power and control relationships between person and physician.

Like McRae earlier in Chapter 8, Longino and Murphy see a shift in the nature of medical care and the practice of medicine; they differ, however, in their emphasis on aspects of both. Although Longino and Murphy see strains in the current paradigm, they do not see a real shift occurring at present.

The concluding chapter of this book attempts to pull together all of the preceding ones. It discusses the difficulties the authors faced in writing their chapters: where to draw on materials that would stimulate their thinking; how different assumptions lead to different views; and areas of agreement and disagreement among the authors. The line between "what-if?" projections and predictions of the future is blurred. At times different authors predict what they think will occur; in other instances, authors describe what might occur under the condition of a significant change in life expectancy. Most predictions are based on assumptions that the future builds on the past, that there is some degree of continuity. Similarly, our descriptions of what might occur tend to be based on what is already familiar to us. Unlike science fiction writers referred to earlier in this book (Seltzer, p. 11), social and behavioral scientists and practitioners tend to stay within the usual rules of their disciplines and fields. The familiar past, however, may not necessarily be a prologue to the future. The unexpected can take place. In fact, the operative paradox is that the unexpected should be expected. Consequently, predictions are not always accurate nor are "what-if?" descriptions necessarily inaccurate.

Chapter 10

Paradigm Strain: The Old Age Challenge to the Biomedical Model

Charles F. Longino, Jr., and John W. Murphy

The underlying principles of Western medicine are experiencing considerable strain. One of the major reasons the biomedical model has reached an impasse is the growth of the older population, a trend that will continue if life expectancy persists in inching upward, eventually reaching 100 years. This situation provides an unusual opportunity to examine the relationship between population dynamics and ideology, in this case, medical ideology.

The Western biomedical model sets the parameters of Western medicine; this model defines the nature and technique of medical practice. That is, it provides medical practitioners with a focus. But this focus is fairly narrow. In servitude to the biomedical model, the medical researcher and the physician are encouraged to clear away nonmaterial irrelevancies and concentrate exclusively on factors that are physiological. As a result of this emphasis, analysis is moved away from the experiential world of the person, which is intertwined with culture and society.

The biomedical model also relies on an understanding of causation, derived from science, that is essentially mechanical. Repairing a body, in this view, is analogous to fixing a machine. Furthermore, this rendition of causation leads to a remarkably optimistic expectation that each disease has a specific cause that is awaiting discovery by medical research. Finally, because the body is the appropriate subject of medical science and practice, this object is also the appropriate subject of regimen and control. These are the doctrines of the biomedical model.

The challenge to this model comes from several sources, including the process of growing older. The aging of the population, including a potential extension of life expectancy, has brought about an increased prevalence of chronic conditions and the deterioration of physiological functioning. But these problems do not have a precise moment of onset, do not have a single and unambiguous cause, do not have an end that can be easily modified, and are implicated in a melange of factors indirectly related to physiology. Accordingly, the incompatibility between the orthodox medical world view and the chronic illnesses of members of an aging population is undermining the efficacy of the biomedical model. Yet a paradigm shift—a change in the practical and philosophical world view—is occurring that will resolve the strain.

In order to comprehend biomedicine properly, the philosophy that sustains the biomedical model must be outlined. Insight is provided in the following section into the key elements of this model. Most important to remember is that dualism is central to the success of orthodox biomedicine.

Roots of the Biomedical Model

Medicine does not consist simply of the application of sophisticated procedures and techniques. Presupposed by the biomedical model is an image of the individual, valid knowledge, the focus of intervention, causality, and so forth, which are preconditions for the prevailing practice of medicine. A causal historical link cannot be said to exist between these assumptions and the onset of biomedicine (Weber, 1958). Nonetheless, these and other themes support modern medicine.

Certain key philosophical considerations are essential for making sense of how medicine operates as a science. This constellation of ideas might be referred to as the silent side of biomedicine. Foucault (1989), for example, uses the term *episteme* to describe this essential background. An episteme, as he writes, "make[s] possible the appearance of objects during a given period of time" (p. 33).

Viewed from the cultural position of 20th century medicine, during early medical history, from the early Greeks to the end of the medieval period, intervention was quite convoluted. Any complaint could be the result of a combination of factors, both natural and spiritual. A physician, therefore, had to be a soothsayer and technician whose securing a cure involved metaphysics and technique.

Gradually the move was away from religion and toward science. Myth and speculation were replaced by fact. Direct observation, logical analysis, and the dissection of nature were elevated in importance. As a result, the use of medicine would be much more effective.

This change did not occur all at once. The admixture of spirit and nature continued until the arrival of Descartes, who wrote in the early 1600s. He made a theoretical maneuver that allowed nature to be "rationalized" (Weber, 1978). Nature, in other words, could be materialized and transformed into an inert object. Facts combined with judicious reasoning could thus be the cornerstone of medicine. There would no longer be any justification for contaminating facts with immaterial considerations.

The thrust of Descartes' position is the fact that mind, *res cogito*, could be severed from the body, *res extensa* (Carlson, 1975). Matter is thus freed from subjectivity; pristine matter is available for inspection. Like nature, the body becomes an object that is encountered. Factors such as mind, soul, consciousness, and spirit are unimportant and dismissed because of their intangible character. The locus of disease is the body, which is envisioned to be nothing more than a physiological organism.

Following Descartes' tack, other thinkers began making changes that are vital to modern medicine. The belief was spawned that facts could be separated categorically from values. What this meant was that facts were externalized, or thought to be associated with empirical indicators. Physicians could thus safely become empiricists and attend solely to physiological markers. How interpretive factors, related to culture or biography, might affect an illness became irrelevant. The experience of persons was denigrated and treated as illusory (Schwartz & Wiggins, 1988). Only so-called objective factors were considered real.

Consistent with this transformation of nature, the impetus for action was reformulated as causal. Discussions revolved around "causal chains" and "webs of causation" (Norell, 1984). Adopting this imagery enabled physicians to view events as structurally linked. A sound rationale, accordingly, could be understood to underpin the advent of illness. In this way, the most propitious strategy for intervention could be formulated, based on predictable and manipulable causes, rather than arcane connections. Through rigorous research, as opposed to prayer or incantation, the source of a problem can be pinpointed. Hence, diagnostic activity became a scientific investigative process.

What should be accomplished by a medical intervention was also influenced by the acceptance of either-or, or dualistic, thinking. Sickness or pathology was understood to be a condition of disequilibrium, or of nature out of balance. Restoring the body to "normal" equilibrium became the goal of most interventions. Understanding norms with respect to equilibrium was thought to represent a significant theoretical improvement. Abstractions such as the mean, middle way, or justice (*dike*) had existed before, but they were now abandoned in favor of a more concrete explanation of normativeness. Instead of searching for some primordial guidepost for eternal justice, or rightness, norms are thought to be inherent in the physiological system and not outside of it. Normativeness and stability are thus not a mythical problem, but a matter of bringing various structures into harmony (Strasser & Randall, 1981). The etiology of imbalance, accordingly, is relatively easy to identify.

A final element of the rational world view pertains to how knowledge should be acquired. As should be noted, subjectivity or interpretation is a liability in the pursuit of valid data. In order to curtail the influence of the human element, the use of quantitative measures is encouraged. Quantification is believed to be free of moral values and to supply unimpeded access to reality (Ellul, 1964). This claim is also sustained by the dualistic notion that things are either one way or the other (e.g., right or wrong, real or unreal, true or false, without shading). Stated simply, increasingly formalized, quantitative methods are assumed to be divorced from interpretation. Through the appearance of neutrality, the illusion is created that the limitations of perspective are overcome. Truth and objective reality are one.

Derived from rationalism, then, the cornerstone of the biomedical model is the materialization of life. Specifically, humans are approached as if they are simply physiological organisms. But this model does not make much sense unless credence is given to several proposals. Dualism, empiricism, mechanical causality, the equilibrium thesis, and the neutrality of technique constitute the philosophical underpinnings of biomedicine, and these philosophical themes are manifested in the five doctrines of the biomedical model.

The Doctrines of the Biomedical Model

Freund and McGuire (1991) have argued that the ways in which the body is understood are socially constructed. There are cultural ideals that describe the body. No less important, however, are the philosophical developments concerning the body that are historically and culturally based. Emphasized in traditional Chinese medicine, for example, is a balance of vital forces in the body (the *chi*), whose balance and manipulation bring about health. This model is essentially non-material. In light of the previous discussion concerning historical philosophical development, there should be no surprise that in the West, by contrast, the body is understood to be essentially material, and the scientific approach to medicine is overwhelmingly objective and rational. Indeed, the Western biomedical model is predicated on five related doctrines.

The first to arise was *the doctrine of mind–body dualism*. This Cartesian formulation may have been useful as a starting point for biomedical science, but it is increasingly difficult to affirm in the modern practice of medicine. This doctrine is a barrier to understanding the psychosocial component of medicine, including the placebo effect, the connection between stress and illness, the importance of support groups, and the more general relationship between social support and health. Although the doctrine is no longer strictly adhered to, the interaction between the mind and body is still considered to be peripheral to scientific medicine. In some contexts this schism is actually an embarrassment, and many members of the medical science community seem ready for its reformulation.

The second doctrine is that the body is a system of functionally interdependent parts. Usually this thesis is referred to as *the mechanical analogy*, whereby the body is treated as though it operates like a machine. Furthermore, the doctor is like a mechanic. Cassell (1991) has observed that the diagnosis of disease is normally based on the belief that each bodily function (e.g., kidney function) reflects a particular structure (as in the biochemistry and anatomy of the kidney). So when disease is noticed, the structure of an organ is the first place to look for a cause, microscopic or otherwise. The search for tumors is predicated on this framework. The mechanical analogy is also invoked when the cardiovascular system is described as an hydraulic system and the heart as a muscle pump. Thinking that a physician can repair one part of the body in isolation from others, however, is quite a simplistic view.

Third is the doctrine of *physical reductionism*. Simply put, disease is viewed to be isomorphic with the malfunction of physiology. This focus on materialism excludes all nonmaterial dimensions (social, psychological, and behavioral) in the search for causes, and therefore obscures the social conditions or physical environments that contribute to pathology or promote healing. Similar to body–mind dualism, reductionism denies context. The answers are in the body alone.

The fourth doctrine is that the body is the appropriate focus of *regimen and control*. This principal is a logical corollary of physical reductionism. If disease exists in the body, then the body would be the logical locus of treatment. Because of the emphasis that is placed on physiology, a patient has the responsibility to follow the doctor's orders. After all, the physician is assumed to be an expert in this area.

Fifth, and finally, the doctrine of *specific etiology* relates to the idea that each disease has only one cause. This rendition of causality was strongly reinforced by germ theory and the invention of vaccines to attack the microbial origins of disease. The search for "magic bullet" cures, which motivates most medical research, is promoted by this doctrine.

This discussion of the biomedical model has remained at the theoretical level. Perhaps a better way to understand how philosophy has shaped medical practice is to examine briefly the rise of scientific medicine. In their historical settings, the actual impact of certain concepts can be appreciated.

The Flowering of Scientific Medicine

The idea of scientific medicine can be traced back to the 12th century B.C. to a Greek physician, Asclepias, whose followers believed the chief duty of the physician was to treat disease and correct imperfections (Dubos, 1959). Disease theory, however, only developed recently, in the early decades of the 19th century in France (Cassell, 1991). The classification of diseases was a conscious effort to introduce science into medicine. Having a universal classificatory scheme was viewed as essential for securing common understanding among doctors. A natural history approach was adopted, similar to classifying flora and fauna. The attempt to describe diseases followed. Once diseases, which were viewed ontologically as things, were defined and consensus was gained on these definitions, the search for causes, that is, etiology, proceeded apace. Structure and function were at the basis of the search for causes, and the mechanical analogy provided a unifying model of the causal chains. On the basis of a disease's classification, a physician could make diagnoses with regard to a generally accepted etiology. Indeed, a physician could prescribe a therapeutic treatment, or regimen, that would control and cure the disease. Disease classification, etiology, and treatment were disseminated throughout the medical profession, thereby supplying the basis for a consensus that eventually came to be equated with fact and truth.

The decades between 1800 and 1830 mark the shift away from philosophically based classical medicine to scientifically based clinical medicine. Perhaps better than any other event, the invention of the first crude stethoscope by Laennac in 1816 symbolizes the shift in perspective. Before, doctors observed patients; now they *examined* them (Starr, 1982). Furthermore, in Paris they also began keeping statistical records on the effectiveness of therapeutic techniques.

As scientific medicine developed into the mid-1800s, doctors became more detached; they ignored the experience of patients and instead paid attention to physiological markers. To stethoscopes were added ophthalmoscopes and laryngoscopes to strengthen the physician's sensory powers in clinical examinations. A focus on the person was being supplanted by a focus on the body. When the microscope, X-ray, and chemical and bacteriological tests appeared, along with machines to measure physiological functioning, the transition was complete. The patient's subjective judgment was no longer needed. So-called objective evidence was viewed as much more accurate and reliable. The answers to questions posed by disease were to be found in the body, not the mind or the environment. The Cartesian doctrine of body–mind dualism and the related theme of physical reductionism promoted the shift from person to body that characterized the emerging science of medicine.

By the early 1900s, standardized rates and actuarial tables for comparing a patient to populations had been introduced to help physicians make objective judgments, based on the idea of normality. Eye charts, weight-height tables, and IQ tests are examples of the inventions of this period. In each case, normalcy is associated with objective criteria that are devoid of the uncertainty associated with subjectivity. Normal and abnormal, those dichotomous (or dualistic) concepts came to reign supreme in clinical medicine and guided both diagnostic and treatment decisions.

In the 1880s, the organisms responsible for epidemic killers like tuberculosis, cholera, typhoid fever, and diphtheria were isolated. Microbiology allowed physicians to establish the links between disease and cause, between diagnosis and treatment, in a powerful way. So completely were these connections imprinted on the popular mind that germ theory, and the specific perspective on etiology of the biomedical model, came to dominate scientific medicine and raise hopes that disease would soon be eradicated from the earth, or at least from the civilized world. By the 1890s, medicine was actually making a difference in persons' health, although these improvements resulted mostly from prevention and other advancements in public health (Starr, 1982).

Antiseptic surgery was invented by Joseph Lister in 1867, but the method was not perfected and applied broadly until the last decades of the century, when virtuoso surgeons such as Charles and William Mayo gained celebrity status, raising hopes, again, for miraculous outcomes from common killers such as appendicitis and gall bladder disease.

After Abraham Flexner of the Carnegie Foundation visited medical schools and wrote his famous *Bulletin Number Four*, in 1910, scientific medicine became the primary mode of investigating and treating disease. Flexner argued that all medical schools should be closed, except those that trained the scientist–physician. Johns Hopkins and Harvard, rooted in basic science and hospital medicine, were to be the models. This reorganization of medical education had implications beyond the training of physicians. The entire edifice of professional medicine took shape. These changes were consistent with the rise of positivism and the belief in its ability to procure objectively valid knowledge. The result has been the cultural legitimation and dominance of scientific medicine, whose aim was to conquer disease. Most doctors trained after 1920 have a hard time distinguishing between science and medicine. To be sure, medicine's total embrace of science has had profound effects. Nonetheless, by the end of the 20th century, the orthodox biomedical model would be challenged by the clinical demands posed by the growth of the older population in the United States.

The Aging Population and Medical Politics

Pressures on the biomedical model and scientific medicine have come from several quarters, primarily during the second half of the 20th century. Psychology, and particularly psychiatry, have understood the mind–body connection throughout the entire century, and their influence in medicine has been gradual and continuous. The association for psychosomatic medicine became visible in the 1950s, made up of physicians who openly challenged the mind–body dualism doctrine of the biomedical model and foreshadowed developments that came two decades later.

As the nation's level of education increased, the general population was less impressed than before by the "miracles" of science. The failures of science were also evident. For example, President Nixon declared war on cancer and increased funding for cancer research, thus raising expectations that the magic bullets were on their way. Although the 5-year cure (nonrecurrence) rate has risen for some cancers, expectations have been lowered for a real cure in the foreseeable future. "Better things for better living through chemistry" became a hollow slogan to those who were aware of the ways in which chemicals were poisoning the environment. Science is not the beneficent force that it once had seemed. The environmental movement contributed to eroding the high status that science once held.

The loss of wonder at the progress of science seems to have come in the 1960s and early 1970s, when authority of all kinds was being challenged by a baby boom come of age. Medical authority did not escape its challenge. Physicians seemed less like gods, and their sovereign profession came increasingly under fire as a fortification for greed. The escalating cost of medicine, and dwindling access to it, served to underscore a public sense of betrayal by both science and professional medicine. Scientific medicine, to skeptics, looked like the monopolization of professional knowledge, an excuse for keeping prices high and avoiding competition.

The environmental movement and the challenge to institutional authority were corrosive to the unquestioned power and orthodoxy of scientific medicine, but in the meanwhile the values that infused the consumer protection movement were reshaping the doctor-patient relationship. The detachment that physicians had gained in the scientific pursuit of disease seemed to have eroded the personal relationship that, at least in folklore, bonded the doctor to the patient. Dependence on objective laboratory tests, rather than on subjective recounting of the symptoms and life circumstances by patients, made the doctor and patient less accessible to one another as persons. When doctor-patient relationships are not personally satisfying, there are more opportunities for patients to be dissatisfied with treatment. Scientific detachment was no longer offset by unquestioning trust in the scientist-physician by their patients. Malpractice claims resulted, thus increasing the cost of insurance protection for the medical profession, costs quickly passed on to consumers. Corporate medicine may have created the circumstances and the consumer protection movement the values, but the fact remains that the prevailing approach to medicine is commercial, with medical care viewed as a commodity, provided by physicians, with patients as the consumers. The values and attitudes that subtend commercial relationships are pragmatic and self-interested, and not idealistic. This shift erodes further the unquestioned authority of the physician.

In the midst of these cultural changes in the United States, there has been a demographic change occurring that will form the greatest challenge of all to the Western biomedical model—the population of the nation is proportionally aging. The older population is itself aging and is expected to continue to do so. If life expectancy were to climb to 100, the impact of this development on medicine would only be an extension of this trend. Changes described in this section are only the precursors of the dramatic shifts that will occur from the second to the sixth decades of the next century.

The reason that population aging has such a strong effect on medicine is that health issues change during the life course. Epidemiologist Maurice Mittelmark (1993) made this point clearly when he asserted that "Accident and injury are prominent concerns in childhood, adolescence and early adulthood, developing chronic diseases are a central feature of middle adulthood, morbidity and mortality from chronic diseases characterize the period around retirement, and deterioration in functioning, disability and dependency are concerns mainly of old and very old age" (p. 3).

The aging of the population shifts the emphasis from acute disease, accidents, and injuries to chronic disease, and deterioration in functioning. Chronic diseases such as heart disease, Alzheimer's, and diabetes, and chronic conditions such as hypertension, osteoporosis, and osteoarthritis can be managed, but they cannot be cured. Furthermore, with advancing old age, chronic diseases and conditions tend to accumulate. The medical care of older adults, therefore, focuses on the management of chronic disease, and increasingly on rehabilitation, but rarely on cure. The original aim of scientific medicine to discover and conquer disease is thereby sidetracked.

Chronic diseases and functional deterioration also connect the patient to a wide range of socioenvironmental considerations, and, therefore, challenge the Cartesian focus of the biomedical model on the body. Geriatric medicine has tended to have lower status than most other specialties exactly for this reason. The heroic tendencies of scientific medicine are challenged by this situation. In other words, these diseases and conditions require an appreciation of the interaction between a myriad of variables related to the cause and course of the problem that tend to be obscured by the medical model (Kleinman, Eisenberg, & Good, 1978). Chronic diseases and degenerative conditions require the type of expansion in scope that has been anathema to orthodox biomedicine.

However, if diseases cannot be cured, at least physiological functioning can be maintained and sometimes improved. This issue of functionality, or its inverse, dependency, is an important concern of geriatric medicine (Cockerham, 1992). Disability is the limitation of one's capacity to perform normal activities of daily living, that is, to take care of oneself. The impact of an aging American population will be seen most clearly in this area of medical practice. In 1985 Manton (1989) estimated that 20% of persons over the age of 60 had one or more disabilities, with the proportion rising, of course, as this population ages. Even the most cautious projections (Kunkel & Applebaum, 1992) predict more than a threefold increase during the next half century. Thus, population aging presents not only a challenge to the health care industry, but to the health care ideology as well, and to the biomedical model in particular.

Cracks are now visible in the edifice of the Western biomedical model from paradigm strain. It is possible to point to some of the features of an emerging paradigm, one that will be responsive to the health of the growing elderly population. In some circles, this new philosophy is referred to as postquantum theory, while in others the term is postmodernism. At the core of either viewpoint, however, is the rejection of dualism.

The Emerging Paradigm

The emerging paradigm represents a change away from an ontological view of disease and toward a much greater emphasis on the biopsychosocial viewpoint that disease occurs because of interaction between persons and their environment (Foss & Rothenberg, 1987). If diseases are things, in the ontological sense, then they should have a discrete beginning and end. But disease categories are abstractions; they are human inventions; they have no independent existence. They are also static. On the other hand, the story of an illness, including the conditions that contributed to it (within and outside the body), is found in the "life-world" of the patient. Pathophysiology, in short, is dynamic. Therefore, most chronic diseases or conditions make more sense when viewed within a framework that elevates in importance values, commitments, desires, biography, and other interpretive considerations.

Cassel (1991) attributes much of the early theoretical work on the emerging paradigm to René Dubos, who began to write increasingly in the late 1950s and throughout the 1960s about the interdependence of organisms and their environments. In his book, *The Mirage of Health* (1959), he argued forcefully that the adaptation of humans to their environments contained the roots of their bodily afflictions. This is an extreme departure from the doctrine of physical reductionism and mind–body dualism. The claim that the tubercle bacillus, for example, is the cause of tuberculosis, in the absence of environmental factors, Dubos asserted, is naive in the extreme. Intestinal microbes are omnipresent in humans; their attack is triggered by changes in the internal (bodily) and external environments, which are themselves interdependent and evolving. In this way, the body was united inextricably to a wider web of non-physiological considerations. Disease, accordingly, is not autonomous and something that simply attacks the body.

Imagine a case conference in a medical school. The case presented by a professor of internal medicine is about a man, aged 78, who was found unconscious by a neighbor in his fifth floor walk-up apartment in the inner city. When he reached the emergency room, a quick chest examination pointed to pneumonia as the presenting illness. The attending physician expected that the pneumonia was caused by the pneumococcus, a belief later confirmed. The patient was thus treated with penicillin. One of his knees was also swollen as a result of osteoarthritis. He responded well to the drug therapy; his fever came down; his lungs cleared and he was released to go home. This event appeared to be an example of successful scientific medicine.

The case seemed uninteresting to the interns and residents. The diagnosis had been quick and straightforward, the treatment was appropriate, and the patient got well without complications. "But there is more," said the professor. "It is artificial to stop at the boundaries of the body. There is a story here, and none of you discovered it because you did not ask all of the right questions." The man's grief at the loss of his wife caused him to be depressed. He was socially isolated; no social support was available to him. He lived alone and kept to himself since his wife died. The depression caused a loss of appetite. The swollen knee made it very painful to descend and ascend the stairs, so he did not go out for groceries. Malnutrition resulted, which weakened his immune system and made him vulnerable to bacterial infections. Pneumonia resulted.

That is half of the story. In his aloneness and sorrow, he began drinking one night, became intoxicated, vomited, aspirated the vomitus into his lungs and developed a lung abscess, or aspiration pneumonia, and he was brought back to the emergency room just 2 weeks after his release. The students again talked about diagnosis and treatment. The professor shook his head. "Don't you get it?" he said. "By limiting your view only to the disease state, you are missing the other factors in the story. His solitude, his bereavement, his living conditions, his bad knee, his nutrition, and the pneumococcus, infection, antibiotics, and respirator, are all part of the story. The search for the cause of an illness is limited by the classic disease theory. It does not account for all of the facts and until you understand this, you may be able to get a patient out of a hospital, but you cannot keep him out for very long." This hypothetical example, drawn largely from Cassel's examination of the nature of human suffering and the goals of medicine (1991), illustrates the paradigm strain.

The more encompassing strategy, often termed *holism*, is justified by recent developments in philosophy. As Lyotard (1984) writes, "metanarratives" are no longer legitimate. Metanarratives are scenarios that claim an absolute status, because they are believed to be sustained by Divine inspiration, natural law, or some other factor that is immune to situational contingencies. Biomedicine is replete with metanarratives. Because of the emphasis placed on dualism, for example, pathogens, the body, the disease state, and health are treated as autonomous and devoid of interpretation. These are simply realities that members of the medical team are trained to recognize. But are these and related phenomena objective in the Cartesian sense?

The reason metanarratives are rejected is quite simple: Dualism is considered to be passé. Due to recent shifts in understanding language use, objectivity cannot be separated clearly from subjectivity. Derrida's (1976) infamous phrase, "nothing exists outside of the text," captures this new view of knowledge. Language does not merely point to objects but mediates everything that is known. Language cannot be placed aside, so that a view of reality unadulterated by interpretation can be achieved. Because there is no escape from interpretation, Descartes' dream is shattered (Bordo, 1987). Instead of obtrusive facts, all that exist are modes of interpretation. Truth, as Lacan (1977) writes, is derived from language and not reality. This subversion of dualism has implications for medicine that are difficult to ignore. Take the body, for instance. Now the *soma* cannot be viewed as simply corporal matter, or a *Korper*. Phenomenologists have recommended the term *lived body* to describe this new condition (Murphy & Longino, 1992). Because interpretation is ubiquitous, discomfort, pain, or illness should not be associated exclusively with the presence of standard physiological markers. Within this framework, the body and mind are inextricably united; the person is not merely a physiological organism. In this regard, every bodily sign is psychosomatic, and not simply those that cannot be readily explained by biomedicine.

In general, for postmodern philosophers, facts are not objective in the dualistic sense. Because facts are tarnished by interpretation, the usual bifurcation between fact and value cannot be maintained. Instead of being empirically objective, facts are thought to reside within a person's *Lebenswelt* or "life-world." This term has been adopted to indicate that facts are embroiled in the values, beliefs, and commitments that are at the heart of quotidian issues. Therefore, interpretive meanings should be the focus of attention, as opposed to the so-called objective facts of a case. In terms of the *Lebenswelt*, a single empirical referent can have several meanings depending on how reality is constructed by a patient. What is chosen as significant is thus situationally prescribed.

Viewed from within the life-world, patients are persons who are connected to an environment that has meaning. They interpret their condition and respond to it in a variety of ways. Persons are not merely caused to act ($A \rightarrow B$), but they react to events and situations in ways that are believed to be adaptive. Forgetting to tell the social side of an apparently objective causal sequence, accordingly, will obscure the human element that ties variables together. The residents and interns mentioned earlier failed to recognize that the strength of the relationship between factors depends on how persons view themselves, others, and the social context. What appeared to them to have a straightforward cause and solution was actually a much more complex problem.

Likewise, variables should not be imagined necessarily to be joined in a causal manner. A does not always lead to B in a mechanical manner. This description may be clear and concise, but a key element is missing. A and B, simply put, are also mediated by interpretation. As a result, the interpretive significance must be ascertained before any response to it can be planned. This is not to say that variables are randomly related but that their relationship is cognitive. The strength of the association between *A* and *B*, as mentioned earlier, depends on how persons define their identity, interpersonal relationships, and milieu.

Norms, additionally, are presumed to be "locally determined" (Lyotard, 1984). This is an idea borrowed from René Thom. Illustrated in his work on catastrophe theory, the world is comprised of a myriad of linguistic regions. Within each one, a different language game is operative. Indeed, movement from one frame to another signals a dramatic change in reality. In each locale, different linguistically inscribed assumptions are in place. Rather than an Archimedean point, norms are grounded in the *petite narrative*, or social construction of reality, that has been linguistically instituted (Lyotard, 1984).

As a result, technical rigor does not necessarily generate high quality data. In the example of biomedicine, precision is equated with accuracy. Technical refinement is thought to lead to an improved knowledge base, which can be used to upgrade the intervention process. Improved technique, however, does not automatically make a researcher more aware of how reality is interpreted. For this reason, Habermas (1970) argues that the principle of "communicative competence" should guide research. Instead of striving to become value free, researchers should try to comprehend the pragmatic thrust of language. They should attempt to be value relevant. A physician, accordingly, should try to gain entree to a patient's worldview in order to clarify a diagnosis, rather than rely on more laboratory tests.

In sum, the biomedical model is under siege by many philosophers. With respect to identifying health and illness, interpretation must be recognized to pervade the practice of medicine. Because disease is implicated in a cultural dynamic that pervades the body and every other facet of life, physicians should attend to the experiential nature of a patient's problem. Patients, as well as physicians, have a role in defining their condition. Therefore, the issue is how to create a situation where both viewpoints are given credence.

The Western biomedical model, through its dualistic focus on the body, delegitimizes the power of persons to define themselves in the face of pressure from the medical establishment to provide "objective" definitions. Even though physicians are hardly objective, operating according to the culture of science, they demand submission from patients. Nonetheless some patients are beginning to believe that their opinions are no less valid than those expressed by medical practitioners. A conflict of interpretations is thus mounting because physicians believe they are objective and should have the final word on any medical topic. This position is no longer warranted, however, from a point of view that begins with the person and not the body. Medicine must be democratized if the practices associated with holism are inaugurated on a large scale.

Paradigm Shift and Policy Change

Democratizing medicine seems congenial to a culture that is said to espouse individualistic values. A consistent postmodern philosophy of medicine, however, would stake out a radical position on policy change that would seem quite foreign to most citizens of the United States, because, in the parlance of postmodern theory, reality is "decentered." Or, as Jean Gebser (1985) declares, "the center is everywhere." There would be no longer any places where absolutes, such as those fostered by biomedicine, could hide. If language use extends to the core of existence, then nothing escapes the influence of interpretation. Therefore, absolutes are merely modes of interpretation that have gained widespread acceptance. As noted by Roland Barthes (1986), objectivity is a special case of language use.

Many aspects of medical care would have to be rethought if dualism were honestly rejected (Foss & Rothenberg, 1987), and most of the rethinking would devalue the medical establishment. For example, the justification would be eliminated for physicians to control the delivery of health services. Typically, M.D.s are viewed as dispassionate, rational, and in possession of extremely valuable knowledge. Their *modus operandi* is not necessarily objective, however, but represents one among many ways of conceptualizing ailments. Accordingly, other viewpoints could be introduced without their having to be treated as automatically inferior to biomedicine. Types of medicine competing with one another in a pluralistic environment was characteristic of medicine in America during the early and middle 19th century (Starr, 1982). Orthodox medicine early in this century, like the Catholic church of the Middle Ages, came to dominate the medical scene almost completely, actively defining other approaches to medicine as invalid, ineffectual or even dangerous. A postmodernist philosophy of medicine would undermine medical orthodoxy, encouraging once again input from various members of a community without fear that the practice of medicine would be ruined.

At present, health care is mostly shaped by medical knowledge. When making a diagnosis, for example, a patient's suggestions are not given much credence. Intuition, simply put, is not thought to be scientific and is dismissed as invalid (Kestenbaum, 1982). Abandoning dualism, however, fosters a more encompassing approach to assessment. A diverse body of knowledge can be introduced, thereby allowing a host of options to be tested before a final recommendation is made. For there is no *a priori* reason for limiting input to biomedicine. The interdisciplinary nature of geriatric assessment seems to the most orthodox to be a step in the direction of democratizing medicine. From the radical stand staked out by postmodern theory, however, this single attempt to be pluralistic would be only a small step in the direction of democratization.

Moving away from the issue of the power of the medical profession, a postmodern philosophy of medicine seems especially relevant to the central concern of this chapter. When dualism is operative, as it is in the biomedical model, the focus of medical intervention is primarily the body (Jonas, 1966). Physiology is presumed to be immune to interpretation and to be factual. But as physicians assess the expanded entity called a lived body, many variables, formerly criticized as intangible, are understood to affect behavior. The mind, biography, surrounding environment, and culture, for instance, are a few considerations that become very significant in a non-Cartesian world. Given the unity of subjectivity and objectivity, the locus of intervention should extend beyond the confines of physical nature.

Physicians are blamed regularly for overmedicating patients. But considering the prevailing dualistic image of the body, this method of treatment makes sense. Due to the obsession with disease, nonmedical options are assumed to be fraudulent. A more holistic practice of medicine clearly would be warranted, however, if the body were understood to be tied to culture. In this sense, treatment can be redefined so that medicine can become more culturally sensitive. Chiropractic and folk medicines, for example, would no doubt begin to play a larger role in treatment, as they did before the hegemony of orthodox medicine in the United States.

If a total paradigm shift were to occur and an antidualism philosophy of medicine were to take root, there would be dramatic changes in assessing patients. Physicians appear to be dependent on medical technology in order to make a sound diagnosis. The use of laboratory tests has proliferated for many reasons, including the need to get the best "second opinion" available. But these devices do not have a monopoly on reason and, in fact, tend to obscure the experiential side of illness. Accordingly, if sensitivity to a patient's needs were a priority, there would be no justification for establishing technology as the sole centerpiece of diagnosis. The search for knowledge would be enlarged to include a variety of so-called qualitative sources—key citizens, diaries, oral histories of communities, folklore—that may clarify a patient's cultural and personal situation. Clues for diagnosis would not be restricted to traditionally conceived objective facts about the body.

Descartes was worried that an "evil genius" was trying to deceive him about the true nature of reality (Bordo, 1987). Mind–body dualism, thus, represented an attempt to avoid this deception. By becoming dualistic, Descartes reasoned, subjectivity would be isolated and controlled, and thus attention could be devoted to acting objectively. Any factor that was not deemed objective, therefore, should be relegated to the periphery of the knowledge acquisition process. To Descartes and subsequent dualists, objectivity is associated with discrete, readily measurable pieces of data. Anything that defies this simplistic definition is given scant attention.

In the realm of medicine, however, this dualism has fostered some practices that have become problematic. The body became an object that could be known accurately only by technical, medical experts. In the end, the human character of illness was eclipsed, while medical practice was shrouded in a mantle of authority and removed from public view.

To establish a serious antidualistic philosophy of medicine, the required political agenda is a radical one. According to this viewpoint, the institution of medicine could not be appreciably improved without a shift in political outlook, and the reallocation of financial and other resources. However, the new agenda would not be simply economic, but also philosophical. National health insurance of any kind would not be an improvement, for example, unless some important philosophical changes were also witnessed.

The praxis of an antidualistic philosophy of medicine, therefore, would focus on empowerment through a change in culture and self. This philosophical stance would argue that people must begin to believe that their body is not an object that operates solely according to the laws of nature, and that social and cultural correctives can be undertaken that promote health. In other words, health care could no longer be viewed as within the purview of physicians and drug companies solely. Furthermore, persons would be urged to believe that they have a right to the knowledge that has been reserved for medical experts alone. In this way, real prevention programs could be inaugurated. In general, persons would be given the latitude to participate fully in every facet of their treatment, from defining health to making a diagnosis.

The aim of this final section is to demonstrate the revolutionary nature of a postmodern philosophy of medicine. Democratization, far from being adaptable to modern medical culture, is quite antithetical to it in many ways. Suggesting that the improvement of health care in the United States depends on the democratization of the culture of medicine is a hard and prophetic statement.

Conclusion

The purpose of describing the radical policy changes that would be required for a complete shift in paradigms is to make a specific point. Tempering the biomedical model is not a paradigm shift. Mere observation that the sovereignty of professional medicine is waning is not sufficient. Sensing a growing openness to holistic medicine, particularly among older Americans, is not what is meant by a true paradigm shift. These are examples of *paradigm strain*, cracks in the walls of the Western biomedical edifice, and the vast industry that has grown up around it.

A true shift from a dualistic to an antidualistic paradigm would require a change so monumental that the traditional image of scientific medicine that triumphed in this century would be obliterated, and something quite different would have to be erected in its place. Such dramatic alterations may someday occur, inch by inch, if not suddenly. Adopting postmodern philosophy would promote these changes. Social forces such as those instigated by the demographic imperative that challenges the Western biomedical model and the biomedical establishment that dualism has nurtured may be opening the way for more profound changes that can now be envisioned, including the true democratization of medicine. If life expectancy should suddenly jump to 100 years, the immense pressures on medicine that would be brought on by increased patient demand could trigger a paradigm shift of this magnitude.

R. D. Laing (1973) once claimed that psychiatric patients would probably be helped more by an epistemologist than a psychiatrist. There is a sense in which epistemology and practice cannot be separated. One implies the other. The movement that has been witnessed during the past 20 years and has challenged the biomedical model and broadened the scope of medicine is supported by certain epistemological principles that are difficult to ignore. And if this epistemological side of medicine is given serious consideration, a new approach to delivering medical care may be on the horizon. This conclusion may sound strange to those who believe that medicine is an especially practical discipline. Nonetheless, a change in philosophical worldview is essential to a socially responsive approach to medicine.

References

Barthes, R. (1986). *The rustle of language*. New York: Hill and Wang.

Bordo, S. R. (1987). *The flight to objectivity*. Albany: State University of New York Press.

Carlson, R. J. (1975). *The end of medicine*. New York: Wiley.

Cassel, E. J. (1991). *The nature of suffering and the goals of medicine*. New York: Oxford University Press.

Cockerham, W. C. (1992). *Medical sociology*, (5th ed.). Englewood Cliffs, NJ: Prentice Hall.

Derrida, J. (1976). *Of grammatology*. Baltimore: Johns Hopkins University Press.

Dubos, R. (1959). *Mirage of health: Utopias, progress, and biological change.* Garden City, NJ: Doubleday.

Durkheim, E. (1983). *Pragmatism and sociology.* Cambridge: Cambridge University Press.

Ellul, J. (1964). *The technological society.* New York: Random House.

Flexner, A. (1910). *Medical education in the United States and Canada* (Bulletin No. 4). New York: Carnegie Foundation for the Advancement of Teaching.

Foss, L., & Rothenberg, K. (1987). *The second medical revolution.* Boston: Shambhala.

Foucault, M. (1989). *The archaeology of knowledge.* London: Routledge and Kegan Paul.

Freund, P. E. S., & McGuire, M. B. (1991). *Health, illness, and the social body: A critical sociology.* Englewood Cliffs, NJ: Prentice Hall.

Gebser, J. (1985). *The Ever-present origin.* Athens: Ohio University Press.

Habermas, J. (1970). Towards a theory of communicative competence. In H. P. Dreitzel (Ed.), *Recent sociology* (2nd ed., pp. 115–148). New York: Macmillan.

Jonas, H. (1966). *The phenomenon of life.* New York: Harper and Row.

Kestenbaum, V. (1982). Introduction: The experience of illness. In V. Kestenbaum (Ed.), *The humanity of the ill* (pp. 13–20). Knoxville: The University of Tennessee Press.

Kleinman, A., Eisenberg, L., & Good, B. (1978). Culture, illness and cure. *Annals of Internal Medicine, 88,* 251–258.

Kunkel, S. R., & Applebaum, R. A. (1992). Estimating the prevalence of long-term disability for an aging society. *Journals of Gerontology: Social Sciences, 47,* S253.

Lacan, J. (1977). *Ecrits.* New York: W. W. Norton.

Laing, R. D. (1973). The mystification of experience. In P. Brown (Ed.), *Radical psychology,* (pp. 109–127). New York: Harper and Row.

Lyotard, J. F. (1984). *The postmodern condition: A report on knowledge.* Minneapolis: University of Minnesota Press.

Manton, K. G. (1989). Epidemiological, demographic, and social correlates of disability among the elderly. *The Milbank Quarterly, 67,* 13.

Mittelmark, M. B. (1993). The epidemiology of aging. In W. L. Hazzard, E. L. Birman, J. P. Blass, W. H. Ettinger, & J. B. Halter (Eds.), *Principles of geriatric medicine and gerontology.* New York: McGraw-Hill.

Murphy, J. W., & Longino, C. F., Jr. (1992). What is the justification for a qualitative approach to aging studies. *Aging and Society, 12,* 143–156.

Norell, S. (1984). Models of causation in epidemiology. In L. Nordenfelt & B. I. B. Lindahl (Eds.), *Health, disease, and causal explanation in medicine*. Dordrecht, The Netherlands: D. Reidel.

Schwartz, M. A. & Wiggins, O. P. (1988). Scientific and humanistic medicine: A theory of clinical methods. In K. L. White (Ed.), *The task of medicine*. Menlo Park, CA: The Henry J. Kaiser Family Foundation.

Starr, P. (1982). *The social transformation of American medicine: The rise of a sovereign profession and the making of a vast industry*. New York: Basic Books.

Strasser, H., & Randall, S. C. (1981). *An introduction to theories of social change*. London: Routledge and Kegan Paul.

Weber, M. (1958). *The Protestant ethic and the spirit of capitalism*. New York: Scribner's.

Weber, M. (1978). *Economy and society*. (Vol 1). Berkeley: University of California Press.

Chapter 11

What Does More Life Add Up To?

Mildred M. Seltzer

Τhis concluding chapter will attempt to highlight, without being comprehensive, some of the material presented in previous chapters. It begins with a reprise of the book's purpose and what can be learned from the authors' speculations and continues with a brief review of several scenarios describing a society of centenarians. Each author was asked to describe from her or his disciplinary or professional perspective what impact a life expectancy of 100 years would have on society by addressing the following areas:

1. family,
2. interpersonal relationships,
3. individual development,
4. politics and policy, and
5. labor force participation and retirement.

Each of these topics will be reviewed separately. Practitioners were also asked to consider how the nature of their profession and practice would change. All of the authors were asked to describe research they would undertake if their own life expectancy were 100 years. What kinds of research questions would be asked, what designs used, and how would the researcher's own increased longevity affect the conduct of her or his research?

The authors' speculations were based on different assumptions and resulted in the development of a number of different scenarios. Some descriptions showed a society different from the present one; others described one that would be an extension of today's. Discussions were occasionally prefaced by the comment that "it [consequences, changes caused by increased life expectancy] boggles the mind" (Atchley, p. 41; Troll, p. 79; McRae, p. 23; Shenk & Keith, p. 102). Although several authors deal implicitly with how political and practice ideologies might change, only Chapter 10 by Longino and Murphy deals specifically with this topic.

Reprise and Overview

In 1972, Neugarten wrote "If the average life-span were to go beyond 100, especially if this were to occur in the relatively short period of a few decades, the effects upon the social fabric are presently unforeseeable" (p. 438). After raising a series of questions that would need to be answered if such an event occurred, Neugarten points to the lack of attention given these questions and adds, "Whatever the reason for the neglect, gerontologists should themselves take the lead in opening the issues to a public discussion" (p. 439). Some gerontologists have done so. They have been interested in the impact the demography of aging has on a society. They have also been interested in projecting the effects of population aging into the future. In a proactive society, such projections can then provide a basis on which to plan for the future. Our society, however, tends to react to changes rather than plan ahead; our policy makers and planners tend to be descriptive, present-oriented people rather than anticipatory planners. As a consequence, the data demographers and gerontologists make available are not used to full advantage.

Subsequently, Neugarten and Maddox asked what would happen if we increased life expectancy and improved the "vigor and productivity" of late life (1981, p. i). They observed that old age as we now know it would be very different and that gerontological research should be concerned with what old age "...*will become*..."(p. i). Research alone cannot accomplish everything; without research, however, we cannot bring about necessary changes.

The authors in this book meet the essence of the Neugarten (1972) and Neugarten and Maddox (1981) challenges. They describe what some of the social and personal results might be in a society in which the average life expectancy is 100. Although they do not prescribe what could or should be done, the authors' speculations contain some useful ideas for the proactive planners and gerontological research personnel. Three issues permeate virtually every chapter:

1. discussion of Fries, hypothesis concerning the compression of morbidity,
2. the meaning of age as a marker, and
3. the availability of formal and informal support systems.

Economic and political policy issues undergird all three.

The importance of the first issue, the compression of morbidity, relates to the nature of late life. The Fries hypothesis (Fries, 1984) assumes that old age is not characterized by a long period of extreme frailty and disability; rather, only a brief illness precedes dying. If this is an accurate picture, then concerns about financial and social supports are minimized. On the other hand, if increased longevity means increased duration of frailty and disability, then societal and personal costs become a crucial political issue. As Hendricks notes, "The social policy implications of any gains in life expectancy [without better health] are staggering and mere tinkering will not serve society well" (p. 55).

Closely related to issues of morbidity are data suggesting the Gompertz function does not perform as predicted in extreme old age, that people are not dying at the predicted rate in old age (Manton, 1992). Consequently, our population of the extremely old continues to grow numerically.

There is agreement that the crucial issue is whether increased life expectancy means merely postponing frailty and disability to a later chronological age or eliminating the declines of old age. As Friedsam points out in Chapter 9, the emphasis is on conditions under which we reach the terminal phase of life; what awaits us there is left hanging and unexamined. In the best of scenarios, if health is good most other aspects of old age are, at a minimum, tolerable. It is when old age is associated with poor health and frailty that problems arise. At that point questions are raised about who provides care, at what cost, where, how and for how long, with what resultant tensions and social policy implications. Alternatives to the present patterns of caregiving are based on maintaining current components of the system and raising questions about how these would fit together and be organized in a long-lived society.

Given good health and sufficient money, old age is not too bad and is certainly better than the alternative. In anticipating what awaits us if health deteriorates, Friedsam describes hospices with and without walls, the institutionalization of dying, and a weakening of the taboo on the right to die. Atchley also suggests the weakening of constraints on suicide with the result that programs of planned and assisted suicides could increase. He emphasizes, however, that euthanasia for social reasons rather than as an act of mercy is a "...frightening possibility." McRae reinforces this stance against suicide, taking a firm position against starting down the "slippery slope" (p. 32) by permitting physician-assisted suicides.

Several of the authors discussed issues of health care rationing. Friedsam observes that without an explicit policy we could continue the kind of institutionalized rationing we have at present. Currently we are already discussing explicit rationing and in some instances, implementing such a policy.

Most of the authors ask who will care for parents and children when both generations are very old. Friedsam reminds us that some research indicates that some older people would prefer not to be taken care of by their families. Dunkle and Lynch suggest that formal social services will become increasingly common, although Shenk and Keith, Hudson, and others raise questions about the financing of such programs. In fact, a common question in most of the chapters concerns the costs of care for the large numbers of very old people. Who will pay? To what extent will people be willing to pay? What is the likelihood of rationed care? To what degree would the increased numbers of old people lead to intergenerational conflicts, both personal and societal?

In most descriptions, then, there is a strong correlation between the individual author's scenario and the assumed nature of the last years of life. If living to be 100 means either postponing currently experienced frailties until a later age or extending the duration of illness and frailty, then the scenario tends to be depressingly unpleasant and negative. If, on the other hand, we can live to be 100 with minimal decrements until shortly before death (as in several of the scenarios), then a life expectancy of 100 is an encouraging situation offering exciting opportunities to experience new stages, phases, roles, and relationships. It is a most positive scenario. Essentially, the majority of the authors echo an old motto: "If you have your health you have everything." (Of course, good economic health helps, also.) Good health at any age, and particularly in old age, has an impact on more than life satisfaction. It affects every area of life. Because providing health care in late life has become a current issue of great importance, the poor health of large numbers of very old people would have a tremendous impact on social policies, human service delivery systems, family support systems, and labor force characteristics, to mention only a few of the affected areas.

The second issue, the meaning of age, is discussed by almost all of the authors. Shenk and Keith make this issue one of the major cornerstones of their chapter as will be discussed later in this chapter. The chronological definition of old age would change; rather than 65, 75, or 85, the boundary could be set at 90 or 95. We would find new words to describe various stages of old age. The use of age as proxy would be less reliable and therefore less common. The life course would be remapped.

The availability of formal and informal supports is a third theme found in most chapters. Chapter 7 by Dunkle and Lynch deals with social work's role in providing a range of formal support services for an old population. Friedsam's discussion about long-term care describes possible and probable systems of care in a long-lived society. A discussion of support systems is an integral part of many authors' descriptions of family life and friendship patterns. In fact, in much of current gerontological literature, including some in this book, old age, support services, and health care have become, if not synonymous with one another then certainly inevitably linked. This bundling of topics is not the result of a conscious gerontological conspiracy. It is related to some of the factors Longino and Murphy and Shenk and Keith discuss in their chapters: the biomedicalization of aging, family bias implicit in our human services and welfare programs and policies, and our homogenization of old age and the aged population.

Scenarios

The authors' descriptions of a society of centenarians ranged from a Panglossian vision to one almost as dismal as Swift's description of Luggnuggian society. Scenarios were based on different assumptions, from Atchley's use of current census projections to Hudson's creation of eight scenarios based on dichotomizing three major variables. There was considerable agreement among them, regardless of basic assumptions about the causes of longevity. All describe a society characterized by great population diversity in age and ethnicity. An old population that ranges in ages from 65 to over 100 represents two or three generations. Their cohort experiences will be sufficiently different from one another that the term *old* will either have many meanings or become meaningless. It will definitely become even more elusive than it is currently. Living to be 100 would also be a significantly different experience than it is now. At present, a centenarian is the rare survivor, the recipient of Presidential birthday messages, and the object of television coverage. A 100-year-old feels extraordinary. Troll asks at what age would one become extraordinary in a society where reaching the age of 100 is a common experience?

As already discussed, in most scenarios, issues of health care are salient. In part this may reflect our society's current preoccupation with the cost and proposed changes in our health care delivery system. In part it may reflect the continued bipolar picture of aging: The old are identified either as sick, frail, and poor, or as a new privileged class of active, well-to-do old people.

Many of the authors' assumptions are based on current demographic and economic realities. Others are anchored in our existing social system and its components. For example, most of the authors are concerned with issues of caregiving. There appears to be inevitable association between caregiving and the family as a social institution. Although the nature of the family would continue to change, presumably caregiving would continue to be a family responsibility, usually the task of women. Caregiving activities would be affected by the numbers of those needing care, those available to provide such care, labor force participation, and family structure. Caregiving would be supported by governmental activities, new technologies, and new health care organizations, just as they are now. The relative importance of each component might change, but system components remain much the same.

Friedsam, however, calls attention to gerontology's limited vision of the future and of the consequences of marked demographic changes. He observes that gerontologists either do not anticipate or are not concerned with the possibility that our society would require fundamental structural changes should life expectancy increase dramatically. He decries the "business as usual" approach that characterizes our present attitude toward issues of social change. I would describe that business orientation as *laissez-faire*. Hendricks also urges us to move away from a "mere tinkering" approach; to recognize…"that all social institutions will be fundamentally restructured to accommodate the changes" (p. 57). [brought about by the impact of increased life expectancy].

Atchley provides a reality orientation to his speculations about the nature of a centenarian society by drawing on three Census Bureau scenarios for future mortality rates (a high life expectancy, a medium one, and a low one). The first assumes a continuation of current trends in longevity; the second anticipates a slowing in longevity trends; the third holds current rates constant with an increase in AIDS-related deaths. All three scenarios show a projected increase in the oldest–old population with, therefore, the likelihood of a dramatic increase in the number of centenarians. Pointing to the usually conservative underestimations made by the Bureau of the Census, Atchley observes that the actual numbers of very old may well be higher than those projected. Current figures also indicate that active life expectancy will increase, thus resulting in a less disabled oldest-old population. Certainly, previous efforts in anticipating increased life expectancy and its consequences for our society underestimated future numbers of old people. Neugarten and others (1975), in anticipating aging at the turn of the 21st century, projected two sets of figures, based on different mortality assumptions. The more conservative figures expected the population aged 65 and over to reach 26.5 million; the higher estimate was 35.5 million. The first figure is based on 1968 mortality rates, the latest year for which mortality rates were then available. The figure of 35.5 million was based on the assumption that age-specific mortality rates would drop 2% per year after 1970 for all people aged 20 and over. (Neugarten, 1975). Additionally, it was predicted that in the year 2000, men who reached 65 would live to 83; 65-year-old women would reach 86. We now know these are overly optimistic life expectancy predictions. Instead of 18 years, recent figures estimate white male life expectancy at 65 is about 15.2 more years; a black male's 13.6 years. A white woman of 65 can expect almost 19 additional years; a black woman, 17 years. As has been noted in previous chapters, the 1990 population age 65 and over numbered 31.1 million, thus the actual figures fall between the lower and higher predictions cited above.

The CoRad report (Havighurst, 1969) projected a population of 28.2 million people 65 and older in the year 2000. As noted above, we were already some 3 million over that in the 1990 census reports. Population figures are rarely, if ever, exact; similarly, predictions of the future have a margin of error.

Hudson, in chapter 6, describes eight possible scenarios, each resulting from a combination of three dichotimized variables: the status of the economy, advances in biomedical research and health behaviors, and demographic trends. Table 6-2 delineates each scenario. As is evident, each scenario has different parameters and consequences, ranging from quite positive to extremely negative. In the best of all possible situations, there is strong economic growth, major biological advances and health promotion behaviors, and a large, healthy very old population who would make few demands on society. It would be, in Hudson's words, "… a world of economic and physical harmony" with a minimum of social and political pressures (p.116). At the other extreme, the economy is stagnant and the aged population is growing in size and in frailty. Under such circumstances we might well end up with a war of all against all.

Shenk and Keith's scenarios are based on two differing perspectives of age as a marker. In the first, old age continues to be a generalized marker. In this case, old age would remain a distinct period of life, although roles would be redefined and new ones created for old people. In the second scenario, the meaning of age is significantly more pliant, and the period of old age becomes more layered. Roles and responsibilities would change for each successive age category, with each having its own characteristic ones. The authors make two assumptions regarding the nature of the increased life expectancy: (a) the additional years are relatively healthy ones, and (b) there will be a system of health care rationing based in part on chronological age. They dismiss a third assumption, that the extended period of life would be characterized by extreme frailty, although they do not say why they reject this possibility. Given the two assumptions and the two different uses of age as a marker, they develop four scenarios. These two views of age combined with two more variables—prolongation of good health, versus extension of a period of frailty and the rationing of health care on the basis, in part, of chronological age—result in four different scenarios.

McRae describes his three different scenarios as idealistic, nihilistic, and a potential future reality. In the latter, women will continue to outnumber men in old age; there will be a range of vigor, and the final months of life will be characterized by increased morbidity.

The Family

It is clear that there will be increased diversity in family arrangements. Family structure is changing now and would continue to change in the centenarian future; informal support systems and living arrangements will differ. Authors speculate about the nature of five- to eight-generation families and reconstituted families. How would the informal support system be affected? What happens, for example, if a parent of 100 requires help from an adult child of 75 or 80? What are great-grandchildren's responsibilities to great-grandparents? Atchley suggests that the longevity revolution could make family support of the very old a less predictable activity than it is currently. At present, family ties are characterized by two qualities: moral compulsivity and voluntarism. He asks what moral obligations these great-grandchildren would feel for their great-grandparents.

Although gerontologists have a tendency to examine families in latter life primarily as support systems, families are more than systems of caregiving for their aged members. Families are also primary groups that provide socioemotional support to members of all generations. Interestingly, however, only a few authors discussed how the dynamics of marriage might be affected by the increased longevity of both partners. Currently only a small minority among the very old have living spouses. If, however, life expectancy of 100 were common, would people marry latter in life than they now do? If not, and if the gender differential in mortality were to be reduced or virtually eliminated, golden wedding anniversaries would be common. On the other hand, a seventy-five-year marriage might experience some strains. For example, what roles would familiarity, boredom, or habituation play in this dyadic relationship? Projecting the present onto the hypothetical future, Hendricks reminds us, we may find current divorce figures predictive of high divorce rates among long-lived marriages. Hendricks suggests the possibility of serial marriages, which would not be drastically different from current practices in some sectors of society. Should such marital arrangements become more statistically common, they would probably become less titillating.

Because increased life expectancy would affect the many roles individuals play, Shenk and Keith suggest the timing and length of marriage would be affected. One might marry relatively early in life or relatively late. A period of widowhood might extend for 30 years before a remarrige. Presumably temporal norms would have changed so that current "appropriate" times to marry, to go to school, to raise a family, to have a career, to retire, or any combination of these, would no longer be valid.

Issues of reciprocity in old age are often dealt with in terms of responsibilities of the younger for the older; the reverse is rarely considered, except with respect to matters having to do with death, or the care of developmentally disabled or mentally ill adult children. Moreover, responsibilities are more frequently dealt with than are rights in intergenerational relationships. Several of the authors did discuss family responsibilities in terms of younger generations for the oldest generation; few discuss the oldest generations' responsibilities for younger ones. Shenk and Keith touched on the possible roles and relationships of grandparents, great-grandparents, and great-great-grandparents vis-à-vis their various generations of grandchildren. If we define specific levels of old age, these authors suggest that grandmothers, for example, would have different and specific responsibilities for each successive generation of grandchildren.

The authors discuss some of the complexities of multigenerational families. An increased number of living generations results in both quantitative and qualitative changes. For example, as the number of living generations increases, the potential number of interpersonal relationships increases exponentially. Numbers affect the nature of relationships. In general, the greater the number of people and relationships, the more norms governing relationships become formalized (Mott, 1965).

Interpersonal Relationships

Troll discusses how an increase in centenarians would provide more age peers in their social convoys and consequently, less need to turn to younger people to provide social support. She also raises questions about how others associating with centenarians perceive them and how these perceptions affect the centenarian. Currently, the oldest-old she describes are those without many living family members and friends. In a long-lived society, relationships would also be long-lived. The affective component and nature of relationships would change over time. As Troll illustrates, time might heal all interpersonal rifts.

Some of the same or similar questions raised above regarding the impact of duration on marriage are equally applicable in the discussion of other kinds of interpersonal relationships. How does length of time affect friendships? Do duration and familiarity increase predictability? Do they breed contempt, indifference, boredom or, does longevity strengthen the ties that bind? To what extent does the need for novelty affect long-term relationships? Would friendships be primarily among age peers or would they cross age categories?

Troll suggests that with a large number of centenarians around, the death of friends and other age mates would occur later in life. Many would be growing old together and, as a result, there could be a "culture of the oldest-old" (pp. 76–77) in which one would have age mates with whom to have fun and to share values and interests.

Some of the scenarios discussed in previous chapters suggest the possibility of intergenerational conflict. How would this affect interpersonal relationships both within and external to the family? How are interpersonal relationships affected by an economy of scarcity in which there is a scarcity of all resources?

Individual Development

Several of the chapters contain discussions about what we mean when we refer to "development." Citing Kastenbaum, Hendricks reminds us that situational factors shape whatever intrinsic developmental factors exist. What is viewed as adult development "may be nothing more than a reflection of career and family transitions and other involvements in the world" (p. 65). Atchley writes that if we define development "...as the continued evolution of adaptive capacity, then development could be expected to continue to the very end of life" (p. 44). Troll also speculates about some developmental concerns in very late life. Atchley, Hendricks, and Dunkle and Lynch agree that few gerontologists give sufficient attention to the developmental issues of very late life.

Hendricks, in particular, emphasizes the importance of new perspectives and concepts. He challenges us to consider the inadequacies of current ways of gerontological conceptualizing. He warns that attempts to use current ways of thinking about middle and old age in anticipating the characteristics of development in a society of centenarians are doomed. We need new ways of thinking about these many issues. This echoes Friedsam's concern of gerontologists' limited vision about the future.

Hendricks focuses on relationships between social structural contexts and individual life courses. He examines the limitations of gerontological theories in explaining what happens when the aging processes remain relatively the same but the life course, transitions, turning points, transformations, and social structure change. What is the source of identity in the face of these changes? Even expected transitions require the individual to reconfigure personal resources in order to regain equilibrium. Hendricks stresses the importance of maintaining a sense of mastery over situations. He views this as more important in differentiating among the very old than chronology or biology. Atchley also deals with the importance of a sense of sovereignty of control over one's life.

Atchley, Hendricks, and Troll particularly make the point that increases in longevity affect our time horizon. The life cycle assumes new dimensions; there are new "possible selves" (Markus & Nurius, 1986), new "expected life histories" (Seltzer & Troll, 1986). There are opportunities to develop new roles, to achieve new developmental stages. Because a time perspective is essential to the perceived continuity of self, there would also be changes in perceptions and concepts of self. Troll, for example, describes the self-perceptions of the currently very old, noting that at least two factors affect these self-perceptions: their own expected life history and that of others who are also survivors.

Atchley expects that the time horizon for planning would change. The increased time horizon can create uncertainty about the future and the nature of aging. Individuals can become fearful about an uncertain future and the possibility of becoming disabled for an extended period of time. These uncertainties and fears could result in feelings of anxiety and depression. Like Hendricks, Atchley points out that the life course for extremely late years is poorly mapped, leading to further ambiguities and uncertainties about roles and life events and, thereby to increased anxieties.

Troll raises questions about cognitive development in very late years. Current findings show that many of the extremely old of today have remained very cognitively competent. At the same time, she asks whether we have the capacity to record and integrate the knowledge and experiences of a century; whether we are "programmed" to be able to do so.

Most of the authors ask as many questions as they answer. This is not surprising, given the complexity of the issues raised by increased life expectancy. However, the questions they ask contain within them ideas and suggestions for further research and planning.

Politics and Policy

Hudson's entire chapter is written from the viewpoint of a political scientist. One of the first things he points out is that it would be essential to reconsider age-related public policy in a society of centenarians. We would redefine when "old" begins and what it represents or stands for as a proxy. We have already begun reconsidering. We are, for example, phasing in different ages of eligibility for Social Security benefits.

The politics of aging have changed in the past 60 years. Originally the passive recipients of policies and legislation, the old have become increasingly active on their own behalf. One factor in bringing about changes has been the increasing diversity of the older population. It has become more and more difficult to talk about a homogeneous old population, to speak on behalf of all older people as some are wont to do, or to making sweeping generalizations about the circumstances of the aged. Diversity can only be expected to increase in a society of long-lived people. Given the diversity, given our constricting economy, and the increasingly tenuous nature of intergenerational understandings, Hudson points out the probability of further changes in the ages for age-based criteria as well as the establishment of additional eligibility requirements for various programs and services. In order to plan effectively for an uncertain future with unknown needs, Hudson recommends the development of some contingency or risk analysis plans.

Troll becomes highly speculative in suggesting the possibility of war between the long-lived and short-lived peoples. She also suggests, playfully we hope, the politics that could be involved in such conflict. She discusses the possibility of centenarians creating their own organization, the equivalent of an American Association of Retired Persons for centenarians because the needs and concerns of 100-year-old people would be significantly different from those 65 or 75 years old.

Friedsam, equally speculative, describes a political scenario developed by Wheeler. It is a society based on the assumption that the method of extending life will be a scarce resource. A gerontocratic society will exist, characterized by intergenerational and interclass conflict as all attempt to obtain the life-extending technique. "Indeed, the only function of the young will be to become old" (p. 173).

As noted earlier, most of the authors discuss a national health care policy, policies regarding health care rationing, and assisted euthanasia. Programs and policies relating to human services and their underlying philosophies are touched on in all of the chapters on practice (Part III). Dunkle and Lynch discuss one specific role of social workers, that of developing and implementing policies relevant to the needs of older people. McRae and Friedsam discuss the politics of medicine and long-term care, both observing ongoing changes in this area and among interest groups that urge specific changes. Longino and Murphy review how policies are shaped by and reflect prevailing philosophies and paradigms.

Labor Force Participation and Retirement

Issues of work and retirement are horse and carriage to our gerontological minds. It is also difficult to dissociate work and retirement from politics and policy. In fact, it is difficult to separate areas of life from one another, except artificially and for purposes of discussion. Scientists study specific and limited areas of our lives; that is not the way we live.

A drastic change in our life expectancy affects when we enter the labor force, how long we remain in it, at what age we retire, under what circumstances and how retirement is financed. Current theories such as the "'life-cycle' theory of saving" (Atchley, p. 38) do not fit the facts of our lives today, let alone for a world of centenarians. In such a world, more people can be expected to outlive their financial resources, a constant concern of today's older population. Hendricks observes that retirement as we now know it may become a thing of the past. As he remarks, "It requires a greater leap of faith to assume things will remain constant than it does to predict something different" (p. 58).

The authors ask a series of wide-ranging questions relating to productivity, education, achievement motivation, and its peaking. They ask about job obsolescence, career changes, age of retirement, and the possibility of eliminating age as a retirement criterion and substituting instead functional criteria. This last point is not unfamiliar to academicians, many of whom are currently engaged in debates about maintaining the tenure system and the relationships of tenure to age and to retirement in the academy.

Several contributors, including specifically Friedsam and Hendricks, observe that the nature of work itself is changing. One area, however, that will be important in the future, regardless of increased life expectancy, will be caregiving. If life expectancy increases to 100 with the likelihood that there will be at least some period of disability during one's life, then there will be a need for additional caregiving services with more men and more older workers employed to provide that care.

In all of the practitioner-oriented chapters, it is clear that the authors predict more employment opportunities for working with old people and the need for more adequate education and training for those who will work with the very old as their clients or patients. Dunkle and Lynch and Friedsam, in particular, observe how the increasing diversity of our population and the differential access to education will affect staffing in the human services industry.

Practice

Three chapters focus on how the professional practices of social work, medicine, and long-term care would be affected by a life expectancy of 100. Again, there are several scenarios that provide the background against which practice occurs. As Friedsam points out, the nature of practice will be related to the kind of "fourth age" we typically experience. In one instance, rehabilitation and activities are irrelevant because death occurs within a short time after its warning signals are given. On the other hand, Atchley points out that our definitions and use of rehabilitation may well change if life expectancy is increased. The likelihood, however, is that all three areas of practice will continue as they are now, changing slowly, and as Friedsam avers, haphazardly, as we continue to depend to a large extent on informal caregiving for those in need of help. In part, slowness of change in this field is related to the nature of cultural change in general; in part, it reflects measured response to different pressure groups.

Shenk and Keith describe additional obstacles to change. We are a future-oriented society and consequently do not value the old or seek their involvement in bringing about change. Instead, we look toward our children, the hope for the future. As a consequence, we leave the care of the old to the family. Additionally, we use a medical model in our view of the old and of aging with the result that we have a relatively paternalistic system of care for them. By contrast, these two authors describe Denmark's system for providing care to its older population. That system is less paternalistic and more egalitarian than is ours. Services are provided to enhance older peoples' competencies and strengths and to maintain people in their own homes, rather than to facilitate dependence and institutionalization.

In the United States, much of social work, long-term care and medicine is based on the assumption that the "expert" knows what should be done, not the client or patient. Dunkle and Lynch emphasize, however, that it is a function of social workers to empower older people to become more active in seeking their own goals. The act of empowerment, however, is implicitly based on the assumption that one group is powerless and another gives them the tools to become powerful.

In McRae's potential future reality of centenarians, Medicare will not exist; there will be universal health coverage. The underlying theme throughout the health care system will be cost containment and preventive medicine. There will be rationing in virtually every aspect of care: available beds, medication, surgery. There will continue to be dependence on family assistance. Patients may well age concurrently with their physicians, resulting in greater familiarity between patient and physician. In general, McRae and Friedsam anticipate more changes in medicine and long-term care than do Dunkle and Lynch in social work. Friedsam points out, however, that in all probability (Friedsam distinguishes between probable and possible scenarios), our policies will continue to depend on informal care in tandem with somewhat disorganized formal services. We will, however, continue to call for coordination of a continuum of care much as the knights of the round table sought the holy grail. The problems Friedsam anticipates and the eventual monopolization of long-term care formal services he predicts are less than satisfying, but very possible.

Longino and Murphy discuss principles undergirding Western medicine in their examination of the relationship between demography and medical ideology. The biomedical model is based on an analogy to a machine; the body as machine is given into the hands of a repair expert. That expert is grounded in rational, logical, positivistic, dualistic, deterministic Western scientific philosophy. A change in this kind of approach requires at a minimum a dramatic political shift, probably more nearly cataclysmic than dramatic. It requires a postmodern philosophy and the reallocation of resources and responsibility. The patient would become central, the physician and drug companies peripheral. The changes envisioned could only be accomplished by a complete paradigmatic shift, not the touching up, slight shifting around that Friedsam notes will probably occur in our health care system.

Research Proposals

Many of the research ideas are implicit in the authors' expositions. Atchley's list of questions, for example, constitutes what he refers to as a "catalog" of research topics that "represents the barest hint of the...research topics connected to the longevity revolution" (p. 45). McRae's research agenda is dichotomized: "the conventional and the totally speculative" (p. 160). Because of his own research interests, he describes potential research about Alzheimer's disease primarily in the areas of causal factors. Turning to the speculative, he considers cures for Alzheimer's disease through fetal transplants and cell regeneration. Even more speculative research about the nature of longevity and the possibility of life-span extension is proposed. McRae points out, however, that financing for research may be limited, particularly in a society of scarcity, because people may be unwilling to support research that enables people to live longer.

Troll makes a vitally important point: One's own age and experience affect one's interests in general and one's research in particular. She suggests that the long-lived nonretired psychologists who maintain interest in research might well change their research focus in late years. Drawing on her own experiences, she discusses how research interests often reflect the age and circumstances of the researcher. For example, as gerontologists began to experience caregiving situations in their own families, they began to examine it as a research topic. If people doing research suspect that age and gender affect their achievement opportunities negatively, they study ageism and sexism. Consequently, as psychogerontologists age, they may emphasize research about care with dignity and issues of control or mastery. They will be more interested in issues emphasizing the strengths and independence of extreme old age rather than caregiving and generational equity issues. Hendricks reminds us, however, that the same social factors that give rise to the social construction of old age determine the realities of research funding. Consequently, certain research topics and methods will not be favored.

As noted earlier, Hendricks also calls for a reexamination of basic gerontological concepts and methods in order to conduct more adequate research about age and age-related issues. We need to move well beyond descriptions to causal factors that accurately reflect the realities of social life. Both he and Atchley emphasize the need to move away from a linear-based, deterministic methodology that stresses incremental change and limited interaction among variables. Both stress the need for new theoretical and conceptual perspectives. Hendricks also suggests gerontologists draw on current, nongerontological theoretical and methodological approaches to help achieve a better understanding of the meaning of adulthood: chaos, systems, and catastrophe theories among them.

Because anthropological research is time-intensive and comparative, Shenk and Keith see the increased life expectancy as providing anthropologists with greater possibilities for research. They could engage in extensive comparative research, studying a number of cultures in depth during their professional careers, instead of relying on secondary sources for bases of comparison.

A major theme in Friedsam's chapter is the need for research in order to cope adequately and constructively with a world in which there are large numbers of old people. Given a number of possible futures, gerontologists must create a real future. His call reiterates Neugarten's earlier one in 1972 and reinforces Beatty's (cited in chapter 2 of this book). Essentially it is a call for research in the service of policy and planning. Other authors in this book take similar positions; few call for research as an end in itself. However, this priority on applied research is not shared by others in gerontology, particularly those in the biomedical sciences.

In the authors' chapters we see a degree of continuity in research topics; the specific focus may change but the general topic area remains the same. In 1990, at the Gerontological Society of America's (GSA) annual scientific meeting, Hickey said that a gerontological Rip Van Winkle returning to the 1990 GSA meeting after a 25-year sleep would be "overwhelmed with the extent of growth and change in this field while at the same time impressed with our continuing fascination with the interacting biological, behavioral, and social processes of aging, despite vastly different views of what constitutes the 'study of aging'" (Hickey, 1990). The language may change but the issues remain the same. Some of the material in this book reinforces his comments. We rarely experience radical changes in our approaches to our disciplines, let alone a totally new vocabulary to describe totally new phenomena. It is a long time between paradigmatic shifts of any proportion, as Longino and Murphy make clear. Much of the speculation in this book about "what if" we lived to be 100 is based on what is. As several of the authors point out, our tendency is to assume that what is will continue; things will not be unchanged, but the change will be gradual and incremental. Our beliefs come from the past, although we live in a world of the present. At the same time, the authors in this book would probably confirm the gratitude expressed by Riley and Riley: "Fortunately, too, as members of an aging society we have been given not only added years, but also the privilege—too often taken for granted—of thinking about such problems [related to aging] and participating in the attempts to solve them" (1986, p. 75). Certainly their presence in this book substantiates this attitude.

Concluding Remarks

It is often the editor's prerogative to ask or to discuss the meaning of the material in a book. In this instance the meaning seems relatively clear: It is important to anticipate and consider what might happen to our society should life expectancy reach 100. The individual authors have done this with panache and intellectual vigor. As social scientists and practitioners, the authors remembered and reminded the reader that social change usually occurs slowly and that not all parts of a society change at the same rate. They also reminded us that there is considerable lag between individual experiences and change in social institutions. We can, therefore, only make some limited statements about the nature of a centenarian society. Whatever we say, however, is necessarily based on specific assumptions that may or may not be accurate. Even if we could predict or describe with accuracy many aspects of such a society, we could not anticipate everything because we do not know all of the significant variables. If we did know them, we would not know how they would interact with one another and how changes in one would affect the others.

There are, nonetheless, some themes that bear repeating because they reflect our many needs. First, we need to plan for the eventuality of such a demographic shift. In doing so, it is essential to recognize that all social institutions would be affected. Certainly, such a shift would change the meaning of age, that is, its use as a marker and criterion of eligibility for services and programs. It would revolutionize our life cycle maps and the temporal dimensions of social and psychological life. Second, we need to refine our concepts and develop research strategies that can tell us something beyond statistical descriptions and in vitro lives. We need new paradigms and models not only for academic disciplines but also for service delivery systems. We need to recognize that the we (the experts) and they (the old people) dichotomy has outlived its usefulness if, indeed, it was ever useful. We need to remember Friedsam's quotation from Shaw, "Long life is complicated, and even terrible; but it is glorious all the same." And, we need to face those facts without fear and with sustained hope.

References

Fries, J. F. (1984). The compression of morbidity: Miscellaneous comments about a theme. *The Gerontologist, 24,* 354–359.

Havighurst, R. J., Chair. (1969). Research and development goals in social gerontology: A report of a special committee of the Gerontological Society. *The Gerontologist, 9,* (4, Pt. 2): 1–90.

Hickey, T. (1990, November). Continuing themes in an environment of change. Paper presented at the 43rd Annual Scientific Meeting of the Gerontological Society of America, Boston.

Manton, K. G. (1992). Mortality and life expectancy changes among the oldest old. In R. M. Suzman, D. P. Willis, & K. G. Manton (Eds.), *The oldest old* (pp. 157–182). New York: Oxford University Press.

Markus, H. R., & Nurius, P. (1986). Possible selves. *The American Psychologist, 41,* 954–969.

Mott, P. (1965). *The organization of society.* Englewood Cliffs, NJ: Prentice Hall.

Neugarten, B. L. (1972). Social implications of a prolonged life-span. *The Gerontologist, 12,* 323.

Neugarten, B. L. (Ed.). (1975). Aging in the year 2000: A look at the future. *The Gerontologist, 15,* (1, Pt. 2): 1–40.

Neugarten, B. L., & Maddox, G. L. (1981). *Our future selves: A research plan toward understanding aging.* NIH Publication No. 80-144. Washington, DC: U.S. Government Printing Office.

Riley, M., & Riley, J. (1986). Longevity and social structure: The potential of the added years. In A. Pifer and L. Brontë (Eds.), *Our aging society: Paradox and promise* (pp. 52–77). New York: W. W. Norton.

Seltzer, M. M., and Troll, L. E. (1986). Expected life history: A model in nonlinear time. *American Behavioral Scientist, 26,* 746–764.

Taeuber, C. M. (1993). Sixty five plus in America. Valletta, Malta: International Institute on Aging.

Index

S͟P *Springer Publishing Company*

HANDBOOK OF THE HUMANITIES AND AGING

Thomas R. Cole, PhD, **David Van Tassel,** PhD, and **Robert Kastenbaum,** PhD, Editors

"... (this book) addresses aging as an integral part of the substance of the humanities—the arts, philosophy, literature, religion, history—this is, aging in the humanities; and vice-versa, the contributions of the humanities as an essential part of understanding aging, that is, humanities in aging."

—From the Foreword by **T. Franklin Williams,** MD

Contents:

Aging, Old Age, and Elders in History
A View from Antiquity: Greece, Rome, and the Elders, *T.M. Falkner and J. de Luce* • The Older Person in the Western World: From the Middle Ages to the Industrial Revolution, *D.G. Troyansky* • Old Age in the Modern and Postmodern Western World, *C. Conrad* • Aging in Eastern Cultures: A Historical Overview, *C.W. Keifer.*

Meaning and Spirituality in Later Life
Aging and Meaning: The Christian Tradition, *S.G. Post* • Aging in Judaism: "Crown of Glory" and "Days of Sorrow," *S. Isenberg* • Islamic, Hindu, and Buddhist Conceptions of Aging, *G.R. Thursby* • Fairy Tales and Spiritual Development in Later Life: The Story of the Shining Fish, *A.B. Chinen.*

Artistic Expression and Representations in Aging
Images of Aging in American Poetry, 1925–1985, *C.H. Smith* • Old Age in Contemporary Fiction: A New Paradigm of Hope, *C. Rooke* • Walking to the Stars, *M. Winkler* • The Creative Process: A Life-Span Approach, *R. Kastenbaum.*

Humanistic Gerontology: The State of the Art
The Older Student of Humanities: The Seeker and the Source, *D. Shuldiner* • Literary Gerontology Comes of Age, *A.M. Wyatt-Brown* • Aging in America: The Perspective of History, *C. Haber* • Elders in World History, *P.N. Stearns* • Bioethics and Aging, *H.R. Moody* • Wisdom and Method: Philosophical Contributions to Gerontology, *R.J. Manheimer.*

Afterword
Integrating the Humanities into Gerontologic Research, Training, and Practice, *W.A. Achenbaum.*

1992   512pp   0-8261-6240-1   hardcover

536 Broadway, New York, NY 10012-3955 • (212) 431-4370 • Fax (212) 941-7842

SP *Springer Publishing Company*

VOICES AND VISIONS OF AGING
Toward a Critical Gerontology

Thomas R. Cole, PhD, **W. Andrew Achenbaum,** PhD,
Patricia L. Jakobi, PhD, & **Robert Kastenbaum,** PhD, Eds.

A critical gerontology requires more than a simple elaboration of existing humanistic scholarship on aging. This exceptional work introduces a basis for genuine dialogue and collaboration across humanistic, scientific, and professional disciplines.

Contents:

1993   368pp   0-8261-8020-5   *hardcover*

536 Broadway, New York, NY 10012-3955 • (212) 431-4370 • Fax (212) 941-7842

 *Springer Publishing Company*

SOCIETAL IMPACT ON AGING
Historical Perspectives

K. Warner Schaie, PhD
W. Andrew Achenbaum, PhD, Editors

This volume will facilitate the creation and dissemination of historical scholarship in gerontological research among the social, behavioral, and biomedical sciences.

Contents

1993   280pp   0-8261-8200-3   hardcover

536 Broadway, New York, NY 10012-3955 • (212) 431-4370 • Fax (212) 941-7842

Possum Hollow

Book 2

Levi B. Weber

Herald
Press

Scottdale, Pennsylvania
Waterloo, Ontario

Library of Congress Cataloging-in-Publication Data
Weber, Levi B., 1911-
  Possum hollow / Levi B. Weber
    p. cm.
    ISBN 0-8361-9126-9 (bk. 1 : alk. paper)—ISBN 0-8361-9131-5
    (bk. 2 : alk. paper)
    1. Weber, Levi B., 1911- —Childhood and youth. 2. Farm
life—Pennsylvania—Lancaster County. 3. Farm life—
Virginia—Amelia County. 4. Mennonites—Pennsylvania—
Lancaster County—Biography. 5. Amelia County (Va.)—
Biography. 6. Lancaster County (Pa.)—Biography. I. Title.
CT275.W3526 A3 2001
974.8'15044—dc21   00-053940

POSSUM HOLLOW, BOOK 2
Copyright © 2001 by Herald Press, Scottdale, Pa. 15683
    Published simultaneously in Canada by Herald Press,
    Waterloo, Ont. N2L 6H7. All rights reserved
Library of Congress Catalog Card Number: 00-053940
International Standard Book Number: 0-8361-9131-5
Printed in the United States of America
Book and cover design by Jim Butti
Cover art and inside illustrations by Joy Dunn Keenan
Layout sketch of "Our Farm" by Suzanne Hinson
House photo from Levi B. Weber

10 09 08 07 06 05 04 03 02 01   10 9 8 7 6 5 4 3 2 1

To order or request information, please call 1-800-759-4447
(individuals); 1-800-245-7894 (trade). Website: www.mph.org

To my wife,
June Elizabeth Weber

Without the encouragement I received from June, I would never have written *Possum Hollow*. When she heard me tell stories to the children, she would often say, "Why don't you write about it?"

She knew it wouldn't be easy because she had written a book, *The Tribe of Jacob*, stories about her mother's family of fifteen children growing up in the Shenandoah Valley of Virginia.

June was always glad to read my manuscripts and suggest changes or corrections before they were given to the typist. Thank you, June!

❤ ❤ ❤

Contents

Preface

The stories my family told about the old days were so interesting that I always wished I had been there too. That's why in later years I began to write about my own childhood near a little village in southern Virginia.

Pleasant memories are easy to recall. My "kindergarten" was meadows, streams, birds, and flowers. My brother and sisters were my teachers. Papa and Mama enjoyed watching our games and activities, only imposing restraints when we went beyond accepted rules. Those youthful ways changed when we moved from that quiet southern community to busy Lancaster County, Pennsylvania.

When a few of my short stories appeared in our local school and church monthly magazine, some of my friends suggested that I write a book about those days. So that's what I did. The earliest event in the stories is my parents' marriage day in 1897. The final event is a hundred years later, August 1997, at our family reunion near Lancaster, Pennsylvania.

I have named this series of books *Possum Hollow.* This is the second volume.

I wish to acknowledge several people who were

helpful to me in writing these stories. My wife, June, carefully read all my manuscripts, correcting spelling and offering helpful suggestions. My typist, Susan Wilmoth, typed all my stories, keeping them cataloged and stored in her computer. I also thank many others who encouraged me to write.

—*Levi B. Weber*
  Newport News, Virginia

Settling into
Possum Hollow

1

Finding the Farm

It was June, and school was out. Papa had told us, "I'm looking for a place somewhere near Lititz that we could afford to buy."

"How will we do that?" Momma wondered.

"Wait with patience," Papa said.

That evening, we children were sitting around on the front porch and steps, talking and worrying about moving again. Papa and Mama were away for the evening, and Granny had gone to bed.

"I bet we'll be moving to some dumb place that has a lot of pigs," moaned Esty.

Finally big sister Eva said, "Let's stop worrying and talk about the good times we had down in Virginia. Worrying just makes us feel sorry for ourselves."

So we chatted about the games we had played and the playhouse Brother (Franklin) had built. Helen remembered our secret hideaway under the ferns that we called Corn Dale, and the fairy stories she used to tell us younger children.

Eva told about going to Richmond overnight with her teacher, Miss Percival. Brother mentioned Vernon Lynn's self-propelled wood-sawing outfit and the copperhead snake.

Esty, next older than I, reminded us of how we thought the strange sounds in the bushes came from the Old Frozen Lady.

I told my favorite story about how Papa had taken me to Beaver Pond Mill, where we ate our lunch together in the rowboat.

Our talking went on until it was growing dark. "Okay, Levi," Eva said, "it's time for seven-year-olds to get to bed. The rest of us should settle down, too. Daddy doesn't want us to stay up late."

We went to bed in a brighter mood; everything was going to be all right.

For some time Papa had been looking around for a farm to buy. Our lease on Emmalene Eshleman's farm would soon expire, and he didn't want to renew it. I could tell that Mama was getting worried, because she was singing more than usual.

Then one afternoon Papa returned from looking at yet another farm. We thought something was up, because he wasn't talking about it. At supper that evening, he announced, "I've seen a farm that might be just the one for us. We'll drive us out to see it on Saturday."

On Saturday, Mama, Papa, Brother, Esty, and I loaded into the Model T. The car was too small to hold us all, so Eva and Helen stayed home with the baby, Mary Elizabeth. We drove to Lititz and turned

OUR FARM AT POSSUM HOLLOW
1918

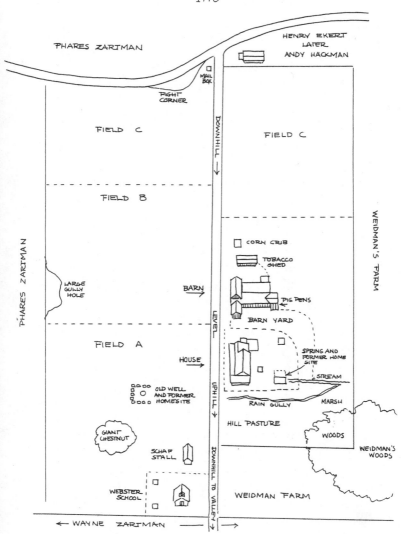

right, taking the Lititz Pike out past the Zion Home hill and on to the village of Lexington.

There we took off to the left on a country road, passing a little cemetery, then a cluster of neat farm buildings on the right. At a point a short distance past those buildings, he said, "Now, beginning here, these fields are part of the farm we're looking at. Notice that bunch of locust trees and bushes up there? That's not part of it. That's called 'the Fight Corner.' It's a no-man's land."

At the Fight Corner, the road turned sharply to the left. Several hundred yards further, Papa turned right onto a dirt road and stopped, with the engine idling. "This road goes right through the middle of the farm. That little house on the left isn't part of it. That is Zartman's tenant house."

We crawled out of the car, and Papa stretched out his arm, pointing to the fields. They were full of weeds. The rail fences on both sides of the road were sagging and crowded with brush.

"Where are the house and barn?" Mama asked.

"Oh, they're on down the road."

Where we had stopped, the fields and road were level. But after we drove a short distance further, the road dropped steeply downhill. Now we could see the buildings becoming more defined as we approached. At the bottom of the hill, the road was level again, but everywhere else the land was hilly.

Papa stopped the car, and we got out. Strung out before us, we saw a huge unpainted barn surrounded by sheds and outbuildings. All the buildings were to the left of the road. Next to the barn was a house, separated from the barn and sheds by a cattle yard.

The house was hard to figure out. It required reflective study.

"Don't be too quick to judge the buildings until you see everything," Papa said.

"*Everything* is the word all right," Mama responded. "It looks like *everything* is here. But where is *everybody?*"

"Oh, nobody has lived here for seven years," Papa said. "This is the old Shreiner Farm. The old folks moved out to live with one of the children. They rent the fields for summer pasture."

Many years before, the barn had been built with hand-hewn timbers and wooden pins. Then the owners added numerous large wings and attached sheds. "Look," Papa pointed out, "see how carefully they built, fitting the timbers together exactly right?" Since Papa was a carpenter, he appreciated precise construction work.

The barn roof was covered with old wooden shingles, and the siding was of broad, well-weathered, vertical planks. Paint had never been applied to the barn. Some of the outbuildings had been painted red.

"How big is the farm?" Brother asked.

"Forty-seven acres."

Mama looked at the clutter of buildings and said, "Why did they need such a mess for just forty-seven acres?"

"Well," he said, "we could take down some of the buildings we don't need."

The word *we* prompted Mama to say "We?"

"Yes," Papa said, "we bought it. But wait till you see inside the house."

"I can wait," Mama said, with a touch of irony.

The barn stood right against the road, and the house was set back about fifty feet. Like the barn, the house had an early colonial start. Through the years, owners had added to it, section by section. It stretched along parallel to the road.

The center was a simple two-story house with attic and cellar. That was extended to the left with a smaller two-story wing, set over a cellar but without an attic. To the right someone had attached a two-story flat-roof wing, also with a cellar. This addition projected eight feet forward from the other part. Here a front porch began, extending the full length of the house.

On the far left side was a huge added summer kitchen, stretching to the rear. It ended with a large authentic colonial bake oven, still in mint condition.

Later we cataloged the whole space: six upstairs rooms plus the attic, seven rooms downstairs, and six in the cellar. There were eight outside doors and a total of seven stairways. We counted four chimneys but no fireplaces. No electricity. No plumbing. The house had been painted many times and was chipping and peeling.

"Let's go inside," Papa said. He unlocked the door, and we entered the parlor. There in the middle of the floor was a huge pile of broomcorn seed. A dozen large brown rats slowly retreated to the next room. Papa quickly promised, "We can get rid of the rats all right!"

"Henry, as long as you looked," Mama asked, "why did you buy *this?*"

"Well, nobody wanted it, and we got it for only $2,700."

"Do you know this will be the ninth time we have moved?" Mama said thoughtfully.

"Yes, but this can be the last. We'll make a nice place out of it."

"Well," Mama said, "we can set up the cookstove in the summer kitchen to keep the rest of the house cool in the summer while we cook and can food."

"Yes," agreed Papa. "Then in the winter, we'll move the cookstove back into the regular kitchen, where we'll be eating. That way it can help warm the house better."

"We'll also need a parlor stove, and maybe also a little stove in this room next to the kitchen," Mama suggested.

"I'd like to put a hot-air furnace in the cellar sometime," Papa added. "Then we could have a heating grate right here in the middle of the house."

"That sound's good," said Mama. "Some steady coal heat would help to warm this big house in the winter."

While the rest were looking around inside the house, Esty and I went out the back and saw something the rest didn't. There was a large flowing spring, a hillside meadow, and a huge forest stretching down below, in the valley.

On the way back to Emmalene Eshleman's farm, there were many questions and a lot of conversation. Esty and I talked mostly about the stream and the woods. "Maybe we can have a pond like the one we had in Amelia," Esty said.

That evening at the supper table, Mama asked, "Why didn't any of the Shreiner children want the place?"

Papa smiled. "Well, you know how some people are. They all thought the place was *verhext* (bewitched)."

"Don't tell Granny," urged Eva, with a laugh.

After more discussion, Papa said, "I think *Possum Hollow* will be a good name for the old farm."

That old farm was the beginning of things to come: some happy, some sad. Once again our lives moved along into new experiences.

2

Moving Day

We were moving again. This time, instead of traveling a long distance by train, we had only five miles to go. As usual, Papa was patiently working out the details. Our lease had another month to run, so that gave us plenty of time. Also, since Granny had gone back to live with Aunt Alice again, she wouldn't be involved in this move.

The first thing of importance was cleaning up the old house at Possum Hollow. For help, Papa hired Henry Mease, a neighborhood acquaintance. When we finally began to move, the house was clean and ready.

The order of moving our possessions was important. First, all furniture and machinery not needed for daily living was gradually moved during and after the cleanup. Then, the day before finally leaving the Eshleman place, Papa removed the backseat cushion from the car to make room for freight.

Several trips were necessary to move everything

needed in the kitchen. There were utensils and jars of all kinds of fruit, vegetables, and jelly. Mama had baked a variety of cakes, pies, bread, and cookies—enough for a week.

Because the cooking range would be out of operation for a day, she packed a big picnic basket to keep us eating. She often expressed her energy and determination across the kitchen range. We would not go hungry.

The large kitchen at Possum Hollow had a big walk-in pantry with lots of shelves for jars, cans, and other supplies. The baked things were packed in wooden boxes because of the rats and mice Most of the jars of canned food would be placed on shelves in the cool cellar of our new home.

The final day of the move required precise planning. Early in the morning, Papa took all the women and little Mary Elizabeth to Possum Hollow. Returning with the car, Papa proceeded with the last big move. He hired two men with their two-horse wagons. With our rig, we made a three-wagon train.

Piled high with furniture, the wagon train moved slowly through the edge of Lititz and out toward Lexington. I sat in the first wagon with Papa. The horses moved slowly, the wagon creaked, and the wheels rattled on the gravel.

I remembered long ago when I had seen the horses and carriages in old Mr. Maxie's funeral cortege down in Amelia. At the tollgate, Papa said to the man, "This is a moving. I'm paying for the next two wagons."

Turning left at Lexington, we drove on past the Fight Corner and then turned right and went down the hill to what was now home. Because of the grade, the brakes were drawn, giving a screeching sound as we bumped over stone ridges crossing the road.

Esty was standing on the road in front of the house. When she saw us coming, she ran to tell the others. When we came to a stop, they were all waiting outside.

The horses were uncoupled from the wagons and taken to drink at the spring below the house. After the men tied them to a rail fence, they all gathered around and helped with unloading and placing the furniture in the right rooms.

There was laughter and jokes, all in Pennsylvania Dutch (German). We were in a bilingual community. When the work was finished, Mama brought out some cookies for the men. She gave each of them a tumbler. "Here's lemonade, all the way from Eshleman's," she said as she dipped it from a kettle.

The men hitched the horses to the wagons and turned around to leave. Papa had to return with them to bring the car from Eshleman's. Since it was late in the day, he told Mama not to expect him in time for supper.

Henry Mease went with them, too. He lived near Lexington. We stood on the road awhile, watching them climb the hill. Then Brother put our wagon away and took the horses to the stable.

As we assembled in the kitchen, Mama stood quietly, trying to figure out the next move. Then Eva took charge: "Let's not fool with the stove this evening. There's enough lunch left in the basket for supper. We can open a can of pears and finish the lemonade."

She got us all around the table just like it was a real supper. Then Mama took hold of the situation again. "Nall [meaning Brother], after supper you and Levi go and bring in wood from the pile and corncobs from the shed. We'll have a real good breakfast in the morning."

When we finished supper, things got quiet again. It was getting dark, and night sounds began. "Hey!" Brother cried out, "what did they mean when they said this place was *verhext* (bewitched)?"

"That doesn't mean anything," Eva said. "You shouldn't talk about it now, anyhow."

Then Esty wondered, "What was that?"

"What was what?" Brother asked.

"I heard something."

24

"I wish Papa would get back," Mama said. Then she lit the lamp.

Finally Papa returned. He brought a bag of graham crackers and set them on the table for us. He had stopped in the grocery store at Lititz and bought a few things, such as a large tin bucket with a lid for carrying water. Our well had become polluted with trash during the years it wasn't used. We would be getting our drinking water from neighbors until it could be cleaned up.

We avoided going upstairs to bed as long as possible. Eventually Papa said, "Time for bed! You know your rooms. Let's go."

Papa and Mama had a room upstairs to the right. Eva and Helen's room was at the head of the stairs, and Esty had a room by herself on the left. Brother and I had a room next to Esty, at the end of the house. We had a separate stairway. We felt isolated. Besides this, there was a little cubbyhole door that opened into a forbidding space under the roof.

Each room was provided with a night lamp. Night lamps had no stand. They sat on the flattened bottom of the oil reservoir and had a loop handle on the side, like a cup. After the night lamps were lit, Mama blew out the kitchen light, and we went to bed.

Brother and I used a lantern. We didn't mind. Lamps were more for girls anyway. I finally went to sleep while trying not to hear sounds from the cubbyhole.

"Time to get up!" It was Papa's regular get-up call and sounded like old times. I woke up and wasn't scared. Night was gone. We hustled downstairs.

Mama had frying pans on the stove, and the girls were setting the table. Papa took us out and showed us how to take care of the horses and cow. He showed us the chicken shed and how to care for the hens.

By the time we were finished with morning chores, breakfast was ready. We sat around the table at our usual places. Papa reached for his Bible and read some verses selected from the "Daily Readings" in the *Sunday School Quarterly*. Then we bowed our heads in a silent blessing.

The breakfast was special: hashed brown potatoes, fried eggs, and slices of homemade bread with butter and jelly. Mama cut extra-large pieces of shoofly pie. There was coffee for the grown-ups and cocoa for the children.

Nothing quite equals a good breakfast together. The first day at Possum Hollow was off to a good start. It was beginning to feel like home.

3

Exploring

Although everything was different at Possum Hollow, there was also a feeling of unity. What had at first seemed confusing became simple harmony. The first timbers hewn by pioneers so many years ago began a story of patient labor that through time gave hope and comfort to many families. Now again, after recent years of neglect, there was hope. Papa's imagination turned Possum Hollow into a place of excitement.

Our first project was to clean the polluted well. The pump was located in the back hall, between the summer kitchen and living room. The well was directly below, in the basement. Papa hired a well digger to do the work.

The well digger climbed down into the well without a ladder, bracing himself against the walls. By using the pump and a bucket hooked to a rope, we soon emptied the well.

Trash removed included rat bones, a dead squirrel, and the wooden remains of the rotten well cover. We pumped it out as much as we could for several days. Then Papa took a sample of the water to the Health Department. We were told it was clean but that we should boil our drinking water for two weeks and then bring another sample. That also proved to be pure and safe to drink.

We waged an ongoing battle to get rid of the rats. They had owned the place for years without being challenged. Brother and I devised several trapping methods.

One trap was a metal barrel filled with water to within a foot of the top. Brother anchored bait on a small block of wood floating in the center. The block was kept in the center by a string tied to a stone at the bottom of the barrel.

We leaned a board against the outside of the barrel, giving the rats an easy way to move within sight and smell of the bait. I sprinkled chaff and dust on the surface to hide the water. When rats tried to walk on the water and reach the bait, they drowned.

At night we also set steel traps in the chicken house feed bins. Early in the morning while the chickens were still roosting, we removed the rats and traps.

The rats had a regular run between the tobacco shed and the barn. Papa was a good marksman with a rifle. He loaded his 22-caliber Savage with "shorts" and picked off rats crawling along their run. These methods, along with careful use of rat poison, eventually took care of the rats.

During the first weeks after our arrival, we

explored the mysterious buildings and the outlying areas of the farm. Everywhere we looked we saw surviving bits and pieces from the past. Behind the house we found the remains of a kitchen backyard garden. Among currant and gooseberry bushes, old garden paths were still visible.

In one corner an old smokehouse stood sturdy and strong. It was a combination of art and utility. For several years we used it ourselves.

Just below the garden, breaking into the downward slope, there was a rectangular drop, probably the remains of an old cellar. Along one side was a stone-lined reservoir filled with flowing spring water. It was four feet wide and extended about thirty feet, forming what must have been part of a foundation. This would have been typical of many old houses or log cabins that had springs in their cellars.

Other explorations took us up the road past the house. Here the road led up a small hill that crested just before another gigantic drop to a valley below. This high point was the boundary of our farm. At the hilltop and on the right of the road, to our surprise, were the remains of *another* former building site.

Sometimes Esty and I did the exploring, but this time Brother was along, too. We walked around slowly, trying to figure it out.

Just beside the road was an A-roofed shed in excellent condition. We found a door and went in. It was empty except for some old hay covering the floor at one end. Beside it in the field we found a large pear tree and a lot of raspberry and spice bushes clustered around a stretch of broken-down fence.

Not far from these, an old well was covered with

a few fence posts, to keep people and animals from falling in. The ground was littered with bits of old plaster. Close by and part of what must have been a yard, an old broken-down woodshed lay on the ground.

Brother walked around, looking at everything like a budding archaeologist. He picked up a stone and went to the well. Creeping up to it, he found an opening in the posts and dropped the stone.

"Hey," he called, "there's water down there. I heard a splash."

Then putting his face close, he hollered down into the well: "Hello! Hello!" He turned to us: "It echoes just like the one in our house!"

Right next to our line fence stood a one-room country school. Years earlier, the site for the school and playground had been carved out of our farm. A wooden rail fence enclosed the area. Brother got us to go along with him onto the school grounds and look around. It seemed like trespassing, but we went anyway.

"After all," he said, "we'll soon be going to school here."

That remark didn't sit well with Esty: "You mean all three of us will be in the same room?"

We went in the front gate together and looked all around. It was Sunday afternoon, so we weren't sneaking away from work. The spot where the building stood had been leveled, but the playground was hillside. We wondered how the children would keep from losing a ball at recess.

Large black oak trees were shading the schoolhouse. In one back corner of the yard, on the high side, was one outhouse. On the lower back corner was another. We knew, of course, that one was for boys and one was for girls. We tried to figure out which was which. There were no identifying signs.

"What will happen if we get them mixed up?" I wondered.

"Don't be so dumb," Esty said. "We'll just go where the other boys and girls go."

We stood and looked around for awhile. The school was at the crest of a long and rather steep slope down to a valley below. The old dirt road past the school was deeply eroded between steep banks. It descended in a gentle curve to a cluster of houses and barns below.

Among the buildings was a large three-story stone structure housing the local grain mill. Behind the mill was the usual millpond, supplying the waterpower.

That evening at the supper table, we told about our discoveries. "There is a little story about that A-roofed shed and the school," Papa said. "Many years ago the school was damaged by fire. While the building was being repaired, school was held in that shed. The shed had been used for sheep, so a lot of the old folks still call the school the Schof Schtall (sheep stable).

"Mr. Diehm, one of the school directors, came by the other day," Papa added. "He wanted to see if the school can use water from our place like they did while the Schreiners lived here."

"Isn't there a well at the school?" asked Brother.

"No, and they don't want to dig one, either. I gave them permission. So someone will have to carry a bucket of water over there every day."

The daily task of carrying the water became a valued responsibility. Two boys were selected to take a bit of school time to go and "fetch the water."

There were only a few weeks until school would start. We three younger children knew where we would go, but the girls wanted to continue their high school at Rothsville.

Papa was working on plans for their schooling. He always had a way of making hard things seem pleasant. But he had a long way to go before I would feel good about going to the *Schof Schtall*.

4

Webster School

A laggard is a clock that wants both hands,
as useless if it goes as if it stands.

That was my daily response at roll call, but I didn't know what it meant. Each scholar at Webster's one-room school was given a wise saying written on a slip of paper, to be repeated at roll call. Each week these slips were exchanged among the children. It gave variety.

I could understand, "A stitch in time saves nine" and "Well begun is half done." The difficult ones were just jargon. Miss Rhudy never explained them, and the children were too timid to ask.

Miss Rhudy's singular beauty was canceled out by her stern, no-nonsense schoolroom attitude. She seldom smiled. In the other schools I had attended, the teachers would smile and lower their heads toward us as they answered our questions.

By now I was in the *Second Reader* of the set of Blodget Readers. I was still small, but Miss Rhudy acted as though I were one of the big boys in the *Sixth Reader*. Our classes were also designated as Readers, depending on what book we were using. My sister Esther (Esty) was in the Fourth Reader, and my brother Franklin (Brother) was in the Sixth Reader.

One day Franklin brought his slingshot to school. He had skillfully fashioned it out of some old harness leather and neatly inscribed his initials on one side. At recess while showing it to the boys, he took a pebble and slung it away from the school across Zartman's field. "That's how David got Goliath," he said.

One of the little girls went and tattled to Miss Rhudy, hoping to earn some credit points. It worked as expected. Miss Rhudy walked up briskly, roughly snatched the slingshot from his hand, and threw it in the furnace.

One of the big girls came to Franklin after school and said she thought Miss Rhudy was mean: "She could'a let you took it to home and not let you fetch it back again."

Franklin thought Miss Rhudy didn't like him because he didn't talk like the others. He had grown up in the South. In this area around Possum Hollow, casual conversation in everyday English was often affected by the local German dialect.

Once while sitting at my desk, I was daydreaming about how Miss Rhudy looked a lot like the ladies in the dress section of the Sears Roebuck catalog. She dressed like they did but never smiled. I wondered if giving her an apple or peach would help. I knew I wouldn't dare to do it. But I thought maybe one of the big girls like Florence Zartman could give it a try.

My musing was suddenly interrupted. Miss Rhudy had grabbed little Hanna Weitzel from her First Reader desk and began paddling her. Hanna cried pitifully, sobbing in her small voice, "I didn't go to do it; I didn't go to do it!"

Her two bigger sisters looked on in shocked disbelief. Her crime? She had dropped her book and happened to tear a page when she picked it up.

In the Miles Snavely affair, however, Miss Rhudy deserved and received high praise. Miles was called "Miley." Everybody would say, "Miley said this" or "Miley, can we play this game or that?" He was bigger than Miss Rhudy and owned the playground.

One time I made the mistake of calling him "Miley," not realizing it was a title reserved for his peers. He shoved his balled fist against my nose and said, "Here, smell my onion!" as he slowly rotated it, bringing tears to my eyes.

Miley discovered how to get extra recess time. Shortly before recess, he would raise his hand to go to the outhouse. He would then extend his leave until recess. When Miss Rhudy became aware of it, she refused to let him go out. She told him to wait until recess. That made him mad.

To get even, he carefully relieved himself on the floor under his desk. The golden stream flowed toward Miss Rhudy on the floor. When she saw it, she said with controlled anger, "Miles, come here!"

Right beside my desk, she grabbed him by the

collar and with her heavy wooden ruler gave him a whipping he would always remember.

Then with a calm voice, she said, "School dismissed for recess. Miles, you stay in and get the mop."

Miles lost some of his playground arrogance. The other boys listened as he tried to brag about it, but the girls kept their distance.

I was learning a lot of things not written in my books. Miles never got me to "smell his onion" again.

The First Year at
Possum Hollow

5

The Parade

Mama went to the phone on the wall, checked the receiver to see if the line was busy, and then cranked the bell for the exchange. Stretching up to the mouthpiece, she called out, "1-5-5-G." That was Aunt Alice's number. Our number was 1-5-7-F.

There were two phone systems: the Bell and the Independent. Mama and Aunt Alice were both on the Independent but on different party lines. They had to ring through the exchange.

It was late in the afternoon of November 11, 1918, and something special had happened. Mama began talking to Aunt Alice in Pennsylvania Dutch. "Have you heard that *der Grieg is verbeigange* (the war is over)?" she asked.

"I've just listened in on the party line," Aunt Alice replied, "and heard someone talking about it."

"That's how I heard it, too," Mama said. "Mrs. Weidman was talking on the line."

Mama and Aunt Alice talked and talked until someone else wanted the line. The Great World War was over!

I was seven and a half. As far as I knew, there had always been war. I couldn't understand what would happen now. The next day at school, I began to find out more. Everybody was excited, and discipline was almost absent. No one wanted to study.

Recess was a riot. All kinds of spicy couplets about Germany and the Kaiser were shouted in full voice. The favorite was this one:

> Kaiser Bill went up the hill
>   to take a look at France.
> Kaiser Bill came down the hill
>   with bullets in his pants.

Lest she seem unpatriotic, Miss Rhudy did little to check the noisy celebration. She dismissed school early.

The *Lancaster News Journal* was full of reports about the fall of Germany and the Armistice. We called it the "Armistick" until we learned the proper pronunciation.

Caught up in the excitement, the Elizabeth Township School Directors planned a school parade. Each school would have its own truck, borrowed from a local business. Our truck came from Zartman's Mill. Eli Zartman's son, Forry, was in Webster School.

The parade was carefully planned. Each truck would include a teacher and all the children who wanted to go along. Our truck was packed full. The parade assembled at Brunnerville and proceeded slowly to Lexington. From there, each truck returned again to its own school.

Everybody was bursting with excitement. Many were chewing gum, not ordinarily allowed in school. Every truck carried some effigy of the Kaiser. Our school's truck had an old stuffed overall suit swinging from the rear canopy. A sign with large letters, KAISER, was fastened to its back.

Miss Rhudy took no part in the hilarity. Without the bastion of her schoolroom, she was uncomfortable. The old solid-tired trucks bumped along, blowing their horns, with clarions sounding. Shouts and singing were accompanied with tin whistles and popping firecrackers.

The parade ended, and we were back again, unloading at Webster School. Miss Rhudy jumped down from the truck as sedately as possible. I had never seen her jump before.

Not until we were quieted in our seats and ready for dismissal did Miss Rhudy again assume her usual dignity. She made a short patriotic comment that was overshadowed by her strict pronouncement: "Tomorrow we will be back to regular rules and behavior."

We knew what that meant. The parade was over. Miss Rhudy was again Miss Rhudy.

6

Winter at Possum Hollow

Six months had elapsed since we had left the Eshleman farm near Rothsville. Approaching winter gave an urgency to our preparations. Papa was losing his usual patience, and Mama admitted that she was "*schusseling* (bustling)" too much.

We prepared stables in the central section of the sprawling barn. Two horses and two cows—our entire livestock inventory—didn't need much space. The small chicken house was insulated by stacking old corn fodder against the outside walls.

Feed was in satisfactory supply. In the few months available, we had harvested a crop of corn and mowed hay from an old hay field. Papa bought enough "short-feed" (chopped-up grain) at Zartman's Mill to carry us through a possible snow blizzard.

The livestock was provided for, but Mama was concerned about the house. "I think we need another stove," she said.

The large eat-in kitchen with its cooking range was, if anything, above average. The pump was in an inside vestibule. That was certainly better than most of the neighbors' back-porch pumps. But there was only one other stove for the remaining seven rooms—three rooms downstairs and four rooms upstairs.

"One stove is enough," Papa delcared. "We can keep warm in the kitchen and then go straight to bed."

Winter came early, as expected. Papa laughed as he told us, "Someone said the woolly worms predicted a long, hard winter."

The woolly worms were right. It snowed, and we shoveled walks. It snowed again, and we shoveled again. Snowbanks along the walks were piled shoulder high, and still it snowed. As we walked across snow-crusted fields, we could see small holes where field mice lived below the snow, in a world all their own.

The kitchen range and the parlor stove did not heat seven rooms. They reduced the cold in only two or three of them. The classic upright shiny parlor stove with its isinglass-paneled doors did the best it could. We warmed up in the kitchen and dashed to our bedrooms. With us we took heated corn bags and preheated nightshirts (pajamas came later).

Water froze in glasses left overnight. In the morning we reached from under the covers and pulled in our clothes, to warm them. We became skilled at rapid dressing.

Snow always affected school. Helen rode the jitney bus to Rothsville, where she was a senior in high school. She missed many days. Eva was at home, taking time off between college sessions. Snow didn't bother her.

At good old Webster, no school was ever missed. We all walked to school, bundled up like Eskimos and dragging our sleds. Sledding or coasting was part of school just as much as our Blodget Readers and 'rithmetic books. Almost everyone had a sled. We compared the different brands.

The Weidman boys had King of the Hills. We had Lightning Guiders. Front guider yokes were on the newest sleds, for steering. Old ones didn't have them; they had to be bumped around corners. Only little children used the old kind. Grown-ups were ashamed to be seen on the old style of sled.

There were also other no-name repainted sleds. One special sled was called the Flexible Flyer. It had "chilled runners" slightly grooved for better control. No one at Webster had one, but they all knew some lucky child who did.

At recess some of the big boys would take their sleds to the high point of the playground, near the boys' outhouse. They would run and take belly flops on the sleds, beginning a long run and coasting almost to Zartman's Mill. The course took them past the school, over an abrupt bank, and down a steep, winding road to the valley floor. It took ten minutes to return.

One day some big boys intentionally started the trip too late to return during recess. Miss Rhudy made them stay in during the next recess.

One night the moon was full, and the Weidmans were coasting in the fields again. Sometimes Franklin and I coasted with them. Tonight Mr. Weidman was with the boys, Clarence and Ike. I always envied the Weidman boys, because our Papa never coasted with us.

This time we were coasting in our fields. We would begin up near Ekert's and gradually, gaining momentum, fly past our sheds, ending down at the creek. Walking back and listening to Mr. Weidman tell about the old days was as much fun as going down the hill.

On one of these trips, Franklin was sledding at high speed and hit a partly exposed board right behind our sheds. His sled upset, causing a big pile-up. Franklin hurt his leg, so we stopped and went home.

At home, he carefully pulled down his heavy woolen stocking to look at his leg. We couldn't believe what we saw. His leg was a mass of blood. We could see a big red gash on his shin, with the white shinbone visible.

Mama called Dr. Long at once. He said Franklin should be brought in right away, even though it was seven o'clock. Papa cranked up the Model T while Mama wrapped towels around Franklin's leg.

It was five miles to Brickerville, where Dr. Long lived. The Model T was equipped with tire chains, so the trip was without incident.

The next morning we learned that the wound had required three stitches and that Franklin would have to stay off the leg for seven or eight days. He was instructed to change the bandage daily. He could reuse the bandage after sterilizing it on the hot stove lid.

Franklin didn't go to school or work for a week. I envied his special privilege. After a week, the doctor removed the stitches. Franklin could go back to school again if he was careful.

At school Franklin received special attention. The Weidman boys added to the saga with expanded versions of the accident. The fact that I had been riding on his back and was also in the accident was not noticed. I was only seven years old and emerged unhurt because I was thrown into a snowbank.

Winter had begun, but this would turn out to be a special winter for us.

7

The Flu

By late December, winter had stabilized. Drifted roads were shoveled enough for automobile traffic. Sleighs were needed only on country sideroads. I was glad because now we could drive to Lititz Mennonite Church at Christmastime.

At church, we were always given something for Christmas. Everyone, old and young, received a small box of hard candy and an orange. The box had a string handle and was decorated with Christmas tokens. Mama and Papa emptied their candy into a dish and set it on the table as common property.

Mama kept a close watch over little Betty's box. She was only two years old. Her real name was Mary Elizabeth, but "the girls" (Eva and Helen) had established the change. *Betty* was so natural for the little black-haired, brown-eyed tot that the name *Mary Elizabeth* was almost forgotten.

About the same time, the girls began to call Papa

"Dad" or "Daddy." One of the old ladies at church said, "That's not proper because *Dad* or *Daddy* is not used in the Bible. *Father* would be proper."

"Why do you say 'Papa' at your home?" Eva asked her. "That isn't in the Bible either."

"Well, that's different," the lady replied.

We kept calling Papa "Dad," and that's how it remained. In Pennsylvania Dutch the word for "Daddy" (*Daadi*) was often used for a father or a grandfather. So it seemed strange for the lady to object.

Clear weather stayed until after Christmas. Then one Friday morning a severe blizzard blew in from the west. The children struggled to school in their *Tuttsell* (bag-type, pullover) caps, with scarves covering their faces. The weather was so severe that Miss Rhudy dismissed school early.

The three Snavely children and Sam and Ruth Smith were grouping together. They lived several miles away, over the hill. They were trying to decide whether to go by the road or to cut across the fields. They were worried because Ruth had an artificial leg and would have difficulty.

"Ruth can spend the night with us," offered my sister Esther (Esty). We lived only about 300 yards away.

Everyone, including Miss Rhudy, said that was an excellent solution. Sam would explain it when he got home. While the others faced a rough walk home, little ten-year-old Ruth came to stay with us. Eva made a place for her at the supper table, beside Esty. Ruth seemed like one of us.

When we bowed our heads for the blessing, Ruth

folded her little hands. After supper she offered to help with the dishes. The evening was cozy and warm, and there was a special air of friendliness. Then the phone rang. Mama went and took the call. She said "Hello" and then just listened.

Whoever was on the other end of the phone was doing all the talking. Mama's face showed a mixture of anger and concern. She finally found a chance to talk. All she said was "It is no trouble at all." Then, after more patient listening, she said, "Well, it would have been hard to get permission first."

Little Ruth was nervous. She knew the caller was her stern papa.

"Ruth, everything is all right," Mama said after she was off the phone. "Sam explained it at home. Your papa will come for you in the morning."

Mr. Smith came for her on foot at eight o'clock in the morning. He wouldn't come in. He waited outside for Ruth to get bundled up. Then, without a word, he began stomping home, with Ruth limping along behind.

News began to surface about an influenza epidemic raging in Europe after the war. Everyone was worried that it would come here too. In fact, some isolated cases of an odd form of pneumonia had already taken some lives. It might have been flu, as it came to be called.

In the late fall, little first-grader Helen Ekert had died from it. I remember her lying in her small white casket. She looked like a little sleeping doll. About a month or so later, Dad took us to his brother Amos' funeral in Reading. He had died of the same thing.

Then late that winter, flu struck our neighborhood full force. All at once, I was flat on my back in bed, beside my brother, Franklin. We both had the flu. Everyone else in the family seemed to be upstairs in bed, too. No one was downstairs talking or making any sounds.

Dr. Long came by about every other day. He went from room to room, rattling his thermometer in its sterilizing bottle. He felt our pulses, took our temperatures, and left more ugly medicine. Everything we ate tasted awful. Hot milk with toast or soft-boiled eggs all tasted the same—just like something rotten.

Sometimes Mama was the one who cared for us and sometimes Eva. Dad even helped to feed me once. I remembered almost nothing about those days when I had the flu. I didn't even remember about "going potty."

Finally, one day the doctor said I was better and could get out of bed. When I tried to stand up, I fell flat on the floor. I was so weak that Mama had to dress me.

The epidemic was over. Spring was in the air, school was back to normal, and no one in our family had succumbed to the flu.

One evening after work, Dad was reading the paper, as usual. He looked up and started to read a headline. "It says here that more people in the world died from the flu than in the war! We should all be thankful that we were spared. Now let's try to forget the hard winter and get ready for spring."

8

The Tobacco Year

Snow was beginning to melt during the day, only to freeze again at night. Deep ruts began to form in the muddy country roads, making some almost impassable. The township hired Wayne Zartman to shape up the worst roads with his four-mule road scraper. He was allowed tax credit since there was no cash available in the township budget.

Snow and sledding was finished, and coaster wagons came out of storage. While sleds were only for play, coaster wagons were useful for work and play.

It was fun to pull the wagon up the hill to the mailbox and coast down again with reckless speed. There were no brakes. We sat in the wagon, tilted the handle back over the wagon bed, and steered by twisting the handle back and forth.

Franklin made a special high-speed coaster using old metal baby-coach wheels. There was no seat; we just laid down on it.

One evening at the supper table, Dad talked to us about work. "There is going to be work for everyone. From now on, work is going to be your play. Useful work can be even more fun and give a deeper feeling of happiness than play."

He quoted his much-used saying: "Happiness is a state of mind and not of circumstances." It was difficult for me to apply this principle when I tried to compare coasting with pulling weeds.

Once when I had to pull milkweeds, Dad told me, "Imagine you're killing giants." That didn't help much. David had only one giant to kill, and there were hundreds of milkweeds.

This would be our first full year on the farm. Though Dad thought tobacco was a bad use of land, he decided to raise some this first year to "pull the ox out of the ditch." The farm was already equipped for raising and processing such a crop.

Since it would be a year before cash was available from the tobacco, Dad had planned for other sources of ready cash. We would raise a variety of vegetables for the retail "curb market" in Lancaster. The barn and sheds also had room for more cows and chickens.

Dad carefully explained the program: "While we work the tobacco, other planting and marketing can still go on. In the fall and winter, there will be butter and eggs for sale. Then next spring, we will sell the tobacco. If we all work together, it will not be necessary to raise tobacco again."

A cup full of tiny tobacco seeds was enough to start things rolling. It was like rolling a ball, because the seeds were balled in an old piece of woolen cloth.

The ball was soaked in warm water for about ten minutes. Then we hung the ball by the stove to germinate. The seeds began to swell and crack their shells.

It was urgent that the seeds be sown before sprouts appeared. We sowed the seeds by stirring them into a sprinkling can full of water and sprinkling them over the prepared bed. One cup of seeds could provide enough plants for several acres of tobacco.

We had carefully spaded and raked the tobacco beds, so they were ready. But since they had not been used for several years, it was necessary to steam them. This process would kill all weeds and fungus.

Everything in tobacco country is standardized for raising tobacco. It was easy to get the beds steamed. A man at Brunnerville had a steam traction engine and the necessary pipes and pans. A day and time were set.

At seven o'clock on that day, we heard the shrill whistle of the engine as it passed Phares Zartman's and came toward us. It was the signal to get ready. The engine came lumbering and puffing down the hill like a train locomotive, hauling along pipes and pans in a trailer. It took a half-hour to put the engine in the right place and set up the pans.

A pipe was attached to the steam valve on the boiler. Four eight-foot sections were needed to reach the pans. The pans were placed upside down over the beds to corral the steam and heat the ground. The pipeline was about four feet above the ground. It ran across the lawn and then elbowed down to the pans.

Before setting the pans, Dad handed the steam man two eggs. He buried them eight inches deep and spaced about six feet apart in the center of the bed. He marked their locations with two small stones.

After all these preparations, the man went to the engine and turned the valve open. He watched carefully to be sure everything was right. Then he took a bag of Red Man chewing tobacco from his hip pocket and stuffed some in his mouth. He extended the bag to Dad and said, "*Wit du en bissel* (do you want a little)?"

"No, thanks," Dad replied.

After the steam man chewed the tobacco into his cheek, he spit out a big blob of tobacco juice. He looked at Dad thoughtfully and said, "Henry, I guess you know the Schreiners never had any luck with tobacco."

Dad made no comment.

The man walked to the engine, looked at the steam gauge, and checked his watch. He blew the whistle and said, "It's eight o'clock; we should be finished at four." He discharged some more tobacco juice. Some dribbled down his chin, and he didn't wipe it off. Then he pulled an old chair out of the engine cab, found a shady spot, and settled down.

At noon Mama had to call Franklin and me twice for dinner. We could hardly break away from the steam engine. The man had been telling us all kinds of stories about steam accidents. "Stay away from hot pipes!" he warned.

At the table I kept asking questions until Dad said, "All right now, keep quiet and eat."

I had to ask one more. "Why did you bury the eggs?"

He explained carefully: "I always respect intelligent questions like that. We must be sure the ground has been hot enough for long enough to kill the weeds and germs. If the eggs are hard boiled when we finish, we know everything is all right."

I risked one more question: "What will happen to the eggs?"

"Just go ahead and eat," Dad told me.

After dinner I ran out to take a look at things again. I was so interested in the engine that, failing to see the steam pipe suspended above the ground, I crashed right into it. My nose was badly hurt. Mama put salve on it, but it didn't help much. It was sore for a long time.

Four o'clock finally came, and the whistle blew again. The steam valve was closed and dismantling began. The men wore gloves because of the hot equipment.

First, the pans were set aside so the eggs could be examined. The man dug them out with a trowel. He cracked their shells and squeezed them. "They're hard, Henry," he said as he handed them to Dad.

"No, you keep them," Dad responded.

Franklin and I hoped the man would give them to us, but he didn't. He stuck one egg in his pocket. After spitting out his tobacco, he squeezed the other egg into his mouth with two bites.

The steaming job was successfully completed, and we helped to load the equipment. With another blast from the whistle, the man was on his way.

The bed was ready for seeding, and the seed was

ready. In the morning, Dad sprinkled the seed and covered the bed with tobacco-bed muslin. That coarse cotton fabric would cover the small plants until they could survive in normal weather.

So far, farming tobacco had been fun. The work part was still to come, but somehow there would be a way to work in the idea of "killing giants."

9

The Growing and Learning Season

The tobacco seeds germinated into small plants that were planted in rows out in the field. We did the planting by hand, for all four acres. Dad had said, "It wouldn't be worthwhile to buy a planter for just this one year."

Next to the tobacco field was the section we called the truck patch. It had colorful rows of Early Jersey Wakefield cabbage, Golden Bantam sweet corn, peas, snap beans, tomatoes, red beets, lettuce, radishes, and other market vegetables. There was a little of each and not too much of any one vegetable. We made staged plantings of some things to have an ongoing supply.

These would all be sold in Lancaster at the Saturday Curb Market. Our stand was near the corner of Duke and Orange streets.

During the planting everyone but the baby was busy from morning till night. Little two-and-a-half-year-old Betty was just old enough to need watching. She had outgrown her homemade playpen. It was like a prison, and she would climb out of it.

As an aid to babysitting, Mama bought a little sulky. It was just a baby seat with two little wheels and a handle to pull it. We fastened Betty in place with a seat belt. As a child restraint, it was a failure. She only wanted to be pulled around. If left alone, she simply opened the belt and got out. Then she loaded in her four dolls and pulled them around outside the house.

Betty had four dolls: two rag dolls, one doll with a china head, and a partly broken rubber doll left over from playpen days. When its belly was squeezed, the whistle embedded in its back still gave a little peep.

Helen gave names to the dolls: Dickalicka, Mertz, Weedly, and Minnie. The china doll was Weedly, and the rubber doll was Dickalicka. The rag dolls somehow shared the other two names.

Betty left the dolls scattered at random but seemed to like Dickalicka the best. At night she usually laid them in a row by the wall and covered them with a little blanket.

Dad wanted to plant a row of sweet potatoes. Since growing them was a specialty, we had to go to the sweet potato man to buy plant starts. Dad took me along. We followed the country roads about three miles to his farm.

Near his house, Dad stopped the car along the road close to the plant bed and waited for someone to come. When no one appeared, Dad blew the little wheezing horn. Soon a lady came out and spoke to us. "The mister is out in the field, and I didn't see you-uns. Vat do you-uns vant?"

Dad said, "I want to buy two hundred sweet potato plants."

"Vell," she said, "that iss easy. I'll pull them myself." She looked ready for work. She wore a large rag "slop-bonnet" with an ample frill to protect her neck. A large gunnysack work apron was tied around her rather full waist. Her dress looked like it was about worn out. She was bare footed.

"Chust set your basket down," she said. "I'll hand you the plants, and you count 'em. I'll trust you."

Sweet potato beds are underlaid with fresh horse manure to generate heat. The manure is covered with several inches of dirt, on which the sweet potatoes are spread. A layer of earth covers the potatoes to hold the heat and to support the sprouts. Pulling the sprouts can become messy, especially after the bed has been worked over for awhile.

The lady knew her job. She stepped right into the bed and began to pull. She held down the sweet potato with one hand to keep it from coming up with the sprouts. Muck oozed through her toes.

As she handed bunches of sprouts to Dad, he counted them out loud as he put them in the basket. When we were finished, she wiped her hands on her apron and placed the money Dad gave her in her apron pocket.

As we turned to leave, I saw her pour water on her feet from a sprinkling can and wipe them with her apron. Then she returned to the house, wiping her hands once more on her apron.

On the way home, I asked Dad, "Who was that lady?"

"She's the sweet potato man's wife."

I pondered the word *wife*. I had not come across it in my school reader and had never noticed it in conversation before. The lady with her unusual clothing and bare feet became my unconscious definition of the word *wife*. It somehow remained stored in my mind for later use.

The next day we planted sweet potatoes and pulled our first radishes.

10

The Invisible Paint

Eva was going to Millersville State Normal School (MSNS) and was home for the summer. She helped in the fields, picking peas and beans and going along with Dad to Lancaster Market on Saturdays.

Helen had graduated from high school and would also be going to MSNS with Eva. They were in training to be teachers. This summer Helen was helping Mama in the house and doing a lot of sewing.

Ever since she was a little girl, Helen had worked with the sewing machine. Dad told her he would get her a good sewing machine and help her go into business as a seamstress, but she wanted to teach school.

This summer, her sewing skill was in demand at home. Eva needed a new dress for school, and so did Helen herself. Esther needed a Sunday dress, and her other dresses needed to be let out (lengthened). Betty was growing and needed some little-girl dresses. Mama made her own dresses and sewed in the winter.

With all the sewing going on, I heard about many kinds of cloth goods: dimity, crash, voile, pongee, gingham, organdy, and others. I heard about rickrack, piping, flouncing, and backing. Sewing was fascinating. It was a household division apart by itself.

Helen's work was neat and always fitted perfectly. She was careful and never got excited.

Marketing was going well. We always had a variety of vegetables neatly prepared for display. Dad outfitted the Model T for carrying the produce. He removed the backseat cushion from the car and fastened wooden racks to the rear roof upright supports.

Dad parked our market car at the curb by our leased sidewalk space. He formed a market stand by laying the side racks across several bushel boxes. Our family usually sold out their produce by midafternoon and came home in time for Eva to clean up the car for Sunday.

In the evening after supper, when we had settled down, Dad would have us all come to the table to count the market money. He would empty the moneybag on the table and separate the bills and change according to their kinds. Then he carefully counted, starting with ten-dollar bills, if any, and on down to the pennies.

One time he let Esther count it, but she got mixed up. Once there was almost thirty dollars. When Dad had counted it all, he would say, "Well, that is what the family wages were this week." He explained that some of it had to be allowed for seeds, fertilizer, and the grocery store.

It made me proud to be included as one of the wage earners. He told us that if we made enough money, maybe we could buy a truck for market next year. A Ford truck might cost $175, and that was a lot of money.

I liked Eva and Helen. When I asked them questions, they would answer and try to help me understand. One time I heard about some invisible paint. Eva suggested, "That must have come from a fairy tale."

Helen explained, "Maybe there is something like it. *Invisible* means you can't see something that is right there in front of you."

I was especially interested in the stories going around about the old folks that used to live here. These stories had things in them that were claimed to be magic.

Up in a little loft in the tobacco shed, Esther and I had found some old, smelly paint buckets. Maybe the Schreiners (who used to live here) had left some invisible paint. They had painted a lot of hex signs and put one above every door and opening in the barn and sheds.

Dad had torn some of them off, and Franklin and I found a pile of them one day when we were looking around in an old shed behind the barn.

"Don't pay any attention to them," Dad said. "They're not for us. We didn't put them there."

However, Franklin and I went around and collected a lot of them. They were all exactly the same.

A little thin piece of board, three by four inches, was designed to be nailed above the door, always with three nails. Behind the board, placed so the nails wouldn't hit them, was a piece of paper carefully folded to form a triangle. When the paper was unfolded, there was a poorly written message with some of the words spelled wrong:

gode the father
gode the Son
gode the holy gost
The blood of Jesus
X X X

"The papers were supposed to keep evil spirits out of the barn," Eva told us. "But I don't think using the Bible that way is right."

I kept two of them in a matchbox on my private shelf. Franklin, Esther, and I each had a private shelf in a little recessed bookcase in the living room.

I didn't tell Esther about my interest in invisible paint. She would have made a joke out of it. But I went exploring around the old paint cans in the loft. One can way back in the corner was half full of something.

I got an old paint paddle that was lying on the floor and pushed around in its gummy contents. I was able to push through the scum and discovered there was still some liquid paint there. It was pale blue and smelled funny. My imagination convinced me that this was magic invisible paint!

I secretly went about setting up a test. I took a little block of wood up in the loft and planned to paint it invisible. Nearby I saw an old bag of pig hair and some rags. Using the paddle and a rag, I smeared the block with a coat of paint. I was excited! In the dim light, I could hardly see the block.

I left the block to dry and returned the next day. I could still see it but not well. I rubbed on another coat. Maybe that would do it. However, the next day I was still able to see it but not really good. I reasoned that I could see it because I knew it was there.

The next day was Saturday. In the living room, Eva and Helen were working at sewing. I told Helen about my project and asked her, "Come to the kitchen and see if you can find where I've put the invisible block on the floor."

She came and walked all around, looking carefully. Finally she happened to step on the block and said, "Oh, there it is!"

Then I knew I had found invisible paint! But just as we were finishing the experiment, Esther came in. She squashed all my hopes for a successful outcome. Esther laughed and said, "I see the block. Helen is just being nice to you."

Summer was a busy time. Even so, Franklin, in what little spare time he had, worked at building a small dam. It was located right below the barnyard, where the small creek flowed down to the woods. We all remembered the little dam down at Amelia. That's where we had played with Charlie Wallace, the duck, and had seen frogs.

Franklin worked hard on his dam, starting at the ends and finally finishing in the middle, where the stream ran. It took the new pond several days to fill and run over the wooden trough Franklin had made. Now we had a dam again. The girls even came down to look at it.

Then one night a big thunderstorm raged, bringing torrents of water. The ditches along the road emptied through a gully and into the stream. The dam Franklin had worked so hard to build was broken right in the middle. He looked at it, cried a little, and said, "If we had time, we could repair it again. Most of the dam material is still there."

By then, Franklin was beginning to worry about school. He was in the upper reader at Webster School and had a decision to make. The law said he had to go to school until the end of his fifteenth year. That meant he would have to repeat his classes or go to high school.

The girls persuaded him to go to Rothsville High, and Dad agreed. But Franklin was troubled. He became nervous around a lot of strange people. It was that way with him sometimes at church.

Summer had several weeks left before school, and there was an uneasy feeling among us. Esther and I would have a new teacher at Webster. Franklin would be going to high school, and Eva and Helen would be away at MSNS. Things would be different.

I thought about it sometimes in the evenings. When I was little, Mama had taught me the "Now I Lay Me Down to Sleep" prayer. After I entered the second grade, she told me, "You're getting bigger. Now you should pray the Lord's Prayer, 'Our Father which art in heaven.' You can add some things, like saying what you are thankful for."

So I would always add, "And I am thankful that

our family is all together." Once I heard a preacher talk about that. I wondered if, after school started, I could still say our family was together. I also thought about the dam. Maybe we could still fix it before school.

11

Church and Sunday School

Every Sunday morning, we went to Sunday school and church. There were three congregations in our district—Hammer Creek, Hesses, and Lititz. We went by turn to both Hammer Creek and Hesses. Each met every other week on different alternate Sundays.

Lititz was a village church and had services every Sunday morning and evening because it had electric lights. The others were country churches and were planning to install Delco light systems to replace their naptha (white) gas lamps.

Going to church was important to Dad. We were among the first to arrive and about the last to leave.

When we first moved to Possum Hollow, most of the people in the churches were strangers. Getting to know them was easy. I associated them with their automobiles, and the horses and buggies some of the old folks still used. The way they dressed also reflected different personalities.

The most interesting way I came to know them was by how they sang. Some men sang bass and some tenor, while others sang the melody with the sopranos, but an octave lower. A few sang in a steady monotone, the same in every song.

Since men and women sat separately, on opposite sides of the church, it was a little harder to pick out who sang soprano or alto. I noticed that old ladies never sang alto. That seemed to be a specialty among teenage girls.

I enjoyed four-part singing and tried to sing like the men. Once Dad explained to me that I was still a little boy and should sing along with the girls. When I got a little older, I would have a voice like the men.

Sunday school was a lot nicer since I had grown out of the little children's class. We still had a lady teacher, but the class was all boys. Next year we would have a man teacher. Instead of picture cards, we had our own Sunday school book and didn't sing little children's songs. We learned about good people and bad people in the Bible and how we should always be good.

I wondered what "being good" was like. If we weren't bad, did that mean we were good? Sometimes when I was afraid in the dark, Esther said it was because I was bad. But she also was scared in the dark sometimes, even though she thought she was good. She didn't say bad words or tell lies, so I guess she was good.

Maybe even grown-ups were scared in the dark

but were brave about it. I tried being brave, but it didn't help much.

When we first moved to Possum Hollow, Franklin didn't like to go to church. He said strange people in closed places made him feel sick. When it was time to leave for church, he would beg to stay home.

Dad would have none of it. He would take Franklin by the arm and drag him, crying, to the car. He finally got over it, enjoyed going to church, and was learning to sing bass. Some of that old fear came back again when he thought about going to high school.

This summer we went to an all-day Sunday school meeting at Metzler's Mennonite Church. These meetings were held in different churches from time to time in the summer. There was a morning session, an afternoon session, and usually one in the evening. Each session began with about fifteen minutes of congregational singing, followed by a talk.

I liked these meetings because it was a day off from work. I enjoyed the singing and the hour recess at noon. Everyone brought their own lunches, and the church provided coffee. Noon recess on the grounds was a time to visit and meet people.

At noon I got acquainted with a new boy my age. We walked around, looking at the different cars parked on the grounds. There were Buicks, Fords, Durants, Chevrolets, Overlands, and one big Chandler. We came to a new Chevrolet with a little boy sitting at the steering wheel. He was pushing around at the wheel and making automobile sounds.

"Do you usually drive your Chevy?" I asked him.

He grinned and replied, *"Nee, awwer ich will mol browiere wann ich gross bin."*

Just then his mama came, smiling, and translated for us. She didn't need to. I knew he had said, "No, but I want to try it once when I am big."

The people were singing in the church, so it was time to go in. The new boy and I sat together near the back and picked up a songbook. In his child's voice, he began to sing tenor. It sounded good, so I began singing tenor, too. I had never tried to sing anything except soprano since Dad had told me about children's voices. Now as I sang, my voice matched his and it felt good. I already had learned about singing and different clefs and notes.

I had learned about that last summer, when we went to a singing at the Millersville Mennonite Church. Eva told us that the singing was scheduled, and Dad took us there. Franklin and Betty stayed home with Mama.

A young man named Chester Lehman conducted the meeting. There were about a hundred people, and he had them divided into four groups, one for each voice part. He explained about notes and rhythm, and led us in selected hymns. After that, I could follow the notes that carried different parts of the harmony.

By this time, I always sang tenor. But as I followed the lower notes on the bass clef, I knew bass was what I wanted to sing when I grew up. One of my favorite hymns was "Glory Gates." It had real high tenor notes in the refrain:

Oh, the glory gates are ever open wide,
Inviting the world to come;
Oh, the glory gates are ever open wide,
To welcome the weary home!

The Second Year at
Possum Hollow

12

Back to School

It was Wednesday afternoon. Eva and Helen were packing for college. They would leave for Millersville State Normal School on Friday. Franklin and Dad were in Lexington at Althouses, making arrangements for his jitney trips to Rothsville High. Esther and I were fooling around and talking about going to Webster, which would start on Monday.

Little Betty, now about three years old, was bumping around and in the way with her kiddie car. Things were in a mess. Mama told Esther and me to get out of the house and take Betty with us.

At the supper table, we were all talking about school. Eva would have the same roommate again, her friend Agatha. Helen didn't know her assigned roommate. Franklin knew about Rothsville School because he had been there before.

Dad told us that a girl named Anna E. Young

would teach at Webster. She went to the Brethren Church near Elm. Her uncle was one of the school directors in our township.

On Monday, Franklin walked to Althouses for the jitney ride, and Esther and I went to Webster. We were given desks a little farther back in the room because we were bigger now. The smallest ones were always up front.

Miss Young was a nice teacher. She liked us and smiled when she talked. Miss Young played the organ and sang with us from the "Institute" songbook. We got a new Institute songbook every year. Each year school was closed for a week so all the teachers could attend a teachers' conference at Lancaster. Friday afternoon was always open to the public. That was when the new Institute songbook was introduced.

For entertainment, a men's quartet sang a funny song in which each one was supposed to be a pie. The first tenor was a cherry pie, the second tenor an apple pie, the baritone a pumpkin pie, and the bass a "big pot pie." The song went along, starting up high with the cherry pie and ending deep down with a booming "and I am the big pot pie." The people clapped.

This year's songbook was named *The Wreath*. It was distributed to the audience, and we all helped to sing some of the new songs. There were ballads, play songs, and hymns. One of the numbers we sang was "Hunting Chestnuts."

There's a place I know where chestnuts grow,
So big and round and brown,

Hanging high up in the leafless trees,
Burrs so sharp and round.
Old Jack Frost out walking sees them there,
Blows his icy breath in air,
Burrs crack open and the chestnuts fall,
In showers on the ground.

We also sang one of the hymns, "God Speed the Right." Near the end of each verse, the title was repeated with the word "right" held on a long high note. A lady sitting behind me sang so loudly that I turned around to look. She smiled at me real sweetly as though I were a little baby.

The songbooks were sent to the schools, where each child would buy one. The price of fifteen cents was marked inside the cover. I counted the songs and found ninety-one, including the two on the outside back cover: "The Star Spangled Banner" and "My Country, 'Tis of Thee."

This year the government made a law that no one could buy or sell any kind of "strong drink." There was a lot of talk in schools and churches about the evils of drink.

One day two ladies came to the school door. Miss Young invited them in and introduced them to us. They were members of the Women's Christian Temperance Union (WCTU).

The ladies talked about how bad things happened when people got drunk and asked us to take a pledge never to drink strong drink. We all raised our hands and pledged that. To help us remember it, one of the ladies taught us a short pledge:

Say *drink* six times;
We'll drink cold water pure.
We'll never touch the wine;
We'll drink cold water pure."

We all shouted:

Say *drink* six times;
We'll drink cold water pure . . .

She stopped us and said, "No! You must repeat *drink* six times like this." She lifted her hand and said "drink" six times, counting it on her fingers. We tried again, almost shouting:

Drink, drink, drink, drink, drink, drink—
We'll drink cold water pure.
We'll never touch the wine;
We'll drink cold water pure.

School was more fun this year. The biggest boys and girls were out of school, and little first-year children were up front. I was in the fourth reader. We were studying short division and fractions. I already knew all the multiplication tables. Esther was doing long division and learning poems.

In the evenings, Mama didn't help me with my reading any more. We used to sit together in a big chair with the reader in her lap. She would put her arm around my shoulder and sometimes tickle my neck.

We had read about "Leary the Lamplighter." He was a friendly neighbor who took care of the village street lamps. Leary helped people and carried messages. One time he found a pet kitty that was lost. He was always doing something nice. Mama began to call me "Leary" sometimes.

All schoolchildren had to be vaccinated for smallpox. For my shot, Dad took me up to Brickerville, to Dr. Long. I was glad to get the shot because the other boys and girls at school were going around showing their "vaccinates" with the little celluloid turtle shells taped over the scabs. I wanted to be like the rest.

Dr. Long had me sit on a chair and roll up my left sleeve. He went to his wife's sewing basket and got a needle from the pincushion. It had a piece of thread hanging through the eye.

Dr. Long scratched a place on my upper arm until it bled. He dropped some medicine on it. After punching it some more with the needle, he taped a little turtle shell over the sore. He said, "Don't worry if it gets sore; it's supposed to. That's how you know it took."

The next day at school, I could show my "vaccinate" too. The regular term for it at school was *vaccinate*. Dad told me that after it was done, it was called "vaccination." I believed him, but at school I called it my vaccinate. I didn't want the others to make fun of me.

13

Hunting Chestnuts

Dad bought a shiny New Holland gasoline engine. It was mounted on a special wagon, with little iron wheels so it could be pulled from place to place. We would use it for belt power around the farm.

In the old farming style, farmers had used rotary horsepower machines to convert power from horses pulling in a circle. That power went to a transfer unit with gears to run a flywheel and a belt, thus furnishing rotary power for equipment like a threshing machine or a buzz saw.

Later a steam engine would go from farm to farm with the threshing machine. Now we were entering the era of gasoline engines.

Often people had turned or run smaller machines by hand. Now this was changing. Dad said we could put a belt pulley on the big corn sheller and maybe on a washing machine or butter churn.

Right now, however, we had a buzz saw with a belt pulley. Dad had bought it at a farm sale to use with the new engine. We were ready to cut firewood.

At one Saturday breakfast, since Franklin and I were both home from school, Dad announced, "We're going to saw wood with the new engine. There's a big pile of discarded fence posts and rails below the barn, in the meadow. That's where we'll set up the saw rig."

"What do you mean by *rig*?" I asked.

Dad would always explain such things to us. "When several pieces of machinery are worked together, it's called a *rig*. When a rig is put together for temporary use, it is called a *setup*. When the threshing rig comes, the men set it up."

We used a horse to pull the engine close to the pile of posts. Next we placed the buzz saw beside the pile at a convenient place and fastened it down with stakes driven into the ground. Then we moved the engine into position so the belt pulleys were lined up at the right distance.

We put the belt on the pulleys and tightened it by pressing a rail between the engine and the saw to hold them apart. Then we used stakes to anchor the engine.

Franklin filled the reservoir with water, and Dad poured gasoline into the gas tank. The grease and oil cups were checked, and we were ready to go.

"Well crew, let's go to our posts," Dad said with mock dignity. "This is how we'll be organized: Franklin, you help me with the posts and rails at the saw cradle, and Boy, you take hold of the sawed-off piece and throw it away on a pile."

I couldn't believe he called me "Boy." That's what he always used to call Franklin! Now I wasn't a little boy any more!

Dad took the crank and spun the flywheels. When the speed was right, he turned on the switch. The engine began to pop, and we were ready. Dad and Franklin put a log on the cradle and pushed it into the saw. The saw whined and the engine began to pop, pop, pop real fast.

I grabbed the first piece and threw it away to begin the woodpile. I remembered the time long ago in Amelia when Vernon Lynn sawed our wood. I had to stand at a safe distance. Now I was helping; it made me feel good. We sawed till the dinner bell rang.

After dinner we sawed awhile until Dad said it was enough. I looked at the big pile of sawn wood. It had taken only a few hours to saw enough for the winter.

"Well crew," said Dad, "let's take down the setup and move the rig to the shed." He took off the belt and rolled it up. Then he took off the saw blade and hung it on a big nail in the shed.

The water in the reservoir was real hot. After draining it, we pulled and dragged the engine and saw into the shed. I wondered who would carry all the wood to the woodshed near the kitchen. I was afraid it would be me.

After supper I explained to Esther about the rig, the setup, and the crew. She was afraid *she* was going to be the one to bring the wood to the shed.

Then Mama surprised me: "Bringing in the wood is your job, Levi."

Each of us had a special job of our own, and from it we earned spending money. This was my first real job. She said I would get fifty cents.

I began to make plans for my new job. I could use the wheelbarrow since the wood pile wasn't far from the shed. It might take a day or two for me to stack the wood in the shed, and then I would have my fifty cents. Now I was part of the regular children. Betty was the only little one. It had been a good day.

That night I slept really well. I dreamed about hauling wood in the big wheelbarrow. I dreamed about the rig and the crew. Then the dream became clear.

I was there, throwing wood from the saw to the pile, when someone came walking toward us. It was Jesus! He was dressed just like his picture on the Sunday school cards. He smiled and said, "May I be a part of this crew?" Then the dream was over. I never told anyone about it.

One day, just as we were going in from school recess, a large van-type automobile drove up to Webster. A young man and woman got out and entered the school with us. They talked to Miss Young, and when we were seated, they told us who they were.

They belonged to the Gideon Society and went around as a husband-and-wife team, giving out Bibles and booklets. They sang "Jesus Loves Me, This I Know" in beautiful harmony.

Then they gave each of us a little pamphlet carrying the Gospel of John. On the front fly leaf, John 3:16 was printed. A blank space was left where it ordinarily said "the world" and "whosoever."

The lady told us, "You may write your first name in those spaces and read it that way. You ought to read your Bibles every day, just like you read your readers." They sang another pretty duet, wished us "God's blessing," and left.

I took my pencil and wrote "Levi" in the John 3:16 blank places.

One of our favorite songs at school was "Hunting Chestnuts." Everybody liked to scout around and look for chestnuts, but they were getting scarce since the great blight had killed so many trees.

One day Miss Young surprised us: "On Friday afternoon the whole school is going to go chestnut hunting. Forry Zartman says there are some chestnut trees in their woods behind the millpond. His pop says we may go there."

That evening I went to the tool shop and tried to make a belt with a bag attached. I would wear it and put my chestnuts in the bag. I got a piece of harness leather and a little salt sack and tried to cut and rivet together what I hoped would be something special.

The project didn't turn out right, and the outfit didn't fit me. I wasn't good at making things. Franklin always made things that were neat, but mine never seemed to work out.

On Friday afternoon as planned, we all went walking down the hill and out past the millpond to the woods. We found the trees, but there were hardly any chestnuts around. Others had been there before us.

A piece of log was lying under the trees. Someone had used it to shake the chestnuts down. The big boys took the log and bumped the tree branches again. A few chestnuts dropped, maybe a dozen, and that was all.

The chestnut trip was a failure, but we all had fun. The girls were all talking and laughing, and the boys were acting smart.

On the way back, I ran ahead so I could sit in a rowboat tied in the pond near the road. I joined the rest as they passed, and we walked up the hill together.

Miss Young said she was sorry about the chestnuts, but we had a good time all the same. "Hunting Chestnuts" was still one of our favorite songs.

14

The Hothouse

As summer ended, Dad was making plans for raising more vegetables so we wouldn't have to grow tobacco. He had already bought a secondhand tobacco planter to be used for planting cabbage.

Dad had also just finished building a neat little hothouse where cabbage plants could be started. There were several months to go before it would be needed, so it stood there empty.

"It's a pity to have all that nice space go to waste without using it for something," Mama said as she laughed. "If it was a little bigger, I could install some wash lines and use it during the winter for drying the wet clothes."

Then Esther came up with a good idea. "Why don't we use it for a place to husk off the outside hulls of walnuts?"

Hulling walnuts was an awful job. They were messy and stained the hands. Esther and I had just gathered two buckets of walnuts from the trees out back. That's what gave her the idea.

Dad said it would be all right to take care of the walnuts there. On Saturday we carried the two buckets to the hothouse and spread the walnuts on the platforms. We would have to let them soften for a week or two so we could rub off the hulls.

One Saturday when they were ready, Esther and I got busy. We turned two buckets upside down for seats and put on some old gloves to keep the awful stain from our hands. It took us all afternoon to do a good job.

We left the hulled walnuts spread out in the hothouse to dry and become ready for us to crack them. We took the hulls and dumped them on the manure pile.

Mama used a lot of walnuts in cakes and cookies. They were also good in pies and candy. That was one reason Thanksgiving and Christmas desserts were so delicious.

During our discussions about raising a lot of cabbage and sweet corn, Dad said, "We will have to get a truck. The old Model T is not big enough and is wearing out. If we work hard enough next summer, we might also get a new car to replace the Model T."

Then smiling, he joked, "If we can't get a new car, we can just go back to the horse and buggy again. We could go through more snow that way, anyhow."

I knew he was fooling, but what if it would happen? Some people still came to church in buggies, so we wouldn't be completely out of step if we had to do that, too.

I knew we would work hard enough to get a new

car. I wondered whether it would have a self-starter or have to be cranked like the old Ford.

Recently I had heard a man talking about going from his horse and buggy to an automobile: "You know, if I change to an automobile, I want one with a 'self-commencer.' I don't want to break my arm cranking it." We all knew he meant a self-starter.

Now my daydreams were filled with trucks and automobiles. Our old rattly Model T just wasn't fit any more. It was time for change.

The Third Year at
Possum Hollow

15

My New Coat

My overcoat was wearing out and getting too tight, but Mama kept putting off buying me a new one. "Next year you'll be old enough to have the kind the older boys are wearing."

That was the very reason I wanted a new coat. I wanted to look more grown-up and receive more respect. Little boys wore short coats with big collars, while the bigger boys had longer coats with collars more like the grown-ups. Then something happened that settled the coat problem.

Our preacher phoned Mama and told her that a little baby had died, and I was to be one of the boy pallbearers. The funeral was to be in three days, on Friday.

Mama decided to get my new coat in time for that event. It was just before Thanksgiving, and the days were cold. Something had to be done at once.

When Dad came in, she talked to him about it. He

was going to Lancaster on Thursday. He could go to Groff & Wolf, a men's and boy's clothing store, and buy my coat.

Dad never shopped for our clothing before this, and it didn't suit Mama to go along. She got the Sears catalog and showed Dad the style and color that would be nice. The sizes went by age, so I didn't have to go along to try it on.

Because buying the coat took some time, Dad was late in coming home. "I found a nice coat Levi's size," he reported, "and at a discount price."

I watched with anticipation as Mama opened the box. She stepped back with a startled look. "Why, Henry," she said in dismay, "why did you get a green coat like this?"

Dad looked surprised. "The one I looked at was brown."

It didn't take Mama long to figure out what happened. She said with a sigh, "It's just like when you pick green tomatoes with the red ones; you can't tell colors. I should have gone along."

It was too late to exchange it because the funeral was the next day. I would have that green coat until I grew out of it.

The funeral was sad. The parents were a young couple named Martin. This was their first child, and only six weeks old. The first part of the service was in their home with friends and relatives. The child was on display in a little white casket.

As people went to look at it, one lady whispered, "Isn't it sweet, just like it's sleeping?"

Its fine silky hair was red. I noticed that both parents had red hair.

The wind made a moaning sound as the preacher read something from the Bible and spoke words of comfort. The parents cried quietly, and tears came to my eyes, too.

When the preacher finished, the funeral man closed the casket and lifted it in his hands. He carried it out of the house slowly and, with the help of his assistant, placed it on the backseat of his Buick sedan.

We all got in our cars and followed the Buick as the undertaker drove slowly to Hammer Creek Church. There the man and his assistant took the casket into the church by the side door and placed it on a little table in front of the pulpit. After they opened the casket lid again, they disappeared into the anteroom.

We four boy pallbearers sat on the front row without removing our overcoats. Everyone kept their coats on; the church was cool. When the sermon was over, the people lined up and went slowly past the casket, to take a last look at the little child.

After that, the man closed the casket and motioned for us pallbearers to come up front. He helped us take hold of the handles, and we walked in procession out to the cemetery.

When the funeral was finally over, we drove home. Dad, Mama, and I were the only ones of our family who attended.

Thanksgiving arrived, and everyone was home from Thursday through Sunday. Eva and Helen talked about Millersville State Normal School, and Franklin told them about Rothsville High. Rothsville wasn't too bad, the teachers were nice, and his grades were good.

Eva was taking an extra course about rocks and stones. It was called geology, and her professor was Dr. Roddy. I was interested in rocks myself. When I was a little boy at Amelia, Virginia, I collected some special stones. I still had them in a box on my private shelf.

In the evening I brought my box of stones and showed them to Eva. She was surprised because she didn't know I had them. We looked at the stones together.

I had a piece from the mica mine and a piece of crystal quartz. Also, I had saved two gemstones, one red and the other bright green. The green one was the size of a walnut. There were several others, one from the quarry at Eshleman's and some from Possum Hollow.

"May I take them along to show Dr. Roddy?" Eva asked. "He would be happy to classify and catalog them for you."

"Do you really think a professor would be interested in my rocks?"

"I'm sure he would be glad to do it," she said, "and it would help me in class, showing that I'm an eager student."

Of course, Eva and Helen got to see my new coat. Mama gave a little laugh like an apology and said, "Dad thought it was brown. We call it his apple butter and cheese coat."

When Uncle Amos saw it, he had remarked, "*Ei, es guckt wie Lattwarick un Schmierkaes* (oh, it looks like apple butter and cottage cheese)." When apple butter is mixed with cottage cheese as a delicacy, it takes on a greenish hue.

Eva and Helen both said the coat looked nice and made me look grown-up. That almost made me proud to wear it.

That Monday, we went back to school as usual. I was glad about Dr. Roddy and the rocks. The girls also had changed my feelings about my coat. It had been a good Thanksgiving.

One day when no one was around the house, I put on my coat and sneaked into the girls' bedroom. I looked at myself in their big dresser mirror. Taking one of their combs, I smoothed my hair and observed myself.

The coat looked good. I tried to look stern and grown-up. Life was exciting!

16

My First Novel

Thanksgiving was over and Christmas was just around the corner. At school we always had a Christmas tree and gave a Christmas program. We were all so excited about getting ready that it was hard to study and pay attention in class.

Several of the big girls put the Christmas border along the top of the blackboard. Two of them held a long stencil on the board. It had a lot of little holes, forming a band of holly leaves and berries. Two other girls would take blackboard erasers and pat chalk dust through the little holes.

When the stencil was taken away, there was an outline of small dots showing the picture. The girls who were good at drawing took colored chalk and colored in the band of holly leaves and berries.

The Christmas tree was usually cut by permission from Weidman's woods nearby. Three of the big boys would get an old ax from the school cellar and go to select the tree. They dragged it in and put it on the porch until a place was ready for it. After Miss Young and some of the big girls fixed a place, the boys brought it in and set it up.

The trimmings were made by the scholars in drawing class. Once a week there was a half-hour drawing session where everyone could usually draw whatever they wanted. This time, Miss Young assigned different trimmings according to age and ability.

Students made chains from colored paper. They traced stars and bells from patterns and colored them red or green. For the top of the tree, Miss Young cut a big star out of silver paper and pasted it on cardboard.

Everyone had a part in the Christmas program. There were poems, posed and recited acrostics, dialogues, and singing. I had a part in an acrostic and a dialogue. The acrostic was one where nine children stood in a long row holding big letters spelling C-H-R-I-S-T-M-A-S. Each one said a line about Christmas beginning with the letter each held.

My letter was C and my line was easy:

Christmas comes but once a year,
   but when it comes it brings good cheer.

That wasn't hard to learn, but I worked real hard not to lisp when I said "Christmas." I had trouble with lisping.

I took part in a dialogue about Santa's helpers. They were mad because they had to work so hard. So they all got together and decided to go on a strike.

I was supposed to be their spokesman and bring the news to Santa.

As we stood there babbling, Santa came in from the side curtain, all dressed in red and white, and sporting a long white beard. I addressed him in what was supposed to be a stern voice: "You thee, thur, it's this way; all we Thanta Claus helpers have declared a thrike."

We all talked at once about our feelings. Then Santa took over. He convinced us how awful it would be for all the children in the world to be sad instead of happy at Christmas. We were ashamed of ourselves and went back to work, singing a Christmas jingle.

I was ashamed that I still lisped when I spoke my part in the program. At nine years of age, I wasn't supposed to lisp any more.

Eva and Helen were home for the holidays, and we all had a nice time together. Mama always made a lot of different kinds of cookies and candy. Instead of turkey, Mama roasted a big chicken with really good stuffing. We visited around in the house all day, eating cookies and candy until we were almost sick.

Helen gave me a great big book about Robin Hood. It had hard covers and colored pictures. Eva returned my rock collection. Each rock was tagged with a number showing its place on a classification list that gave its name and described its formation.

Dr. Roddy had asked Eva to see if I would exchange the green stone for three different rocks from a volcano in Mexico and one asbestos stone. I thought four rocks from Mexico seemed like a good exchange for one of my stones. Dr. Roddy had already included the four rocks in my classification list.

Eva put my green gemstone in her handbag to take it to him. One thing did bother me a bit when she scratched the gem off my list: I was giving up a gem and receiving four that were just rocks.

I was delighted with my *Robin Hood* book. It had full-page colored pictures of Robin Hood and his friends or enemies. The picture on the front cover was of Robin Hood standing under a tree, talking to a little man. I leafed through the book and looked at all the pictures. There were seven, and each one had an explanation under it.

One picture for page 251 had Robin standing among a lot of dangerous-looking men, thoughtfully holding his bow and arrow. Below the picture the caption said,

Robin, in a ragged and frayed brown tunic and hose, with a hood of similar hue, raised his bow, notched his arrow, and looked for one long moment at the mark.

The picture for page 140 gave me a special feeling. A man was kneeling before a beautiful lady dressed in white and kissing her hand. The caption said,

He bent his knees and kissed the lady's hand gallantly.

I turned to page 140 and read the next sentence:

"I am Robert or Robin Hood, as men call me," he said, "and I think you must be Mistress Alice de Beauforest whom Alan-a-Dale loves so well."

I took the book to Helen, pointed to the word "gallantly," and asked her, "How does one say this? And what does it mean?"

She pronounced it and replied, "When a man was brave and polite, especially to women, he was gallant."

I asked her about Mistress Alice's long name. She said the story took place a long time ago in England, when people sometimes spoke with different words and had unusual names. I would understand the story better if I read it over again.

"A book like this is called a novel," Helen said. "It is a made-up story telling about human experience in a series of events."

I sat down to begin reading my first novel. It began, "It was high noon in summertime, and the forest seemed to sleep." The novel drew me into the story and stimulated my imagination.

17

The Lost Possum

Hunting season was here again. Gunshots could be heard across the fields. Hunters sometimes came through our farm. They were usually from town and wore special hunting coats and caps.

Farmers hunted in their own fields and wore their regular overalls and coats. Some men went way up in the mountains to another county to deer-hunt.

Dad never did much hunting. His shotgun was stuck away somewhere up in the garret. His little 22-caliber Savage rifle was on the shelf in the barn shop. A box of 22 short cartridges was beside it on the shelf. He never used his gun because the rats weren't around any more.

The boys at school were always talking about hunting. I wanted to try it, too. One Saturday afternoon when Dad was at Lititz, I got the rifle to give it a try. Loading it, I walked softly around the edge of the meadow, where the grass was high, hoping to shoot a rabbit in its nest. Rabbits always jumped around when they ran away and would be hard to hit.

I didn't find a single rabbit. My afternoon hunting was a failure. I aimed the rifle at a fence post and pulled the trigger. The bullet made a little hole where it hit the post. This was the first time I had shot a gun.

The sound of the shot and smell of gunpowder reminded me of the time Dad used to shoot rats. Even though I didn't shoot any game, I could tell the boys at school that I had been out hunting.

On Wednesday morning at school, as I was finishing my arithmetic paper, I heard a sound at the door. Miss Young looked back to see what was going on. The door was partly open, and a man was there, motioning for her to come.

After they exchanged a few words, she came right to my desk. She lowered her voice to a whisper: "Levi, there are two men outside that want to talk to you. Go and see what they want."

I was afraid. What would they have to talk to me about? Getting up from my desk, I went back through the door. There stood two big men in hunting coats and caps. One of them had a shotgun. The one without a gun looked down at me and asked, "Did you find a possum lying around anywhere this morning?"

My heart was pounding. I shook my head and replied, "No."

He continued in an accusing way: "Last night we were hunting possums in Weidman's woods, with permission. One got away, and we saw it running up to your place. Are you sure you didn't find it?"

Again I said no.

He looked at me for a moment, rubbing his whiskers. Then without a word, they went down the steps, got into a big and expensive automobile, and drove away.

At noon recess, as soon as I was out the door, I ran home. I didn't want the boys to ask me about it.

When I reached home, Mama asked, "Did someone come to talk to you at school?"

I told her what had happened.

She reported that two men had come knocking at the kitchen door, asking if we had seen a possum around the place. Mama had told them she hadn't seen it but maybe I would know something about it, and that they could find me up at Webster.

By the time I got back to school, I was in a positive mood. When the boys asked about the two men, I was ready to talk about possums. Everyone had a story. They said, "Why don't you look around for that lost possum this evening?"

So I looked and looked, but it was nowhere to be found. Maybe it was still alive or had crawled in a hole and died. What made me feel best was talking with the big boys and having their respect.

18

The Airplane

According to the *Farmer's Almanac*, it would be a snowy winter again. That's what one of the big boys at school said. The almanac was right; there was a lot of snow. We all dragged our sleds to school, ready for fun.

Miss Young surprised us. She brought a sled to school one day. It was a Flexible Flyer! We used to talk about the Flexible Flyer with its speed runners, and now we could really see one.

The sled was not big, but its runners were supposed to be special. They were made of hardened steel, and the bottoms of the runners were slightly arched so that their edges cut into ice and snow. The ads all claimed that it was designed for speed.

Sometimes at noon recess, Miss Young would come out and coast down Wayne Zartman's field with us. I didn't think her sled went any faster than my Lightning Guider.

Coasting was different when Miss Young was along. We acted more polite and grown-up. Forry Zartman couldn't coast with us. He had broken his right arm while helping his pop in the mill. Forry was Eli Zartman's son, and they owned the mill. He carried his arm in a special sling that had a shiny aluminum cradle so it would heal straight. Somebody said his arm was broken so badly that it would always be crooked.

Since I didn't have to study much at home, I would read *Robin Hood* every chance I had. If Dad caught me reading it when I was supposed to be gathering eggs or doing other work, he would take it and lay it up on the cupboard, where it had to remain until the next day.

To make sure that didn't happen, I waited to read the novel until after supper, when the big lamp was lit.

The adventures of Robin Hood completely captured my attention. Since I couldn't read fast, it became an imaginary world to me. My mind reset the scenes as though they were at the Fight Corner thicket or in Weidman's woods.

I played with Franklin's old bow and arrows and imagined I was rescuing Lady Marian as I sneaked through Fangthief Wood. I became so engrossed with the novel that Dad made me put it away for a week.

There was still snow on the ground on Valentine's Day, but we had lost interest in coasting. During our drawing periods, we were all supposed to make valentines to exchange with each other on Valentine's Day.

The older scholars always made real nice valentines and exchanged more of them than the little ones did. There were always special sayings twining around hearts and flowers. We had a favorite and often-repeated verse:

As long as grass grows round the stump,
     you are as sweet as a sugar lump.

This was written below a drawing of a stump surrounded by sprigs of grass. On the best drawings, the stump was brown and the grass was green.

One little girl sent me a valentine with the usual stump and grass drawn well enough to recognize what they were. The writing was good for a little girl:

Arond the stomp arond the stomp,
     you are as sweet as shuger lomp.

Spring came and the snow melted. We began to play prisoner's base and other games. Paraly Over was another favorite: One team threw a ball over the schoolhouse roof to a team on the other side. If someone caught the ball, that team could quickly run around and try to "tag" players on the other team before they got away.

One warm spring day, we were sitting in school with the windows open. In the distance, we heard a sound like an automobile engine. As we listened, it grew louder. Then one of the big boys said aloud, "Hey, that's an airplane!"

Miss Young said we could all go out and look for

it in the sky. None of us had ever seen a real airplane. Everyone rushed out, along with Miss Young. Right there, up in the air, somewhere above where Allen Bomberger lived, was an airplane.

The plane seemed to be high in the sky but was close enough that we could see a man's head in the cockpit. He was wearing a helmet with big goggles. We stayed there watching the plane as it moved out of sight toward Lebanon.

Over the next few days, all we talked about was the airplane. How high had it been? How fast was it going? Could the people as far away as Lexington have seen it at the same time we had seen it?

A new subject of interest was begun—how propellers worked. Some of the boys whittled wooden propellers and brought them to school. Soon all of us were playing airplane instead of automobile. We ran around with propellers on sticks or on the ends of pencils, making airplane sounds, swerving and diving like we imagined the pilots had done in the war.

One day John Zartman pushed his bicycle up the hill to school. No one had ever brought a bicycle to school before, but this was special. He had fitted a large, neatly carved propeller in front of the handlebars. As he rode around the school, the propeller spun so fast it looked like a glass dish. We gathered around to examine it.

John told us the propeller made riding easier, that it helped to pull. I knew he just thought so. It couldn't be true. Franklin had a good propeller he had made, and he had explained how propellers worked. I did not dare to say anything at school, though. The other boys would have either laughed at me or hated me.

Besides, something told me it wouldn't have been polite.

"When a propeller is turned real fast by an engine," Franklin had said, "it can pull the airplane. But when it is pushed by the wind, as on a windmill, it gives power to drive a belt, grind things, or pump water. He was in high school and knew more about machinery.

I was looking forward to summer. Eva and Helen would be home, and Franklin and I would be working together again in the fields. Hoeing weeds or working in the corn and cabbage gave us time to talk about anything we liked. No one would be listening.

There were some things I wanted to ask him. We never talked about serious things when we were in bed at night. I guess it was because Esther's room was next to ours, and she might hear what we said.

19

Zartman's Fire

In many ways this summer would be different from the last. Dad had built a little hothouse in the lower yard. In it we could grow all kinds of vegetable seedlings. He had enlarged the brooder house to raise more chicks and had converted the tobacco shed into a hen house.

What pleased us most was Dad had replaced the old Model T with a shiny new Baby Overland touring car. We had also "made enough," as Dad had proposed last year, to buy a Ford truck.

With the hothouse operating, cabbage plants were ready to set out as soon as the danger of heavy frost was past. Dad warned us all that it was going to be a busy summer.

All the improvements made during the last two years gave me a special feeling of progress. I was glad to feed more chickens and gather more eggs.

When Dad said he was going to get me started at cleaning the stables, I didn't mind. It was hard work, but I had used the big wheelbarrow and four-pronged dung fork before. The job was called "dunging out," and we did it on Saturdays.

Shortly after Eva and Helen had unpacked for summer in their upstairs room, Eva came to me and quietly gave me some advice about being good. I didn't understand it, but I knew it was all right because Eva had said it.

Then she gave me *Two Little Savages,* by Ernest Thompson Seton. It was a book about two boys who played at being Indians in a woods near their house. She said I should take my time and not try to read it all at once.

Eva had applied for a teaching job and had been accepted for a country school in Brecknock Township. Helen would return for her last year at Millersville State Normal School, and Franklin was supposed to return for his second year at Rothsville High. The girls' talk about school was always interesting to me. Franklin didn't like school very much and didn't talk about it.

We all worked hard and enjoyed it. Eva helped in the fields again and sometimes went along to market. Esther helped too but didn't do well. She would take big swings with the hoe and miss the weeds several times before finally chopping them off. Yet she always tried to be careful and do everything right.

Esther seemed to think it was like being good or bad when she tried to do her work properly. When I didn't understand it that way, she would try to explain a Bible verse that was about doing good work.

One time in the spring when I was walking in the pasture, I saw a rabbit jumping up and down and turning somersaults. When I told her about it, she said, "Are you sure you aren't just telling a lie again?"

She was always trying to catch me in a lie. She had an idea that if anything was not repeated or told exactly right, it was a lie. When I talked about the rabbit at the supper table, Dad said, "Rabbits often act like that in the spring, just to have a good time." So I was in the clear.

One day close to noon, I looked up from where I was hoeing in the field. I saw a big cloud of smoke rolling up in the sky from down at Wayne Zartman's place. I dropped my hoe at the end of the row and ran down across the fields to see what was going on. Zartman's big barn was burning!

People were frantically working around the barn, getting the cows and horses out. Wayne was away near Hopewell at a sawmill. A fire engine finally arrived and began pumping water from the millpond, across the road and behind the dam. It was too late for the barn, but all the other buildings were saved.

Finally, when the barn was burned nearly to the ground, Wayne Zartman drove up the back road from Hopewell and saw the pile of burning timber. The smell of burned flesh was in the air. One of the little calves had burned. Wayne stopped the car, leaned over the steering wheel, and cried real loud, just like a baby.

His sister, Mrs. Metzler, came and softly laid her hand on his shoulder. She said gently, "Why, Wayne." Then she stood there beside him until he stopped crying.

During conversations about how to care for the cows, Dad walked up to take part. He offered space we had in our barn to give temporary stalls for the Zartman cows.

Zartmans accepted his offer, and Dad drove them up to see the stable space. We had never used this part of the barn, and it was just what they needed. There were six regular stalls with feeding troughs.

The cows were herded up the road and put in stables almost like the ones they had before. The Zartmans got the stalls ready, using our straw.

From then on, the Zartman women took over, bringing ensilage of their own for feed and carrying the milk home in milk cans. The entire rescue took place as though it had been planned.

I happened to be near when Mrs. Zartman asked Dad in a timid voice, "How much are you going to charge for the accommodation?"

Dad seemed surprised that she had asked and replied, "There's no charge."

There was something about burning buildings that stirred sympathy in our whole family. It came from deep memories of long ago, the summer before I was born, when our own house had burned down in Chesterfield, Virginia.

I remembered again how last year up in Lexington, the Stark's house had burned down. Standing around after the fire, I had heard one man tell another that he saw Mr. Weber hand Mr. Stark

some money, though it was known that Starks had some insurance coverage. Dad had never mentioned doing that. Since then, the Starks had built a new house.

The cause of Zartman's fire was never proved. Someone said he had seen two men leaving the barn before it burned. Others blamed the Deaver boy who worked there. There were other ideas, but that's where the matter rested.

20

Cornfield Conversations

One Saturday afternoon we went to Groffdale Church to hear a foreign missionary tell about his work in India. He shared stories about how people dressed and what they ate. The missionary told about a man-eating tiger that would sneak into the village and try to catch people. He reported times when, because of prayers, lives had been saved or accidents avoided.

The missionary and his wife sang a duet, "Count Your Many Blessings," in a language of India. The stories I liked best were about the dramatically answered prayers and the narrow escapes from tigers and fires.

On the way home, we talked about the meeting. I asked, "Why don't prayers keep people from having automobile accidents or getting struck by lightning?"

Dad didn't say anything, but Esther suggested, "Perhaps nobody prayed."

Last summer a good man had been killed by lightning near Manheim. Someone had said, "It was supposed to be." I was confused. I thought things like that were supposed to happen to *bad* people, not *good* ones.

There were a lot of thunderstorms that summer. Even a barn with lightning rods was struck by a bolt and burned down. A neighbor boy explained about the owner of that barn: "It was supposed to be because one Sunday the man had said, '*Gott verd____ sei* (God d____).' "

In our free time on Saturday afternoons, Franklin began to rebuild the dam on our pasture creek. This time, using scrap lumber, he constructed two parallel bulkheads about two feet apart and filled the space between with dirt. It looked like a fort! "No flood will be able to wash this away," he claimed.

"Because you helped," he told me, "the dam will belong to both of us."

Our pond now was bigger and deeper since we used dirt from the dam pond for fill in the dam. After it gradually filled with water, I practiced skipping stones across the surface. We now had a dam we could be proud of. I tried to think of a name for it from *Robin Hood*.

The rains came and the dam stayed firm. We worked hard during the summer and had little time to fool around or to dress it up around the edges. The girls went down to look at it and praised Franklin for the design and workmanship. Dad said, "That will be a good water supply in case of a fire."

We felt that our project had been accepted as a good part of the farm.

One day Franklin and I were working together, suckering the field corn, talking as we went. The stalks reached above our heads, and the field stretched wide around us. We were tearing off the side suckers so that the main stalks could grow faster and bigger. The quiet seclusion prompted us to chat about personal things.

We began talking about stories the missionary had told. "Why did the missionary have so many experiences and other people didn't?" We talked about things we wished for and never had. "Why are some people rich and others poor?"

Franklin shared a favorite wish: "I've always wanted a bicycle, but Dad said it wasn't necessary."

He remembered the old antique bicycle our neighbor Norman Bomberger had given him long ago. It had wooden handlebars and old gummy tires. The pedals propelled forward but when pressed backward just went around, with no brakes. Riding downhill was an adventure. That antique soon broke up and fell apart.

Franklin asked, "Is there anything you often want but have never gotten?"

I thought awhile but couldn't get the missionary stories out of my mind. "Do you think the missionaries would have gotten a bicycle if they had prayed for it?"

That got us to talking again about praying. Maybe preachers were the only ones who could really pray for things. All at once, I wished there was some secret way I could pray and get answers.

I remembered the picture we had of Jesus kneeling by a big stone and praying. Maybe if I had a special stone for praying, it would help. I told Franklin, "My secret wish is for a special stone to pray beside, like Jesus in that picture."

"That is a good idea," he said, "but stones are really heavy to move."

Franklin was right. But maybe I could find one in a secret place in the woods.

Then Franklin said something I had never imagined: "Jesus didn't pray only at that special rock. He prayed everywhere—at places in the desert, with crowds of people, and in streets."

It was new for me to think of prayer any place except at the table or beside our bed or at a big rock, like Jesus in the picture. Saying the Lord's Prayer at school didn't count as praying; that was just like reciting a poem.

From that time, I kept pondering what Franklin had told me. I wondered how I could learn what to say and how to pray that way. I was too timid to ask anyone about it. I just kept wondering.

One day after a big rain, Franklin and I went to look at the dam. Water was roaring over the spillway. When we got close, we couldn't believe what we saw. The pond behind the dam had completely filled with mud! The silt from the summer rains had done away with all our work.

We knew our opportunity to have a dam was gone forever. I didn't have to keep trying to find a name for the dam from *Robin Hood*.

The Fourth Year at
Possum Hollow

21.

Pancakes and Syrup

Now it was back to school again. Eva went to teach at Brecknock, Helen returned to Millersville State Normal School, and Franklin to Rothsville High. Esther and I, of course, were back at Webster. It was to be Esther's last year there.

My brother was in his second year of high school, and he wanted to take part in the fall field meet. He would try out for the mile run. He set out a practice course in the open field near the house.

Franklin placed three large stakes in a triangle and computed the spacing so that five times around them would equal a mile. He placed his coat and an old alarm clock at the starting stake. In a little notebook from the fertilizer dealer, he recorded the starting and finishing time for each mile.

He practiced until the teacher said his time was good enough to enter the contest. But he needed a gym suit, and Dad wouldn't give him one. "You're going to school to learn, not to run," Dad said.

Then Franklin decided to enter the elocution section. For his recitation, he selected Longfellow's poem, "The Village Blacksmith." His teacher coached him on pronunciation, accent, and phrasing. Once I heard him practicing in the barn. By the time of the field meet, he was ready. I wasn't at the meet, but he told me about it afterward.

Brother was third in line and mounted the platform with confidence. He began,

> Under the spreading chestnut tree,
> The village smithy stands.
> The Smith a mighty man is he,
> With large and sinewing hands;
> And the muscles of his brawny arms
> Are as strong as iron bards.

Franklin got as far as the fifth verse, "He goes on Sunday to the church—," when his old panic problem struck. He had to go down to his seat. The people thought he had simply forgotten his lines. He was deeply embarrassed. Following that experience, his interest in school suffered.

His ability to express his thoughts in writing prompted the editor of the *School Lines* to get him to write short items from time to time. One time he was asked to compose a poem about something that had happened in school. He wrote about a boy who sang a lot in the halls during lunchtime. It went like this:

> Our little Hampton Long
> Likes to sing his favorite song;

While the other boys are mealing,
You can hear his sweet voice pealing.

There was more, but the editor didn't think she should put it in the *Lines*. Hampton might not like it.

Hampton did hear about it from another boy who had gotten a copy. He not only didn't like the poem: he became mad. One time during lunch, he confronted Franklin while he was seated at his desk, eating a piece of pie. Hampton knocked the pie out of his hand and splashed cherries over his face and shirt.

When Franklin told me about it, I asked, "How did you respond?

"Oh, I just cried," he said, "and went to the boys' shed and cleaned up."

Soon after school started, Mama began feeling tired and had to rest sometimes. The doctor had said more rest was what she needed, and Dad had told her to make sure to do that. They finally agreed that she would go to stay at Encks' home in Lancaster for a two-week rest.

The Encks were an old couple who lived in a big house near the Lancaster General Hospital on Duke Street. They rented rooms to people who came out of the hospital and still needed some rest to get stronger. They agreed to take Mama in for two weeks.

"We can get along just fine for two weeks," Dad said. "I'll milk the cows and look after the cooking. Esther will look after little Betty. Levi, you can help Esther with the dishes. Franklin has his regular morning and evening chores."

"Now, Henry," Mama told him, "if it doesn't work out, I'll come right home."

Dad set up our schedules and assigned our tasks. He showed us how they washed dishes at camp when he was in the service. "We made the wash water so hot that the dishes dried themselves. We fished the dishes out of the water with the help of a pancake turner and left them to dry in a drain tray."

Our menu was pancakes and syrup, with some sausage and fried eggs. He bought four different pancake and flapjack mixes. To make it interesting, he got maple syrup, sorghum, and regular molasses, too.

The two weeks went slowly; we missed Mama and her cooking. Dad went to see her often. Then one day, he brought her along home. She was glad and looked rested and full of energy. She sang in the kitchen and would hug and kiss little Betty.

Dad told Mama, "I don't want you to work so hard or you might have to take a vacation again." He repeated his favorite phrase: "Remember, tomorrow is always another day."

"I'll be glad to milk the cows, if you like," he offered.

Mom didn't go for that. "I like to milk," she said. "It's like playing music to hear the milk squirts pinging and plunging in the bucket. Besides, we have only two cows, and I used to milk five all by myself when I was a girl at home."

When Thanksgiving arrived, Mama was working full speed, cooking and baking. Everyone was home and having an exciting holiday. Eva told about Brecknock School, where the children all talked

Pennsylvania Dutch at recess. Helen told about her extra class in botany. She had her hopes set on teaching at Webster the next fall.

I guess Mama worked too hard over Thanksgiving. She began feeling weak and sick again. "You'll have to go back to Encks'," Dad said.

I didn't look forward to another series of meals with chiefly pancakes and syrup. Washing dishes in boiling water didn't appeal to me, either.

Then Dad surprised us with an announcement: "Cousin Bertha, Uncle Jake's oldest daughter, will keep house for us while Mama is away."

We were sorry to have Mama gone again, but it helped to have Bertha there. We always liked to hear her stories. Esther worried a lot about Mama and how hard she had to work.

One time last year, Esther had secretly sent a letter to Mrs. Eckert, a lady who did housecleaning. Esther asked her to come and clean house for Mama on Saturday. Mrs. Eckert had checked it out before she came, and Mama had given Esther a gentle scolding for trying to take the parent's role.

We didn't know how long Mama would be gone, but Bertha assured us that Mama would be all right. Bertha had a nice way about her. We felt comfortable when she was around.

22

Mama at Encks' Again

We enjoyed the stories Bertha told us about things that had happened when she was a little girl. Soon we were telling her our own stories. Esther told my red pepper-cinnamon story.

When I had been in second grade, Mama would punish me for saying naughty words by dusting some red pepper on my tongue. After the dusting I would run to the pump and wash out my mouth.

Then I noticed that the red pepper and cinnamon shakers were exactly the same except for their names. I switched their places on the spice shelf, hoping Mama wouldn't notice.

The next time I said a naughty word, Mama dusted my tongue with cinnamon. When I didn't run to the pump as fast as usual, she caught on right away. As a result, she gave me a tongue dusting of cinnamon *and* red pepper.

By now I knew more about bad words. There were three kinds: naughty, dirty, and swearing. Swear words were evil, and I never thought of using one. Dirty words were about nasty things. Naughty words were the hardest ones not to say. They were the ones I heard some boys saying in the school yard that made the other boys laugh. They would even say a good word wrong so it would sound like a bad word.

I told Bertha about the time when Mama had brought me along from Amelia to meet the relatives in Pennsylvania. We were visiting Uncle Sam's at Farmersville when Uncle Jake came by to say hello.

Not many people had automobiles in those days, but Uncle Jake drove up in an open-body International. It had big wheels and looked like a spring wagon. Bertha laughed when she heard my story. "My six brothers still play around with that old car in the fields."

Dad went to see Mama several times a week. To keep up with the evening chores, he visited in the afternoons. He usually took Esther or me along. Mama always seemed well and happy.

When it was time to go, he would help me with my overcoat and tell me to go and wait in the car till he got his coat on and talked to Mama a little. I would ask him, "When is Mama going to come home?"

"It will be pretty soon," he would say.

About the middle of December, it was my turn to go along. Little Betty would also be going. We drove up to Encks' home and knocked at the door, as usual. Mr. Enck let us in, but we didn't see Mama. Mr. Enck said, "Mary isn't here. She's in the hospital."

Dad simply said "Thanks" and didn't ask any questions. He turned to me: "Boy, let's walk up to the hospital."

We left the car parked there and strolled up the sidewalk to the hospital. We walked in and Dad asked a lady at a desk where Mama was. We followed her directions up some stairs and came to a large room with a number of beds in it.

Dad looked around to find Mama. Then, there in the bed right in front of us, we heard Mama say, "Why, Henry, I'm right here." He had looked right past her bed.

I had never seen Mama lying in a bed like that. She looked different. Everything was white, and her hair was loosely combed, with a large plait stretched out on the pillow. I was wondering about everything when Dad asked, "Is it a boy or a girl?"

Mama chuckled a little. "A boy."

Just then a nurse came, carrying a tiny baby wrapped in a little blanket, and laid him beside Mama on the bed. Mama and Dad looked real pleased and happy. We stayed a little while and then left for home.

When we got home, Dad didn't say anything until we were all together in the room next to the kitchen, waiting for Bertha to put supper on the table. He told us, "Well, Mom will soon be home again, and you'll have a new baby brother."

Esther asked more about this new development before she was satisfied. Bertha acted as if she had always known something about it.

The next morning when Dad was out of the

house, Esther exploded, "Why did Mama have to go and get another baby. She has too much work as it is."

There were lots of things I wondered about but couldn't ask.

Bertha said, "I expect Henry and Mary will name him Henry Junior." That's just what they named him.

23

The Mixed-Up Christmas

Christmas week was mixed up. The Sunday before Christmas, Helen came home from Millersville State Normal School for the holidays. Then on Tuesday, Dad and I went to Encks' home and found out about little Henry Jr. On Wednesday, Eva came home and Bertha left for Christmas. On Thursday, Dad and Eva went to see Mama.

The doctor said Mama could come home on Christmas Day if she was careful and rested. We had everything ready to welcome her home.

Friday was Christmas Eve. As always, we gathered to exchange gifts. We had placed the presents in a basket beside Dad's favorite chair. There he handed them out, reading the tags saying who they were for and who gave them.

Eva gave Esther the book *Rebecca of Sunnybrook*

Farm. Franklin gave me a little Mouse Power electric engine. It ran on a little dry-cell battery. We saved Mama's gifts to give her on Christmas Day.

On Christmas morning, Dad took Eva and went to bring Mama and the baby home. They returned mid-afternoon. Mama and Eva were bundled up and held the baby in the back seat. Helen went out to the car to help, and they all came in together, with Dad carrying the baby.

We gathered in the little room beside the kitchen. The big rocker with cushions had been made ready for Mama. Before she sat down, she gave us each a big hug. The baby was laid in a little basket lined with soft blankets, sitting on Dad's tabletop desk.

Christmas Day was almost gone. We ate cake and cookies that Bertha and the girls had baked. Mama was tired and went upstairs to bed. Dad carried the baby in the basket and followed her.

The rest of us sat around, talking and looking at our Christmas presents. Then we all went to bed, too. As I went to sleep, I was thinking about the little baby and wondering where he had come from.

The next morning was Sunday, and Dad had to go to Sunday school and church. He was the Sunday school superintendent. Eva and Helen stayed home with Mama, Betty, and the baby.

I went with Dad but wasn't interested in the Sunday school lesson or what the preacher said in the worship service. My mind was mulling over all the events surrounding this Christmas. I wanted to be at home, playing with my little engine. When we finally returned from church, the girls already had dinner on the table.

After school vacation was over and the girls left, the rest of us filled in for Mama until she was strong again. We didn't need Bertha anymore.

Things were different in the house. We had to be quiet because of the baby, but the baby could cry as much and as loudly as he pleased. We didn't mind because he had become a part of our home. Little Junior was our brother.

24

Falling in Love with Love

During the winter, when the evenings were long, all of us read a lot. Besides our books, there was the *Lancaster News Journal,* our daily paper; the *Rural New Yorker,* a monthly farm magazine; and the *Youth's Companion,* a monthly magazine for young people.

All of them, including the *News Journal,* had short stories as well as continued stories. They also offered sections of special interest. The part of the newspaper we liked best was the funnies. Everyone except Mama and Eva read them, even Dad. He liked the jokes and the "Rippling Rhymes" by Walt Mason.

As long as I can remember, the funnies were a part of my day. Esther used to read them to me before she could read very well herself. We would spread the paper on the floor and lie down to enjoy

"Mutt and Jeff" and "Jiggs and Maggie." When Maggie would talk a long time with her conversation ending "etc., etc., etc.," Esther would pronounce it "ekt, ekt, ekt" and say that meant Maggie was laughing.

One of the cartoons would end with a little man in the corner of the last picture saying, "Sweep out padded cell." I didn't know what it meant. It sounded like "Swee pout, pad it, sell." One time when Franklin read it to me, he explained the words: "It's like a joke, saying the person is dumb enough for the insane asylum."

Now, the same cartoons were in the paper as well as some new ones. There were the "The Tunerville Trolley" and "Our House." One of my favorites was a little boy's diary called "Little Bennie's Note Book," by Lee Pape. It featured regular items about school happenings and jokes.

One that I always looked forward to was the "Pome by Skinney Martin." One of the "pomes" ran like this:

> Human Beans are people
> Of any age or sex.
> Who rekognize each other
> By the part above their neks.

One time Esther and I got into so much of a hassle over the paper that Dad stopped it for a week.

When it came to reading stories, Esther classified their contents as follows:

Stories about falling in love—"mushy"
Stories like "Elsie Dinsmore"—"goody, goody"
Stories about the wild West and guns—"trashy"

Yet she read them all except the Elsie books. She said she couldn't stand them.

I liked the adventure stories and those about brave men and pretty girls. I tried not to let Esther see me reading those on her doubtful list.

There was one story about a young man working on a ranger outpost at the foot of a mountain. Using a phone, he would contact the ranger station at the top. He didn't know the person there, but she was a woman with a businesslike voice.

Then during a storm, there was an emergency. He had to rescue her. The result was as I hoped. Stumbling down the mountain, they could see each other during lightning flashes for the first time. Finally both were safe in his station, and he said, "Why, how beautiful you are! I thought maybe you were fat and forty."

"I always imagined you were handsome," she replied. "I'm glad the storm got us to know each other."

That was sweet romance! The author didn't mention the unromantic muddy, clinging, drenched clothes.

I had heard somewhere that, at around ten years of age, children begin to fall in love. They don't necessarily fall in love with people; they just fall in love with love. I guessed I was beginning to fall in love with love.

25

Franklin Quits School

The big winter snows held off till January. That was good since it would have been hard to go to Lancaster to see Mama in deep snow. Then it snowed and snowed again. In the fields the snow had crusted hard enough to support our sleds.

I got out my old rusty ice skates and learned to skate on the crusted snow. I had just obtained the skates from one of the boys at school. When I could skate good enough, Dad let me go to Zartman's dam one Saturday afternoon. The snow had roughened the ice, but that made it easier for me. On real smooth ice, I would have fallen more.

One Saturday near the end of January, Franklin let it be known in a quiet way that as of the end of January, he was quitting high school. He had reached the age where he was no longer required to attend school. Apparently he had talked it over with Dad before he told the rest of us.

Franklin liked to study and learn, but he had developed a strong dislike for being in school. When his older sisters heard about his decision, they were sorry but sympathized with him.

He was happy again. He would hum favorite tunes around the house. Dad built on his new attitude and began to talk to him about the farm and some of his plans about building a chicken house. We all could see Franklin's new expression and joyful attitude.

Since it was deep into winter and Franklin had the time, he started a project of his own. He had always liked birds and had books and pictures about them. Over the years, he had collected a lot of bird pictures offered by the Arm & Hammer Soda Company as advertising.

Franklin looked through his books and materials and developed a plan to make birdhouses for sale. He used Dad's carpentry tools and bought his own little scroll saw for fine work. Franklin decided to make wren and bluebird boxes and sell them to the hardware store in Lancaster.

There were three kinds of wren boxes. One kind was for hanging; the others fastened to the side of a building, facing either to the front or side. The bluebird boxes were only for putting onto posts.

Franklin made samples of the various kinds and painted them white, with dull green roofs. When they were finished, he packed them in Mama's large market basket and took the trolley to Lancaster.

On the way, a man from the newspaper noticed him on the trolley and sat beside him to talk. He himself was interested in birds. Picking up one of the

boxes, he checked the dimensions, the size of the hole, and the workmanship.

The newspaper man complimented Franklin for his skill and said the specifications were perfect. Then he encouraged Franklin and wished him well. Several days later we found a little write-up in the paper about a boy and his birdhouse project. Franklin's name wasn't mentioned.

Franklin sold a dozen of the boxes to the hardware store, but he made even more along the way to give to people. He also put some around our house. One hung on the sour cherry tree in the front yard. He nailed another to the house by the kitchen door.

He tried to give one to Millie Eby, the wife of our elderly deacon, Ephraim Eby. They lived in a neatly painted house in Lititz. She thanked him but said she didn't want it because it would just draw birds and mess up her porch.

Franklin wasn't interested in his private shelf any more. He said I could use it. Instead, he put his books and things in the top drawer of our bedroom chest of drawers. He had some books about birds and some special magazines he had saved.

My big brother also had a nice Bible and some gospel tracts. Last year at a revival meeting at Hammer Creek Church, he had stood and gone forward. He often read the Bible and books about the Bible.

I wanted a Bible of my own sometime. All I had was the little Gospel of John that the Gideon man and lady had given me that time at Webster.

26

Another Fire

Melting snow formed little rivulets along the road, only to be frozen again during cold nights. We saw the first signs of approaching spring. The high-pitched caws of crows could be heard again, dying away in the crisp air.

At school there wasn't enough snow for sleds, and the ground was too soft and muddy to play ball. We fooled around inside at recesses until Miss Young chased us out. Spring always seemed slow in coming.

On his regular schedule one Saturday, Dad went to Zartman's Mill for stock feed. He was away a little longer than usual and returned without feed on the truck. His face had a troubled look.

When he got out of the truck, he told me, "Zartman's Mill burned down last night."

"I can't believe it!" I exclaimed. That mill was an important part of our lives as well as of the whole

146

community. We took corn there to be ground, and that's where we bought our flour and stock feed. We even bought gas for our car and truck at their gas pump.

The mill was a three-story structure with the first floor built of heavy stone. The top two floors had a sturdy wooden frame. I liked to watch Mr. Zartman hoist or lower bags with the heavy winch rope. The rope had a chain and hook to wrap around the bags.

When the mill was running, I could hear the mill wheel splashing and feel the vibrating equipment. I remembered one time when we were there in our car and getting gas. Little Betty saw the man lowering bags from the third floor to a truck. She said, "Look, the man is up in him's heaven putting him's bags down."

After Dad told Mama about the fire, he said, "I'll hurry over to Eby's Mill at Lititz for the stock feed. Don't wait for me to get back in time for dinner; I'll be late."

It was three miles to Lititz, and he would have to wait his turn at the mill.

When we had finished our dinner and noon chores, Franklin and I went down to see the burned mill. The stone part of the building was still standing firm, but the top floors were gone. Most of the machinery seemed not too bad to repair, and the sawmill out back wasn't damaged.

We heard the men talking about cleaning up and rebuilding. The mill wheel was undamaged, and most of the first-floor machinery was in place.

At school on Monday, Forry Zartman came to me. He pointed toward the place where the mill had stood and said, "Look, it isn't there any more. Everything looks empty."

It did look empty. Standing on the school porch, we were able to look down and see the Wayne Zartman buildings and the Eli Zartman buildings. A little farther to the right was the Israel Bomberger house and barn. Now the big Wayne Zartman barn wasn't there any more, and the mill was gone.

I was surprised how much little Betty was interested in the news. She wondered about the fire and kept asking questions. Then I remembered that I used to ask a lot of questions when I was little and how my interest in "grown-up things" was often ignored. Betty was four years old, and that's how old I was back when I was asking about things down in Amelia.

Betty would try to repeat adult conversation. She would say, "Absolutel posachibluts (absolutely positively)" and "None of your bizent (none of your business)."

She also used to have imaginary playmates named "Johnny Bend Down," and his brother "Johnny Bend Down, Bend Down." Her current imaginary playmate was "Senschel Weaver."

One time when we were going through an imagination-development exercise suggested in a magazine article, Betty wanted to take part. The exercise was to act as though we were asleep and tell a story as though we were in a dream. That was supposed to free our imaginations.

After we each had told our "exciting" dream story, Betty wanted to tell hers, too: "Time little fairy went out in barn and made so it was sleep in manger." She had combined her fairy tales and Bible stories.

One Sunday afternoon we heard her singing her Sunday school song:

The B-L-E-L-E,
Yes, that's the book for me;
I stand no longer on the Word of God,
The B-L-E-L-E.

If she was actually thinking about her words, she might have imagined a bad boy rudely standing on a Bible. Maybe her Sunday school teacher hadn't explained what the third line meant: "I stand alone on the Word of God." I guess when I had been a little four-year-old, I wouldn't have understood it either.

27

Dad's Compass

For some time talk had been going around at school that Allen Bomberger's older brother, Elmer, was going with Miss Young. We suspected it was true when she began to pay special attention to Allen.

She would correct him more like a mama than like a teacher. Allen didn't have a mama; several years earlier, she had died of typhoid fever. Maybe Miss Young wanted to make up for some of the special discipline and mothering he might have missed.

The news began to leak out that there would soon be a wedding. When everyone knew it anyway, she announced it to us. Along with the announcement, she surprised us by saying, "I will ask you children to help me make our wedding invitations. We can do it during our next drawing period."

Miss Young said a few nice things about us and the school and then asked, "Does anyone have a compass I could borrow for a few days? A compass is something used to draw circles."

No one had a compass to offer. I had an idea that I thought would put me on the good side of Miss Young. Dad had a drafting kit up in the attic. He had used it when he was a builder down in Amelia. A compass was among the shiny instruments in the kit.

One time Dad had used the compass to show us how to make things out of circles. I wanted to tell Miss Young she could borrow it. But I knew I would have to be careful how I told her so Esther wouldn't find out.

After school I walked up to Miss Young's desk and told her, "I can bring you a compass tomorrow morning."

She seemed glad. "Well, thanks, Levi. You're so helpful. I'll only need it for a few days."

When I reached home, I sneaked up into the attic to find the compass. Dad had a box full of things he was saving. There were a few old watches and some old photographs in envelopes.

Among the assorted relics, I found the drafting kit. I snapped open the lid, and there was the compass, just as I remembered it. It was nested in its special compartment among some other pens and shafts, all of professional quality.

I took out the compass, put it in my pocket, snapped the kit shut, and replaced it in the box. Sneaking into my room, I hid the compass where no one could find it; I would take it to Miss Young in the morning.

There was something about it that didn't seem

quite right, but the thought of winning Miss Young's favor was uppermost in my mind.

The next morning I hiked to school early to avoid Esther. I went up to Miss Young's desk and handed the compass to her. She looked at it and thanked me. I could tell that it wasn't quite what she had expected. After trying it on one of her tablets, she said, "Oh, yes, I can use this all right."

Drawing day came. Some were glad to help with the invitations and some weren't. I was among those that weren't. Miss Young handed out some real nice cards. They were better than the heavy paper we sometimes used in drawing class.

She showed us how to make a neat border and a few other little things in the corners. The main part of the card was where she would print the message.

I wondered when Miss Young was going to be finished with the compass. Then one day after school, she came to me and was really embarrassed. "I'm sorry, Levi," she told me, "but I have lost your compass. I bought another one for you. I hope it's okay."

It was a thin children's compass. I think she had bought it at Trimmer's Five & Ten. What could I do? I made no objection and took it home.

That evening I sneaked once more up to the garret. I got the kit and opened it. There, holding the tin toy, I looked at the neat instruments nested in their velvet spaces. I tried to fit the toy compass into the space provided, but it just stayed on top. I managed to squeeze the lid and snap it shut.

I put the kit in the very bottom of Dad's box, under everything else, and hoped Dad would never need a compass again.

My mind was restless, and I was worried. Had I stolen Dad's compass? Because it belonged in our home, was it still stealing or was it borrowing? I didn't dare ask Franklin about it. I had never stolen anything, and I knew it was wrong to steal. I was never even allowed to take something that someone had left behind.

As I mulled this over, I tried to invent a reason or develop a situation that would relieve my conscience, but the matter just lingered in my thoughts. Sometimes I tried to think that the compass was the same as mine, so that wasn't stealing. Then an old saying would come back to me: "If it ain't yours, it must be stealing."

I wasn't mad at Miss Young; I knew she had not lost the compass on purpose. That made me feel a little better. After all, she was guilty too. Finally, I began to forget about it.

28

Money and Banking

Summer was here again. The early plantings of cabbage and sweet corn were maturing; peas and snap beans were blooming. I always liked summer, and I knew this one would be special. In the evenings, Franklin and I would be going swimming and fishing again at Zartman's dam. Dad approved of our evening recreation.

Franklin was reading a book about swimming and diving. Breast strokes, side strokes, and crawl strokes—he tried them all. He liked the jackknife and the swan dives. When he practiced diving, he often belly flopped because the board was too close to the water. I tried the swimming strokes but was scared to dive headfirst into the water.

One evening we two swam until it was beginning to get dark. As we started up the hill toward home, we noticed what appeared to be a small bonfire at the top of the hill. Suddenly it flared up, with large flames shooting high into the sky.

"Hey! That's our house!" Franklin shouted.

I couldn't believe it: "No, it's something else."

"No, it's our house!" he groaned.

We took off, running at top speed.

As we topped the hill, we saw a big fire, but it wasn't our house. Mr. Weidman was there in his field, tending a big brushfire. Our relief was hard to describe. Panting, with our hearts pounding, we stopped to talk with Mr. Weidman.

Franklin told him how we thought it was our house and mentioned that when he was a little boy, our house in Virginia really did burn down. We talked a bit about Wayne Zartman's barn fire and Eli Zartman's mill fire.

"I think the mill will soon be back in business," Mr. Weidman said.

Eva and Helen were home for vacation. It was fun to exchange our stories and experiences. I was always glad when they came home because they often brought us carefully selected books.

This time Eva gave me *Two Little Confederates*. It was about two boys who had lived during the Civil War. Since I had already read *Two Little Savages* twice, a new book was just what I needed. Helen gave Esther *Laddie*, by Gene Stratton Porter.

Our family didn't have many vegetables ready for the first market day. We went mainly to get set up so people would know we were there. Since there wasn't much to do, Dad took me along to help. Later, in the busy time, Franklin would go along. On this trip to the market, after we had set up and put the vegetables on display, Dad strolled up the sidewalk to visit with the other farmers.

While he was gone, a lady came up to me and asked in a nice way, "Young man, I wonder if you might help me? I locked myself out of my house. Would you step up on the porch, crawl through my front window, and open my door?"

I was scared and didn't know what to say. Lancaster was a strange place. I was afraid.

Just then Dad walked up and joined us. The lady explained it to him and pointed to her house right across the sidewalk from us. It was in a set of row houses with neat little front porches.

"We'll be glad to help," Dad said.

She walked with me to the window and explained things to me again.

Crawling through the window was easy because it was close to the floor. Inside, I was supposed to turn left to the front hall, go to the door, and open it. The room smelled like new furniture and had wall-to-wall carpet. The front hall had a smooth tile floor. I had to study the door latch because it wasn't like our old iron latch at home.

When I opened the door, she was waiting outside. "Thank you," she said as she quietly slipped a quarter into my hand.

After it was over, Dad asked, "What would you have done if I hadn't come by?"

I said, "I was scared and hadn't made up my mind."

He responded, "It's always best to be careful when strangers ask for unusual favors. It's easy to get into trouble that way."

When marketing began in full swing, Franklin

was going along to market instead of Eva. She had graduated into her own career. However, she still picked peas and beans in her usual proficient style—"just because I like to do it," she claimed. Franklin enjoyed going to market; it gave him a chance to see the big stores in Lancaster.

One Saturday evening after market, as we were sitting around the table and watching Dad count "our money," he surprised Franklin, Esther, and me. When the money was all counted and arranged in order, he said, "You three children are going to earn a percent of the cash intake as commission."

I didn't know what "percent" and "commission" meant since that was studied in the sixth-reader class. What it exactly meant didn't matter, anyhow; it still sounded exciting.

Dad took his pencil and paper and showed us how it worked. Franklin got the highest percent, next lower was Esther's, and mine was lowest. As Dad said, "It's good for a nine-year-old."

He forgot that I had turned ten on my last birthday. Then he counted out our money. Franklin's pile had some dollar bills and quarters. Esther's was one dollar and some change. My pile had quarters and dimes. We counted our money and fooled around, reveling in our new wealth.

After Franklin and Esther went to put their money away, Dad said to me, "Boy, here I have something for you." He got a little booklet out of his pocket and handed it to me. "I opened a little savings account in the bank for you. Take a look at the book."

There on the front cover in fancy letters it said,

"Lititz Springs National Bank." Right below it in plain letters it said, "Savings Account." On the first page, someone had written, "Master Levi B. Weber, Lititz, Pa., Route 1." I turned to the next page and found it full of lines. On the first line was a date and record of a $1.00 deposit.

"I opened that savings account for you the other day," said Dad. "Always save some of the money you earn. You might need it for a rainy day." That was one of his regular sayings.

Then he smiled. "It's all right to keep a little money for *Schpritzwexel,* but never spend it all." He chuckled when he said *Schpritzwexel* since he often used Pennsylvania Dutch for fun. It meant "spending money."

I had never thought much about banks. Franklin had a little bankbook in his drawer, but I didn't know if Esther had one. Now *I* had one. I could see myself walking up to the bank window with my money. It made me feel grown up.

<u>29</u>

On Growing Up

On Monday, Franklin and I were hoeing weeds in the cabbage field and discussing the often-mentioned topic of "growing up." Some people grew up sooner than others. Some were tall, and others were short.

"That's just the way it is," Franklin said. "They get it from their parents."

Esther had predicted that I wasn't going to get tall because I didn't drink milk. I hated milk; it tasted awful and reminded me of the cow stable.

We decided there were two things that showed when a boy had grown up. One was beginning to shave. The other was changing to long pants. Neither event took place without some difficulty.

Boys were teased about shaving off "peepy fuzz" or trying to act grown-up. If one changed to long pants too soon, that gave others a chance to tease. If changing was put off too long, it was embarrassing.

"Do you remember when the Witters boy changed too soon?" I asked Franklin. "His pants were loose, and the suspenders pulled his waist too high. At church, the boys teased him all across the parking lot to his automobile."

Franklin said he remembered. "I think the boys were also a bit jealous because his daddy had a big and expensive automobile. Anyhow, boys often develop a mean streak when they hang around together. That's one of the reasons I left high school. A bunch of mean-streak boys often made trouble for me."

Then, in a joking way, he said, "We ought to be like the Amish. Those boys always wear long pants."

"In our first year at Webster, do you remember how those in the top class dressed?" I asked Franklin.

They were sixteen-year-olds, three girls and two boys. The girls wore pretty dresses with lace collars, and the boys wore long pants. Instead of playing at recess, they stood around together talking. No one would have even thought of teasing them.

When they stood up front giving their reading lessons, I always stopped my work and listened. Their poems and stories were interesting. Miss Rhudy would help them pronounce hard words and explain their meanings. There was one hard word she didn't explain. I still remember it. Charles Hollinger was reading:

Full many a gem of purest rasereen,
The dark unfathom'd caves of ocean bear.

I asked Franklin if he knew what *rasereen* meant. He didn't know, but he said it might be in the dictionary or maybe Eva would know it.

After supper, when we were sitting around reading or talking, Eva got up and went into the next room. That was my chance to ask her about the word. She was sitting at Dad's desk, working with some papers. I stood there until she looked up from her work.

I always felt safe asking her questions. No matter how stupid they were, she never made fun of me.

On the desk I noticed that Eva had been writing what looked like a list of our names. She smiled and said, "I've been going back and forth so much that I was forgetting how fast we were growing up. I got Mama to help me make an up-to-date list." She handed it to me to read:

1921
Junior—6 months
Betty—4 years
Levi—10 years
Esther—13 years
Franklin—15 years
Helen—20 years

"Eva, why isn't your name there?" I asked.

"Oh, "she laughed and replied, "I know how old *I* am!"

Then I seized my chance. "What does *rasereen* mean?" I asked Eva.

"It's a new word to me," she said. "How did you come across it?"

I told her about the class at Webster and repeated the lines:

Full many a gem of purest rasereen,
The dark unfathom'd caves of ocean bear.

She knew at once what the word was. "Levi, you didn't understand the word; listen:

Full many a gem of purest *ray serene* . . .

She explained the words. It was from Thomas Gray's *Elegy Written in a Country Churchyard*. Then she quoted several lines:

Full many a gem of purest ray serene,
The dark unfathom'd caves of ocean bear:
Full many a flower is born to blush unseen,
And waste its sweetness on the desert air.

Like a schoolteacher, she told about the poem. Gray had written it as though he were walking through a cemetery and looking at gravestones. That particular verse was about good people who did good things and worked hard, but no one recognized how they improved their surroundings. She wondered why Miss Rhudy used that poem.

Eva smiled at me and said, "Don't look sad; it's just a poem. It wasn't written for us. You are young and full of gumption; you're growing up just fine. Lift up your chin!"

Gumption was a word Dad often used in encouraging us to do things.

Summer was going to be fun. There would be hay to make and wheat to harvest and thresh. I was going to "lift up my chin" and show off my "gumption." Growing up was not so bad after all!

As I walked back to join the others, I remembered a remark Eva had made to Mama the other day: "Oh, my! In August I'll be twenty-three. We're all growing older!"

The Author

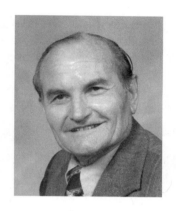

Levi B. Weber, Newport News, Virginia, is a retired building contractor, real estate developer, and broker. In the Possum Hollow books, he tells of his birth in 1911 and his growing-up years in Virginia and Pennsylvania.

During the Great Depression, Weber held jobs on farms, in a commercial greenhouse, and at a dairy. He bought two acres of forest, harvested the timber, and built a four-bedroom house. In 1939 he and his bride, June E. Burkholder, moved in. They have three children.

After World War II, Weber went into contracting, building, and land development. His company built houses around Old Williamsburg, some for employees of Colonial Williamsburg, and notably for Ivor Nöel Hume, head archaeologist at Colonial Williamsburg.

While developing Denbigh Plantation, the remnant of a historic estate on the banks of the James River, Weber's company discovered the remains of the old Mathews Manor, dating back to 1620. Mr.

Nöel Hume conducted the research and cataloging of the artifacts. For Weber's role in locating, studying, protecting, and preserving Mathews Manor, the American Association for State and Local History gave Weber an Award of Merit.

In 1962 he began as a real estate broker. Eventually Weber retired from building and later from realty work. He gives talks about Denbigh Plantation and Mathews Manor at libraries and local historical organizations. He took a writing course at the College of William and Mary, and writes and publishes stories.

Levi and June are members of the Warwick River Mennonite Church. He has been teaching Sunday school for more than fifty years. Weber has served in leading positions in the congregation and in the conference. For eighteen years, he produced the *Rock of Ages* radio broadcast and directed the chorus for it.

Weber has taught teacher-training courses, given talks about Mennonites, and served on the boards of Eastern Mennonite College and Mennonite Economic Development Associates (MEDA). For MEDA, he made five trips to Africa. Weber was a charter member of the Mennonite Christian Leadership Foundation.

He has been active as a board member of the Mennowood Retirement Community and was president during construction of the seventy-room assisted-living addition. In the 1990s, Weber was part of a volunteer task force shaping a Framework for the Future, for the Newport News Planning Commission.

Weber enjoys researching his Swiss-German family background, translating Pennsylvania German pastoral letters of the 1800s, and studying the history and archaeology of old plantations. Earlier he played golf and flew small aircraft. As a passenger with another pilot, he survived a crash in the Virginia mountains and has lived to tell his tales, for the enjoyment of readers.

T